A CENTURY OF HEROES

Edited by

DOUGLAS R. CHAMBERS

CARNEGIE HERO FUND COMMISSION

PITTSBURGH

Dedicated to the 8,764 individuals
awarded the Carnegie Medal in the first 100 years
of the Carnegie Hero Fund Commission,
to those who will be so honored in the years to come,
and to the memory of Andrew Carnegie,
whose idea and gift made possible
the recognition of selfless acts of heroism.

Certain case information accompanies the names of
Carnegie Medal awardees appearing in this book:

C. H. **Carnegie Heroes** are ordered numerically in the
Hero Fund's archives. In accounts of rescues involving
multiple awardees, the award numbers are listed in the
order of the awardees' appearance in the narrative.

☦ This symbol alongside an award number signifies that
the rescuer lost his or her life. Historically, one in five
awardees was recognized posthumously.

FILE NO. Every individual considered for the Carnegie Medal
receives a file number upon nomination. Traditionally,
only one in 10 nominees is selected for recognition.

Published by the Carnegie Hero
Fund Commission and distributed by
the University of Pittsburgh Press.

Manufactured in the United States
of America.

ISBN 0-8229-5866-X

TABLE of CONTENTS

T he massive, fiery steel mills where Andrew Carnegie made his fortune have all but disappeared. What remains as physical evidence of his legacy are the institutions that he created as vehicles for his philanthropy. While the efforts of the foundations he created deserve continuous praise, the aura of Carnegie's legend itself tends to overshadow the earnest work carried on by them today. With this in mind, the centennial celebration of the founding of the Carnegie Hero Fund Commission, commemorated in these pages, deserves the undivided spotlight.

Carnegie would heartily approve the publication of this book. As he once said, "To do things is not one-half the battle . . . To be able to tell the world what you have done, that is the greatest accomplishment." He encouraged the trustees of his many foundations to publicize their work. Yes, it added to his growing legend; however, he hoped such promotion would encourage others to engage in philanthropy. Toward that end, Carnegie also cajoled his fellow millionaires, on one occasion writing retail genius John Wanamaker, "The thought comes to mind—is it not about time that you were beginning to practice distribution?"

There will always be debate as to whether the hard-nosed Carnegie indulged in philanthropy to relieve his conscience or whether he was wholly altruistic. Regardless, in this results-oriented world, there is no doubt in my mind that the results of his benevolence far outweigh the price paid by his laborers and competitors— a conclusion I came to when I witnessed my children playing in Pittencrieff Park, which he gave to his hometown of Dunfermline, and watched them relishing the Carnegie museums in Pittsburgh. Carnegie touched my children, as he has millions of others, in a positive, yet somewhat indirect way. This is not the case for the many lives he has affected through the work of the Hero Fund Commission, for the relationships forged here have been and continue to be very direct and, at times, very personal.

The intimate tone is exemplified by the long-term association the Commission enjoyed with the family of a hero who, in 1910, was part of a rescue team that saved a sailor from the raging surf of Lake Superior. Subsequently, this hero was granted an award of $1,000, which had yet to be collected on his death in 1913. Following a thorough investigation into the family's financial situation, the Commission decided to support his widow and her three young children. Over the next 60 years, in addition to providing financial aid, the Commission supported the family with poignant counseling. This story and others demonstrate how deeply committed the Hero Fund's caretakers are in carrying out Carnegie's desire to honor such heroes.

Carnegie's founding of this institution was a sparkling manifestation of his own evolution as a human being. Consider that in the 1890s, when he was at the height of his industrial power, he made millions of dollars by selling armament and projectiles to the U.S. military. Then in 1898, during the Spanish-American War, he became an avid anti-imperialist who reviled America's military aggressions. Somewhat contradictory behavior, yes. But in the coming years, he did indeed evolve into a pacifist whose heart was crushed by the outbreak of World War I. As a pacifist, the enlightened Carnegie wanted to recognize and reward heroes who were attempting to save lives, as opposed to those soldier–heroes who gain their elevated status by attempting to maim or kill their fellow man. He wanted to show the world that heroes didn't require wars, and hoped to promote goodwill and peace by encouraging citizens to act with moral courage.

While we recognize the brilliance of Carnegie's benevolence, once again, we cannot allow his legend to overshadow the
institutions that carry on his legacy and, in particular, the more than
8,700 individuals whom the Hero Fund Commission has recognized and rewarded for risking their lives. As you will discover,
these heroes have captured the Hero Fund's vigilant attention just
as dramatically as they capture our imagination as we express
wonder at their courage. All of these heroes exhibit the rare quality
of ultimate selflessness that reassures us that the human race is
noble. There is much to learn from them. Honor them.

Peter Krass
Hanover, New Hampshire
2004

MARK LASKOW, PRESIDENT

The Carnegie Hero Fund created this book to honor Andrew Carnegie and the everyday heroes whose extraordinary acts have earned them the Carnegie Medal. It also honors Carnegie's vision of altruistic civilian heroism, a vision whose power and dignity account in large part for the Hero Fund's relevance 100 years later. Carnegie's financial endowment was important, but his insight into the true nature of heroism is the genius that has propelled the Hero Fund across one century and into another.

When Carnegie created the Carnegie Hero Fund Commission in 1904, several of the strongest and sometimes most conflicting forces in his life converged. Yet he shaped his Hero Fund and its mission with a coherent and elegant philosophy that belies its origins in his tumultuous life.

Tumultuous, indeed. Carnegie, born to a working class family committed to radical politics, created himself as one of the world's most successful and aggressive capitalists. Yet rather than renounce his heritage in favor of capitalism, he tried instead to reconcile the two. He did this in part with words—prodigious philosophizing—but, more important, with deeds—prodigious philanthropy.

As we examine Carnegie's life, themes emerge that culminated in his creation of the Hero Fund. As early as 1886, he helped to erect a statue in Dunfermline to commemorate William Hunter, who died there in the rescue of a young boy. Carnegie also established a private pension list, by which he supported those who enjoyed his admiration or affection. Finally, his interest in world peace encouraged him to offer civilian heroes the recognition and support typically afforded military heroes.

The Harwick Mine disaster gave Carnegie a final push to organize the Hero Fund. (That story is well told in these pages.) When he turned his mind to this task, he neatly resolved the varied life influences that motivated him and conceived for it a mission that is simple, morally sound, and fundamentally attuned to our nature as human beings.

Carnegie's criteria for the medal focused on the purest and most altruistic heroism, undertaken with no motive or reward beyond the desire to save another human life. The affirmative test is this: *The rescuer must leave a place of safety and knowingly risk death to save the life of another, without obligation to do so.*

In our time we often use the word "hero" casually to describe sports figures and others who perform competently in their fields of endeavor, but who are usually not subjected to physical risk in their efforts. Carnegie reserved his medal for more serious acts. Beyond that, he and the Hero Fund developed criteria that further illuminate their vision of heroic behavior.

- The award is not made to professional rescuers who act in the line of duty. Police, firefighters, and lifeguards often act courageously in the course of their work, but it is their job to do so, and their services often have their own system of awards to recognize exceptional bravery. For the same reasons, the award is not made to members of the military.

- The award is not made to a rescuer who put the rescued in danger in the first place. The rescuer is under a moral obligation to remedy the situation.

- Rescuers generally do not receive the award for acting on behalf of immediate family members, again because they have an obligation of care. The exception is that an award is possible if the rescuer is severely injured or dies in the attempt.

- The award is not made to children so young, or adults so intoxicated, that they don't understand the risk they are taking.

- Finally, the award is not made if the rescuer saves his own life as well as that of others. For example, an individual aboard a runaway train may show great daring by hanging from the side of the locomotive and reaching among the drive wheels to reconnect a brake line. But the rescuer, doomed as everyone else, did not "leave a place of safety" to perform the act. Indeed, the rescuer would receive a powerful personal benefit (i.e., survival) even if no one else were aboard the train.

In other words, we look for informed, conscious choices (what you might call moral choices) to do very dangerous things that benefit others.

Sometimes rules are just rules. In the case of the Hero Fund, the rules drive home the central question of altruism in general and heroism in particular. Why will humans take mortal risks to save others, when there is no possible benefit to themselves or their own descendants? This confounds scientists and philosophers who study human evolution to understand current behavior. Why doesn't the relentless, morally neutral force of Darwinian selection eliminate from our species any tendency to take heroic but mortal risks? These risks clearly reduce the odds that the hero will survive to produce and care for children. Natural selection should favor those who stand aside and watch. Yet heroes arise among us today as they have throughout recorded history. Something wonderfully unscientific is at work here.

Carnegie hinted that our social evolution—our culture, religion, and civilization—has made it more possible for individuals to act heroically.

I believe that the potential for heroism is a critical component of man's spiritual nature that sets him apart from the other species of God's creation. Remember, though, that the "Carnegie" definition of a hero has a tough requirement of informed and conscious choice.

When Carnegie established the Commission, he made a clear statement of what he considered to be of enduring value in human character. Much has changed in our society since 1904, including many of our values. Through all of that change, it is remarkable that in our modern society we still need heroes, we still find them in our midst, and we still honor their acts and spirit.

Mark Laskow
President

Harwick Mine,
Jan 25 190

by CAROL BLEIER

I

A TRAGEDY DEEP BELOW GROUND
INSPIRED ANDREW CARNEGIE TO ESTABLISH A FUND
TO HONOR THE "HEROES OF CIVILIZATION."

S hortly after eight o'clock on the morning of January 25, 1904, a day that dawned bitterly cold in southwestern Pennsylvania and in the hamlet of Harwick, a mining town 15 miles northeast of Pittsburgh and home to the Allegheny Coal Company's Harwick Mine, a massive explosion tore through the 200-foot-deep mine, claiming the lives of 179 miners, many of them teen-age boys. The accident—"as if the earth had suddenly parted and had broken in two"[1]—still ranks as one of the worst in U.S. coal-mining history. In the following days, the disaster laid claim to two more lives, men who had entered the mine in rescue attempts.

Andrew Carnegie, then retired and living in New York, was soon made aware of the disaster. It touched him deeply. By March 12, only six weeks after the explosion, he had penned a document—a "deed of trust"—that would serve as the philosophical basis for the establishment of his newest philanthropy, the Carnegie Hero Fund Commission. "Gentlemen," it began, "we live in a heroic age."

Southwestern Pennsylvania at the turn of the 19th century was rich in bituminous coal deposits. Numerous mines and company-owned towns to house the miners were developed to feed the great demand for coal by the iron and steel manufacturers of Pittsburgh. Selwyn M. Taylor, member of a prominent city family, was a well-known mining engineer and consultant to coal companies, including the Allegheny Coal Company, and it was he who had drawn the plans for the Harwick Mine. He had equipped it with powerful ventilation, and, by commencement of operations in the latter part of 1902, the mine was reputedly one

(PREVIOUS SPREAD)
MEN GATHER TO
IDENTIFY SOME OF
THE KILLED MINERS
SOON AFTER THE
EXPLOSION AT THE
HARWICK MINE.

(FACING PAGE)
THE TIPPLE OF THE
HARWICK MINE.

of the safer ones. Nevertheless, the industry was especially dangerous. A lack of regulation, limited equipment, and inexperienced miners—often immigrants of differing tongues—led to mistake and accident. The workforce at Harwick was mainly Hungarian, but Italian, Polish, and German miners also labored alongside English and American ones. Contemporary reports also noted that the mine at Harwick was gas-filled and dusty.

AN EXPLOSION THAT SHOOK THE EARTH

On the morning of the disaster, the circulation of fresh air in the mine had been cut off by the formation of ice at the bottom of the airshaft, allowing the accumulation of methane, a highly volatile gas. Coal dust, which is extremely flammable, was also present. A dynamite charge used to break up the coal ignited the deadly combination. In the words of a report by the Department of Mines of Pennsylvania:

> The shot…lighted the gas, which, by the fine particles of coal dust suspended in the air, traveled into every place in the mine like a streak of lightening [sic], carrying destruction in its path, until it finally expended its force up the air and hoisting shafts…. The entire population of the village was in an uproar, and the utmost excitement prevailed. The explosion had been one of terrific force. The tipple, which was built of iron, was wrecked, the cages were blown out of the shaft, and a mule that had been at the bottom of the shaft was caught by the force of the explosion and blown out and over the tipple, a distance of about 300 feet. The accident had destroyed the organization that existed among the officials, as the mine foreman and the fire boss as well as almost all the employees had been killed. The officials who were present and had escaped the disaster seemed to be dazed and without confidence in themselves.[2]

The village suddenly came to know horror, confusion, panic, fear, and dread. Weeping, grieving women and children milled about the mine complex. Scores of caskets filled with bodies burned beyond recognition were soon being taken on sleds to the town's frame schoolhouse, turned morgue. The entire local mine workers organization had been wiped out, and with the mine foreman and fire boss killed by the explosion, there could only be speculation as to what had happened. An investigation into the cause of the explosion quickly got under way.

Harwick
mine
Disaster
January 2, 1904

MANY OF THE KILLED
MINERS, SEVERAL OF
WHOSE FAMILIES
COULD NOT AFFORD A
TRADITIONAL BURIAL,

Adolf Gunia
THE ONLY
SURVIVOR OF
THE HARWICK
MINE
JAN 25

Immediate calls went out for volunteers and aid. When Taylor, 42, learned of the disaster, he hurried from his Pittsburgh office to the site and offered his services. There are conflicting reports on when the first rescue attempt was made. One said it was at 4 p.m., but the two men involved were driven back by the foul air. Taylor and his assistant, James McCann, and another man were lowered into the mine an hour later. Some 40 minutes later, McCann was hoisted in the cage. With him was the explosion's sole survivor, 16-year-old Adolph Gunia. McCann reported that Taylor had collapsed from afterdamp, an asphyxiating mixture of residual gases after an explosion, and that he had attempted to bring him to the bottom of the shaft but had been driven back by the gas. Taylor was soon found and brought to the surface, but he died early the next day. The community was so taken by his sacrifice that many accompanied his sled-drawn casket from the mine to the Cheswick railroad station. A newspaper article said of Taylor: "Himself, he had not a single thought of. His way was to save or die. He died."[3] Taylor left a wife and stepson.

DANIEL A. LYLE

SELWYN M. TAYLOR

Gunia, a German immigrant, lost both his father and brother in the accident. Brought out severely burned—described as more dead than alive—he was semiconscious and at first thought to have been blinded by the explosion. He spent four months in the hospital and bore the resulting deep scars from head to toe throughout his life. Interviewed shortly after he was rescued, Gunia said, "I saw a sheet of flame coming from back in the mine. I ran. Something seemed to hit me in the middle of my back. I fell unconscious and cannot remember anything until McCann picked me up."[4] Eventually he returned to coal mining, but, according to his grandson Bruce Gunia, he never worked underground again, and he discouraged his three sons from becoming coal miners. Adolph Gunia died of cancer in 1935 at the age of 49.

The day following the explosion, coal miner Daniel A. Lyle, 43, answered an appeal for volunteers and rushed to the scene from Leechburg, a small town 15 miles away. Although he suffered asthma and was aware of the dangerous conditions in the mine, Lyle and two other men worked from late afternoon well into the night, going deeper into the mine than other volunteers to look for survivors. The other two men surfaced the next morning and reported that Lyle, like Taylor, had been fatally overcome by afterdamp.

CHAOS AND COMPASSION

The calamity was sensational news, and vivid photos and bold front-page headlines underscored its scope. Charges of negligence and inefficiency arose and were bitterly contested by the government and the coal company. There was controversy over the loss of the fire boss's inspection report and debate about whether the dynamite was misplaced, misfired, or incorrectly tamped. State mine inspector Frederick W. Cunningham and mine superintendent Wilfred Snowden were later arrested on charges of murder and held for a grand jury. Both men were eventually released.

Benevolence developed, as well. The Cheswick Relief Committee was organized and more than $40,000 was soon collected from the general public for the bereaved families. Carnegie responded with matching funds. But it was the rescue efforts of Taylor and Lyle that compelled him to put form to his idea of many years, that of recognizing acts of selfless heroism. A report Carnegie received on Lyle's death noted: "Lyle made a valiant effort to rescue entombed men. He left a widow and five children. What a tragedy that his life had to go with his deed! He was a hero."[5] Carnegie directed that gold medals be struck and presented to the families of the two fallen rescuers "in commemoration of the acts of heroism…wherein they sacrificed their lives in an endeavor to save their fellowman [sic]."[6]

HARWICK'S MINERS WILL ALWAYS BE REMEMBERED

One hundred years after the disaster, the Harwick Mine and miners are far from forgotten, kept in memory by poem and news feature. The *New Kensington Daily Dispatch* in the winter of 1958 ran a series on the explosion entitled, "This Was The Day The Valley Wept." The articles were reprints from a pamphlet written shortly after the disaster to raise funds for the families of the deceased miners. The son of a man who helped bury the dead in 1904 provided the pamphlet to the paper.

Monuments to the miners have also been erected over the years. A stone memorial was placed by the United Mine Workers of America in front of a plot donated by the Allegheny Coal Company for the bodies of many of the miners. It is adjacent to a power plant on the Allegheny River just a few miles from the mine and near where its coal was once burned. In 1996, the Pennsylvania Historical and Museum Commission placed a roadside marker just north of the small road leading to the mass grave. It commemorates the establishment of the Carnegie Hero Fund Commission and the heroic acts following the explosion that led to the Commission's founding. In 1999, the Harwick community dedicated a memorial to all of its miners. It is a large, handsome block of black granite, etched with a rendering of the mine's tipple and shaft buildings, and is situated in the center of a small parklet. Carved into the bricks surrounding the memorial are the names of individual miners.

Crumbling stone walls, a few rails, and some concrete pads—perhaps the floor of the iron tipple—are the only remains of the once busy mine. The entry shaft is covered with a concrete slab and enclosed with a chain-link fence. A cable cordons off a grassy, grown-over roadway leading through a few sparse trees and underbrush to the site. The mine was closed in 1970.

ON JANUARY 25, 2004, MARK LASKOW, COMMISSION PRESIDENT, JUST LEFT OF THE STONE MEMORIAL, AND OTHERS VISIT THE MASS GRAVE TO COMMEMORATE THE 100TH ANNIVERSARY OF THE HARWICK MINE DISASTER.

"…I intend some day to do something for such heroes as we have been reading about. Heroes in civic life should be recognized, as well as those whom governments call heroes because they have distinguished themselves in battle."

Andrew Carnegie

ANDREW CARNEGIE

by CAROL BLEIER

II

"I DON'T BELIEVE THERE'S A NOBLER FUND
IN THE WORLD." — *Andrew Carnegie*

I t crawled up my ain back,"[1] Andrew Carnegie said of the
Carnegie Hero Fund Commission, his unique philanthropic
endeavor to honor acts of heroism. "I cherish a fatherly
regard for it since no one suggested it to me, and as far as I
know, it never has been thought of."[2] He remained interested in the Commission's work for the rest of his life and
took a special pride in its accomplishments. When
he received letters from Carnegie Medal awardees or their families, he acknowledged, "These are the precious jewels of my life.
I love the Hero Fund because it is my ain bairn [child]."[3]

Carnegie's meteoric rise in iron and steel manufacturing
to become one of the richest men in the world at the turn of the
20th century is well known. Not as familiar is the far-reaching distribution of his wealth, and lesser still the establishment of the
Carnegie Hero Fund Commission and his ideas behind it. One of
his favorite quotations was an old proverb, "The gods send thread
for a web begun."[4] Carnegie's web of honoring "heroes of peace"
started gathering threads in childhood.

He was born on November 25, 1835, in the attic of a small stone
cottage in the ancient town of Dunfermline, once the capital of
Scotland. Carnegie cherished his humble birthplace, as he did his
country's ballads, poetry, and the legendary courageous tales of
Scotland's independence. In his autobiography, Carnegie said of
his origins: "Even then, and till [one's] last day, the early impres-
sions remain. ...They are always rising and coming again to the
front to exert their influence to elevate his thought and color his

mind."[5] He found literary heroes such as Robert Burns and heroes among the daring Scottish patriots, particularly William Wallace, and noted: "It is a tower of strength for a boy to have a hero."[6]

More personally, he thought of his mother, Margaret, as heroic. While his father, William, a handloom weaver, toiled in a declining occupation, his thrifty and practical mother took care of the family. She tended a small grocery shop in their home during the day and stitched shoes in the evening. She went on to play a dominant role in Carnegie's business and personal life, precluding his marrying until age 51, after she died. He dedicated his first book: "To my favorite Heroine My Mother."[7]

Carnegie revealed an instinct for his future business ventures while still a young boy in Scotland by organizing his friends to work for him. He kept pigeons and rabbits and wanted his companions to help with their care. Their compensation, since Carnegie had no money, was to bestow their names upon any new rabbits if they would feed them. His plan worked. "Precious knowledge this is for man to possess," he later wrote. "I did not understand steam machinery, but I tried to understand that much more complicated piece of mechanism—man."[8]

When Carnegie was 12, his family decided to follow relatives who had emigrated to America. With borrowed funds, the family, which included Carnegie's four-year-old brother, Tom, found its way in 1848 to Allegheny, a city just across the river from Pittsburgh and now its North Side neighborhood. The area the Carnegies now called home was dismally dirty, overcrowded, and disease-infested. Pittsburgh, without an adequate water system, had been devastated just three years earlier by a major fire. Yet new immigrants, especially Irish, Scotch, and German youths escaping from poverty in their homelands, were willing to take risks and work hard in their new land, where, despite the challenging conditions, they saw unlimited opportunities.

Enthusiastic, self-confident, and likable, Carnegie advanced rapidly from his first job, as a bobbin boy in a smelly, dank cotton mill, making $1.20 a week, to work as a messenger for a Pittsburgh telegraph office. Exhibiting his foresight and a willingness to try new things, he learned Morse code and became a telegraph operator. The job brought him at the age of 17 to the attention of Thomas A. Scott, superintendent of the Western

Division of the Pennsylvania Railroad, who hired him as his clerk and operator. Only six years later, in 1859, Carnegie took over Scott's position. He resigned that job in 1865 at the age of 29 to go into business for himself. "I was determined to make a fortune," Carnegie declared.[9] He chose an auspicious time to build his empire.

Pittsburgh after the Civil War was a busy, prosperous, and growing city. With railroads expanding westward and few or ineffectual government restraints, Carnegie was free to marshal his abundant talents. He accumulated wealth quickly, focusing initially on investing in companies that manufactured sleeping cars, built bridges, and expanded telegraphy. In 1867, a couple of years after he organized the first of his many companies, he left Pittsburgh and moved to New York. There, in a startling show of self-analysis in the midst of his business success, Carnegie sat down at a desk in his room at the St. Nicholas Hotel and reflected on the value of making more money. He wrote a note to himself: "Thirty-three and an income of 50,000$ per annum.... Beyond this never earn—make no effort to increase fortune, but spend the surplus each year for benovelent [sic] purposes.... Man must have an idol—The amassing of wealth is one of the worst species of idolitary [sic].... I will resign business at thirty-five."[10] The note, which surfaced after Carnegie's death, had remained in the desk forgotten. Instead of ending his career at the age of 35, he was about to move into the steel business, which would add exponentially to his wealth.

Though not physically imposing, at five feet three with sparkling pale eyes and a ruddy complexion, Carnegie was a fierce competitor. With innovative thinking and keen insight into human nature, he initiated a vertical business structure headed by family members, friends, and ambitious young men among whom he inspired loyalty. He frequently trusted them to manage his business affairs while he traveled abroad, often for months at a time.

Carnegie focused on new trends in manufacturing processes and techniques. He brought the Bessemer steel process from England to America, lowered the price of steel by keeping production costs down, and reinvested profits back into his businesses for improvements and expansion. He sought to produce the best products at the lowest costs. Carnegie pushed his workers hard; few workers survived in his plants past the age of 40. While he was starting to grow his fortune, he was not thinking of charity. "I was in business to make money. I was not a philanthropist at all. When rails were high we got the highest prices we could get. When they were low we met the lowest price we had to meet."[11]

His business acumen, however, was only part of a multi-faceted persona. Growing up among a lively family of readers and political activists concerned with theology and workers' rights, he became a self-taught Renaissance man who retained lifelong interests in literature, philosophy, and world politics. A voracious reader and a raconteur with a quick wit, Carnegie often expressed strong opinions on numerous subjects beyond his business exper-tise, writing and cajoling kings and presidents, and vigorously promoting ideas that ranged from the simplified spelling of the English language to pacifism. He was, however, pragmatic and adaptable. When Congress declared war on Germany on April 6, 1917, Carnegie wrote to President Woodrow Wilson, "You have triumphed at last. God bless you. You will give the world peace and rank the greatest hero of all."[12]

Although he seldom had doubts in making business deci-sions, Carnegie was periodically conflicted over his prosperity and how he was achieving it. Though not religious, he worried about his soul and self-respect. Another of his favorite quotations came from Robert Burns: "Thine own reproach alone do fear."[13] He was greatly anguished over the Homestead strike and was haunted by it until the day he died. The July 6, 1892, confrontation between workers of the Homestead mill and the Pinkerton National Detective Agency would later cause Carnegie to write: "Nothing I have had to meet in all my life, before or since, wounded me so deeply."[14] He had, paradoxically, great admiration for the com-mon man, choosing his heroes and businesses' presidents from among them. Carnegie also admired those who treated others well. During the Civil War, he met and lauded Abraham Lincoln: "I never met a great man who thoroughly made himself one with all men as Mr. Lincoln. He was the most perfect Democrat, revealing in every work and act the equality of men."[15]

In 1886, Carnegie made his first overture toward rewarding heroic action. He contributed to the cost of a monument erected in a cemetery in Dunfermline in memory of a young man, William Hunter, who died while attempting to save a boy from drowning.

In words very similar to those he used when founding the Hero Fund years later, he wrote, "The false heroes of barbarous man are those who can only boast of the destruction of their fellows. The true heroes of civilization are those alone who save or greatly serve them."[16]

At the age of 65 in 1901, Carnegie sold the Carnegie Company to investment banker J. Pierpont Morgan, who merged it into his recently formed United States Steel Corporation. "An opportunity to retire came to me unsought, which I considered my duty to accept," he wrote to the people of Pittsburgh in a letter published in the newspapers. "I have always thought that old age should be spent, not as the Scotch say 'in making mickle mair' but in making good use of what has been acquired...."[17] The plan to give away most of his fortune had taken root in 1889 when he wrote "The Gospel of Wealth," an essay in which he stated his belief that, beyond providing for a family's needs, excess wealth should be regarded as a trust fund to be used for the benefit of the community.

With this original concept that the rich have a responsibility for the improvement of society, Carnegie encouraged other millionaires to dispense of their wealth. "The man who dies thus rich, dies disgraced."[18] He frowned on indiscriminate handouts, or "soup kitchens," but believed instead that philanthropy should be for those who would help themselves or mankind, and should be organized as rationally and systematically as business. For the last 19 years of his life, he distributed most of his wealth with the same determination and organization that he used to acquire it, hoping it would benefit others and soften the criticism that had pursued him during his business career.

Carnegie's early thinking on heroism remained. A few years after retiring, he was having lunch with his friend, educator Dr. William J. Holland, on a day when news accounts were detailing a dramatic rescue from a burning building. "I intend some day to do something for such heroes as we have been reading about," Carnegie told him. "Heroes in civic life should be recognized, as well as those whom governments call heroes because they have distinguished themselves in battle."[19]

Thus, when Carnegie heard about the tragic coal mine accident in Harwick, he sent some of his former business associates to investigate. He could not get the disaster at the Harwick

Mine out of his mind, especially of the two men who had gone into the mine in separate rescue attempts and also lost their lives. Finally, after years of lamenting how little the world regarded heroic deeds by those in peaceful vocations, the tragedy in Harwick galvanized Carnegie to act.

It was fitting that Pittsburgh should be the headquarters for his new idea. There he could put in place a board composed of men he knew well and trusted completely to run the new institution, such as his second cousin Thomas Morrison and close friends and business associates Robert Pitcairn, Thomas N. Miller, and William L. Abbott.

Although he had left Pittsburgh for New York City 37 years earlier, Carnegie remained deeply involved and interested in the city's well-being: "Pittsburgh entered the core of my heart when I was a boy and cannot be torn out...how best to serve Pittsburgh is the question which recurs to me almost every day of my life."[20] He gave numerous gifts to the city, including Carnegie Institute, which comprises a museum, library, art gallery, and music hall, and a technical school, now Carnegie Mellon University. In a letter to a friend in 1897, Carnegie wrote, "Mrs. Carnegie and I derive the sweetest of all our satisfactions from our Pittsburgh benefactions."[21]

Since Carnegie envisioned the Hero Fund to include pensions for widows and children of deceased heroes, he turned to close friend and former business associate Charles L. Taylor, who then headed two pension funds established by Carnegie. In a letter to Taylor dated March 12, 1904, in which Carnegie touched on several issues concerning the soon-to-be-formed Hero Fund, he concluded, "I have thought over the idea for years, and the Harwick mine disaster brought it to a head, because in the interval I had found you, as the right man wanted, to put the idea into successful operation, another proof that 'The gods send thread for a web begun.'"[22]

Carnegie wanted to do something for those who with little thought risked their lives to save others, sometimes dying and thereby bringing financial hardship on their families. In correspondence, he made it clear that the purpose of the Hero Fund was "for watching, applauding, and *supporting*," emphasis his. The reward, he said, should be for "heroic action wherever displayed and [by] whomever displayed, white or black, male or female— at least this is my hope."[23]

Just as he had kept close watch on his business affairs, Carnegie scrutinized Hero Fund board minutes and maintained constant communications with the Commission. Through telegrams, transatlantic cables, and typewritten correspondence, often with added comments in a blunt lead pencil or black ink in the margins of the letters, he congratulated the board on its work, and urged its members to publicize their efforts and investigate cases quickly. Displaying his sense of humor, after dispensing some advice to the Commission's manager Frank M. Wilmot on how to handle newspaper reporters, he impishly added in the letter to the left of his signature: "No charge."[24]

He gave opinions on who should receive awards, made clear his intention was for "well-proved cases" and not "self-dubbed heroes,"[25] and urged that the Commission should not interpret his instructions too narrowly. In spite of his interference and prodding, he prophetically expected this board of trustees, like all his other boards, to conduct affairs as they saw fit. "Conditions upon the erth [sic] inevitably change; hence, no wise man will bind Trustees forever to certain paths, causes, or institutions. I disclaim any intention of doing so. On the contrary, I giv [sic] my Trustees full authority to change policy or causes hitherto aided, from time to time, when this, in their opinion has become necessary or desirable. They shall best conform to my wishes by using their own judgment."[26]

Carnegie was very fond of the Hero Fund. "It is the fund that may be considered my pet. I used to hate that word, because the children at school cald [sic] me Martin's [his teacher] pet, but now I like it."[27] At another time he wrote, "I don't believe there's a nobler fund in the world."[28] With the success of the Hero Fund, he created similar organizations in the United Kingdom, France, Germany, Belgium, the Netherlands, Sweden, Switzerland, Italy, Norway, and Denmark. All but the German fund remain in operation.

Carnegie died on August 11, 1919, from pneumonia at his summer home, Shadowbrook, in Lenox, Massachusetts. His wife, Louise, lived until 1946, turning over at her death their New York mansion at 2 East 91st to the Carnegie Corporation of New York. It is presently the Cooper-Hewitt, National Design Museum. On the walls of Carnegie's former library, now the museum shop, are some of his favorite quotations, including "The gods send thread for a web begun."

On the last day of the 19th century, Carnegie, still hoping for the existence of only heroes of peace and not of war, wrote: "All goes well, upward and onward. I believe that as the twentieth century closes, the earth will be purged of its foulest stain, the killing of men by men in battle under the name of war and that the profession of arms, hitherto the most and until recently the only profession thought worthy of a gentleman, will be held the most dishonorable of all and unworthy of any being in human form. To kill a man in that day will be considered as disgusting as we in this day consider it disgusting to eat one." [29]

While that belief has not been realized, Carnegie's vision for a better world is being kept alive through the trusts and institutions he endowed. Numbering 22, they were funded with $350 million—most of his wealth—to advance human endeavors in education, science, the arts, and world peace. The largest is the Carnegie Corporation of New York. Among the smallest is the Carnegie Hero Fund Commission, which is still following the Deed of Trust penned by Carnegie in 1904. "My chief happiness... lies in the thot [*sic*] that even after I pass away the welth [*sic*] that came to me to administer as a sacred trust for the good of my fellow men is to continue to benefit humanity for generations untold." [30]

31 May 1905
AN EXCERPT FROM A LETTER
TO CHARLES L. TAYLOR

Your cable made me very happy. You
have made a start, and there is to be
no finish—it goes on forever. There is
not much good to be done in the world
without publicity. You must attract the
attention of the people. This leads them
to think and to appreciate the work that
you are doing, and finally to stir within
themselves the desire to go and do
likewise. In all cases where heroism is
displayed, the action should be prompt
so far as injury is concerned. Your agent
should be on the ground by the first
train, looking into matters.

ANDREW CARNEGIE

DEED OF TRUST

12 Mar. 1904
NEW YORK CITY, NEW YORK
TO THE HERO FUND COMMISSION

GENTLEMEN: We live in a heroic age. Not seldom are we thrilled by deeds of heroism where men or women are injured or lose their lives in attempting to preserve or rescue their fellows; such the heroes of civilization. The heroes of barbarism maimed or killed theirs.

I have long felt that the heroes and those dependent upon them should be freed from pecuniary cares resulting from their heroism, and, as a fund for this purpose, I have transferred to the Commission five million dollars of First Collateral Five Per Cent. Bonds of the United States Steel Corporation, the proceeds to be used as follows:

FIRST. To place those following peaceful vocations, who have been injured in heroic effort to save human life, in somewhat better positions pecuniarily than before, until again able to work. In the case of death, the widow and children, or other dependents, to be provided for until she remarries, and the children until they reach a self-supporting age. For exceptional children exceptional grants may be made for exceptional education. Grants of sums of money may also be made to heroes or heroines as the Commission thinks advisable—each case to be judged on its merits.

SECOND. No grant is to be continued unless it be soberly and properly used, and the recipients remain respectable, well-behaved members of the community, but the heroes and heroines are to be given a fair trial, no matter what their antecedents. Heroes deserve pardon and a fresh start.

THIRD. A medal shall be given to the hero, or widow, or next of kin, which shall recite the heroic deed it commemorates, that descendants may know and be proud of their descent. The medal shall be given for the heroic act, even if the doer be uninjured, and also a sum of money, should the Commission deem such gift desirable.

FOURTH. Many cities provide pensions for policemen, firemen, teachers, and others, and some may give rewards for acts of heroism. All these and other facts the Commission will take into account and act accordingly in making grants. Nothing could be further from my intention than to deaden or interfere with these most creditable provisions, doubly precious as showing public and municipal appreciation of faithful and heroic service. I ask from the Commission most careful guard against this danger. The medal can, of course, be offered in such cases. Whether something more can not judiciously be done, at the request of, or with the approval of, the city authorities, the Commission shall determine. I hope there can be.

FIFTH. The claims upon the Fund for some years can not exhaust it. After years, however, pensioners will become numerous. Should the Commission find, after allowing liberally for this, that a surplus will remain, it has power to make grants in case of accidents (preferably where a hero has appeared) to those injured. The action taken in the recent Harwick Mine accident, where Heroes Taylor and Lyle lost their lives, is an illustration. The community first raised a fund of forty thousand dollars, which was duplicated by me after waiting until the generosity of the community had full scope. Here again the Commission should be exceedingly careful, as in this case, not to deaden, but to stimulate employers or communities to do their part, for such action benefits givers themselves as well as recipients.

SIXTH. It seems probable that cities and employers on this continent will ultimately be placed under similar conditions to those of Britain, Germany, and other European States, and required to provide against accidents to employees. Therefore, the Commission, by a two-thirds vote, may devote any surplus that accrues beyond providing for heroes and their dependents (which provision must never be abandoned) to such other modes of benefiting those in want, chiefly caused through no fault of their own (such as drunkenness, laziness, crimes, etc.) but through exceptional circumstances, in such manner and to such extent as the Commission thinks advisable and likely to do more good than if such sums were given to those injured by accident, where the latter may be suitably provided for by law, or otherwise.

SEVENTH. The field embraced by the Fund is the United States of America, the Dominion of Canada, the Colony of Newfoundland, and the waters thereof. The sea is the scene of many heroic acts. No action more heroic than that of doctors and nurses volunteering their services in the case of epidemics. Railroad employees are remarkable for heroism. All these and similar cases are embraced. Whenever heroism is displayed by man or woman in saving human life, the Fund applies.

EIGHTH. No personal liability will attach to members for any act of the Commission. The Commission has power to fill vacancies.

NINTH. The Commission has full power to sell, invest, or reinvest all funds; to employ all officials, including Secretary, traveling agents to visit and oversee beneficiaries, etc. and to fix their compensation. Members of the Commission shall be reimbursed all expenses incurred, including traveling expenses attending meetings. The President shall be granted such honoraria as the Commission thinks proper and as he can be prevailed upon to accept.

TENTH. An annual report, including a detailed statement of sums and medals granted and the reasons therefor, shall be made each year and published in at least one newspaper in the principal cities of the countries embraced by the Fund. A finely executed roll of the heroes and heroines shall be kept displayed in the office at Pittsburgh.

Andrew Carnegie

ANDREW CARNEGIE
Witness, Louise Whitfield Carnegie

THE FIRST HERO

17 July 1904
SULPHUR POND
WILKINSBURG, PENNSYLVANIA

C. H. 1

Sunday, July 17, 1904, was a warm, sunny day, and as was typical, boys from Wilkinsburg, a small community that borders Pittsburgh on its eastern side, decided to go swimming in nearby Sulphur Pond. The pond was in a deep ravine on a farm and had been created by the dumping of slack from a mine that had been abandoned 15 to 20 years earlier. When the mine was producing, the pond's water was used to operate some of its machinery.

Shortly after noon, brothers Charles and Harry Stevick came to the Baumann home and asked **LOUIS A. BAUMANN, JR.**, 17, and his brother Robert to go swimming with them. They agreed, and on the way to the pond they met up with six other boys, who joined them. Soon after reaching the pond, all of the boys except Charles took a quick dip. A short time later, when the boys were out of the water—Baumann and another boy on one side and the other boys on the opposite bank—Charles decided to dive into the pond. When he surfaced, he cried for help and then submerged.

Baumann immediately dived into the pond, but when he reached Charles, Charles grabbed his leg. Baumann broke free and returned to the bank to regain his breath. He swam back out and dived for Charles, then took him to the surface, but Charles again grabbed Baumann and both submerged. Again Baumann broke free and returned to the bank. A third time he swam out to Charles, that time managing to get Charles close enough to the bank for the other boys, who formed a chain, to drag both from the water.

Charles was unconscious, and thought dead by the other boys, but after several minutes he recovered. Baumann was winded and exhausted from his efforts. He was the first person to be awarded the Carnegie Medal *(see next page).* FILE NO: 201

LOUIS A. BAUMANN, JR.

A 100-YEAR RELATIONSHIP

The case of Louis A. Baumann, Jr. first came to the attention of the Hero Fund in a letter written by his father on September 15, 1904, in which he briefly recounted his son's rescue act. Also signing the letter were six of the young Baumann's friends, who were at the scene and had witnessed the rescue.

Frank Wilmont, the Hero Fund's manager, responded by requesting additional information, and within two days the father wrote back providing a more detailed description of the rescue. The case was then investigated, and, at the May 15, 1905, meeting of the Commission's Executive Committee, the awarding of the bronze medal to Baumann was approved. Eight more medals were awarded that day, including one to Ernestine F. Atwood, 17, the first female awardee. Since the design of the medal and its manufacturer were issues still undecided, it was March of 1907 before Baumann received his medal.

The Commission and the Baumann family have been in contact with each other from time to time since the medal was presented. A long letter from Baumann's brother Robert arrived in 1911, explaining that Baumann was suffering from rheumatism and that his health was worsening. A doctor confirmed the illness in another letter at that time and further stated that Baumann was suffering from a chronic heart condition. Later that year, another doctor sent the Commission an invoice for $3 for a physical examination of Baumann, and the Commission assumed the cost.

It would be 47 years before the Commission again heard from the family. Baumann's sister, Anna, inquired in 1958 about her brother's heroic act, and the Commission confirmed that he was indeed the first recipient of the Carnegie Medal. Twenty years later, brother William wrote to inform that the medal had been stolen. Proof of the theft was provided, and the Commission had a duplicate medal struck.

In 1996, Baumann's nephew, Ronald Hitchon, made inquiry and was sent copies of documents from Baumann's file. In turn, Hitchon in 2003 provided the Commission with additional information on Baumann and his family. He also noted that Baumann died of heart disease at the age of 35 on March 14, 1925, and that his son, James, who was born the previous year, was living in the Arizona State Veterans Home in Phoenix.

Job Pa Sept 15
1904

To Whome it may concern

On the 17th of July 1904 While in swiming
with companions one Charls Stevick got
into the deep Watter and was drownding
Louis A Baumann jr of Penn Township
rescued him after severe strugle. in the
First atempt was taken down with him but
Succeded in getting away and made a
Second atempt and got him out in time
to save his life. he was unconscious when
he got him out. the undersigned Were

Witness
Timothy Welsh.
Arthur Smeltz
Joe Welsh.
Harry Stevick
Robert Baumann.
Louis Möller -

Louis A Baumann

Job Pa

WILLIAM L.
ABBOTT

EDWIN H.
ANDERSON

EDWARD M.
BIGELOW

WILLIAM WALLACE
BLACKBURN

JOSEPH
BUFFINGTON

WILLIAM N. FREW

WILLIAM J.
HOLLAND

JOHN BEARD
JACKSON

THOMAS LYNCH

CHARLES C.
MELLOR

THOMAS N.
MILLER

THOMAS
MORRISON

FREDERICK C.
PERKINS

ROBERT PITCAIRN

HENRY KIRKE
PORTER

JAMES H. REED

WILLIAM LUCIEN
SCAIFE

WILLIAM SCOTT

WILLIAM H.
STEVENSON

CHARLES L.
TAYLOR

FRANK M.
WILMOT

by MARY BRIGNANO

III

When does an institution actually begin? While it is still an idea in the mind of its creator... or when others bring that idea to life?

Perhaps the Carnegie Hero Fund Commission began in earnest on a winter day early in 1904 when Andrew Carnegie summoned two Pittsburghers, Charles L. Taylor and Frank M. Wilmot, to his New York mansion. Taylor (1857–1922), an innovative metallurgist, had been one of Carnegie's "young geniuses," his partners in building the largest steel operation in the world. Wilmot (1872–1930) was a gifted and dedicated administrator. The two were chairman and manager, respectively, of the Carnegie Relief Fund, and they had come prepared to discuss the terrible explosion that had occurred just days ago at Harwick, Pennsylvania. One hundred and seventy-nine coal miners had lost their lives, and two more men had died while heroically trying to rescue those underground.

Carnegie had created his $4 million Relief Fund in 1901, immediately after selling the Carnegie Company and receiving bonds worth $225,639,000 par value of the new United States Steel Corporation.[1] He intended the fund to aid workers injured in "his" mills and provide small pensions for needy, aged employees.[2] In his autobiography he would proudly describe "this first gift of surplus wealth, four millions in first mortgage 5% bonds, upon retiring from business, as an acknowledgment of the deep debt which I owe to the workmen who have contributed so greatly to my success."[3] To oversee the fund, he had appointed Taylor, one of his "original boys, a working, not merely a preaching apostle of the gospel of service to his fellow men."[4]

Now a special bank vault had been constructed to hold Carnegie's bonds, yielding five percent annually, and the "industrial Napoleon" had set off on an exhilarating new campaign: the distribution of a massive fortune "in the manner … best calculated to produce the most beneficial results for the community."[5] He was personally inventing philanthropy on a scale the world had never seen, and with a strategy dear to the heart of this complex, multifaceted man. He aimed to provide "ladders upon which the aspiring can rise."[6] Whether through research, public libraries, technical schools, or museums, Carnegie preached that philanthropy could promote ideas and alter (he would say improve) public attitudes. Only the millions accumulated by a few men like himself and John D. Rockefeller made possible such industrial strength, "scientific" giving.[7]

And he was launching this new philanthropy from a 64-room mansion as innovative as its owner, who was famous for seizing on any new technology that would push his mills to produce ever more steel at ever-lower cost. Built far from New York's then-fashionable neighborhoods, 2 East 91st Street was the first private residence in the United States with a structural steel frame and also one of the first in New York with its own push-button electric passenger elevator. In the sub-basement, a miniature coal car ran on its own railroad track carrying a quarter-ton of coal from the 200-ton bin to the furnace.

Slim and silver-haired, Taylor was still as fascinated by innovation as he had been back in 1880, when the 23-year-old graduate of Lehigh University first arrived in Pittsburgh to help transform the industrial world. A pioneer steel chemist, he went to work at the new, ultra-modern Pittsburgh Bessemer Steel Works at Homestead. Carnegie bought this plant in 1883 — and set off yet another string of "firsts." Coupled with the Bessemer process, the nation's first basic open-hearth furnaces had enabled American steel production to outstrip any other country's by 1890, thanks largely to Carnegie's drive. Then Taylor and others had formulated lighter, stronger steels for new uses. The chemist had been among the first to develop steel for railroad-car construction, an advance that had made railroad transport safer and more profitable … and added millions to the Carnegie balance sheets.[8]

A secretary ushered Taylor and Wilmot into the great man's study, a personal room full of books, portraits, honors, awards, medals, and autographed photographs of kings, emperors, great writers, and statesmen. Beneath the coffered ceiling ran a panel painted with quotations that had inspired Carnegie over the years: "All is well since all grows better," "Thine own reproach alone do fear," "The highest form of worship is service to man," and another, particularly apt for this meeting, "The gods send thread for a web begun." [9] Carnegie was about to announce his plan for a wholly new benevolent purpose—a gift that would be "absolutely unique among the world's philanthropies of modern or ancient times." [10] He had decided to endow a fund of $5 million for heroes and their dependents, and he intended Taylor to supply the thread—the chemistry—that would put his idea into action.

"THE WHOLE IDEA OF MY HERO FUND IS IN THAT POEM"

The disaster at Harwick had struck him forcefully, Carnegie told his friends. He could not get the thought of the heroic would-be rescuers out of his mind, and he wanted to do something for the families they had left behind. These selfless men reminded him of a "true and beautiful poem" by "my dear, dear friend Richard Watson Gilder," the influential editor-in-chief of the *Century Monthly Magazine*. "I re-read it the morning after the accident, and resolved then to establish the Hero Fund," he would write in his autobiography.

Entitled "In the Time of Peace," the poem expressed Carnegie's conviction that just as much heroism was needed to save a life as to take one. The world was continually growing better, he believed, and in the progressive times to come, heroes would no longer be warriors. They would be women, children, scholars— "civic heroes" with "moral courage":

'Twas said: 'When roll of drum and battle's roar
Shall cease upon the earth, O, then no more

The deed—the race—of heroes in the land.'
But scarce that word was breathed when one small hand

Lifted victorious o'er a giant wrong
That had its victims crushed through ages long;

Some woman set her pale and quivering face
Firm as a rock against a man's disgrace;

A little child suffered in silence lest
His savage pain should wound a mother's breast;

Some quiet scholar flung his gauntlet down
And risked, in Truth's great name, the synod's frown;

A civic hero, in the realm of laws,
Did that which suddenly drew a world's applause;

And one to the pest his lithe young body gave
That he a thousand thousand lives might save.

"We have got to show young men that there are just as great battles to be fought in peace-time as in war-time and just as much opportunity for the hero," Carnegie told another friend, Frederick Lynch.[11] "I thought by creating this fund it would be one way of setting the world to thinking upon the heroism of civilization, getting its mind off the association of valor and heroism with war only."[12]

This then was Carnegie's challenge to Taylor and Wilmot: around one unusual idea—a major philanthropic endowment that would promote a new view of heroism—they were to formulate an organization "without parallel in the history of human benevolence." From one inspiring concept they would have to forge a practical and enduring structure. At a time when no large foundations existed as we know them today, they had to organize and administer a new kind of philanthropy...based on a concept that few shared or understood. And they would have to do it in the glare of publicity that always surrounded any Carnegie action.

LENGTHENED SHADOWS

Fortunately, they did not have to accomplish all this alone. When Carnegie finished outlining his plan, he produced a list of 21 individuals he had chosen to serve as his Hero Fund's first commissioners. Within weeks, on April 15, 1904, nearly all would meet for the first time in the Carnegie Building in Downtown Pittsburgh—and few men on earth were better prepared to give flesh to Carnegie's altruistic idea. It seems fitting that they gathered in one of Pittsburgh's first steel-framed skyscrapers, for the structure they forged has endured solidly for a century.

"An institution is the lengthened shadow of one man," Emerson wrote. The Carnegie Hero Fund Commission is in large part the lengthened shadow not only of Carnegie but also those of the founding commissioners. They laid the foundations on which the Commission has carried out its work, and they are a key to understanding why it has endured with little change for 100 years. They created models of organization and set standards of operating procedure. Their achievements changed philanthropy in America.

Although each of these first commissioners stands out, all shared similar traits. Each in his way was an innovator who by 1904 had helped make Pittsburgh the most advanced industrial center in the world at that time—the Silicon Valley of its era. Each had demonstrated unusual ability in managing a business or advancing the newest endeavors of their time—steel, railroads, electricity, and such civic improvements as universities, museums, urban parks, a symphony orchestra, and scientific societies. They were hardheaded, practical men of wide-ranging interests. They welcomed new ideas.

Men who dealt in facts and numbers, the first commissioners were nonetheless captivated by Carnegie's vision of the heroic potential in every human being. Developing a new, large-scale organization to promote a very personal ideal, they became innovators in advancing the systematic analysis, administration, and distribution of great wealth in America.

Handpicked by Carnegie, the first 21 commissioners were socially prominent men who were personally and in many cases intimately known to him. He could trust them to manage his idea and his capital—just as he had counted on his employees to advance his business. Three had risen with him from impoverished boyhoods in Allegheny, today Pittsburgh's North Side. Six had been his partners. Two were related to him through blood or marriage.

Ten—almost half—of them served as trustees of Carnegie Institute, his first major philanthropic enterprise. Established in 1895, this "radically new and different approach to cultural philanthropy" by 1904 comprised the Carnegie Library of Pittsburgh, the Carnegie Museums, and the Carnegie Institute of Technology, today's Carnegie Mellon University.[13]

If the commissioners all knew how to work with Carnegie by executing his ideas with immediacy, they were also comfortable with one another. Many served on boards together, saw each other daily at the Duquesne Club, lived in the same East End neighborhoods, or attended the same churches. Some were related: Taylor, for instance, was married to the daughter of Commissioner Robert Pitcairn, a close boyhood friend of Carnegie.

Most important, the original commissioners were forward-looking men who set great store by science and new technology. They believed in the rational, detailed observation and analysis of information. Several were amateur scientists; one was a professional scientist. Nearly all had advanced or invested in new technologies. In their lifetimes they had seen railroads unite the country and open vast markets. They had watched the telegraph, telephone, and ocean cables shrink the world, and electricity light homes and streets and power great machines. They had witnessed the improvements in health care that followed groundbreaking research into germ theory. Many had helped make steel "the structural metal of modern civilization."[14] They had contributed to civic advances that enhanced their city's image and quality of life—culture and education, safe drinking water, and the amazing display of dinosaur skeletons. They were confident that science was carrying civilization to new heights.

Perhaps what the first commissioners shared most profoundly was their pride in knowing that Carnegie had personally chosen each of them to serve. This fact is crucial to understanding the Hero Fund and how it has evolved. The Commission was and is a uniquely personal organization. Only serving commissioners select new commissioners—and thus there is an unbroken link to Carnegie and his inspiring idea. Commissioners feel and have felt honored to be asked to serve. "There is satisfaction that the work has followed the wishes of the founder, and that it has prospered," a commissioner wrote in 1935. "There is pride that the Fund, in exalting the fine qualities of heroism, has given inspiration and nobility to daily life."[15] "It is a privilege and an honor to serve on this board," agrees Commissioner Ann M. McGuinn today.

Who then were these founding commissioners, who built so lasting and important a structure? On March 12, 1904, Carnegie sent Taylor "a list of suitable persons for the Commission, being chiefly those whom we talked over." The first name was that of Taylor himself, whom Carnegie described as "one of the best men that ever lived."[16] Taylor also became the Commission's first president and served until his death in 1922. Next was Wilmot, who had come to Pittsburgh from New Jersey in 1888 as a clerk for the Pennsylvania Railroad Relief Fund. He was one of only two men with access to safe deposit box 675 of the Hudson Trust Company in Hoboken, New Jersey, where the Hero Fund's $5 million in bonds were stored (the other was Carnegie's longtime secretary, Robert A. Franks, who later became a commissioner). Wilmot would serve as the Hero Fund's manager for 26 years, until his sudden death from a heart attack.

Carnegie's list continued with William Nimick Frew (1854–1915), lawyer, banker, and first chairman of the board of trustees of Carnegie Institute. The only son of a pioneer western Pennsylvania oil refiner who had sold his interests to Rockefeller's Standard Oil Company, the wealthy Frew was a cultural visionary. He played a guiding role in launching the *Carnegie International*, in 1896 the first annual art exhibition in the United States to be multinational in scope. The fact that Pittsburgh, this "center of materialism," could produce such an innovative event surprised the world—and created a new image for the city "at a time when many considered the encouragement of living artists as essential to the nation's progress."[17] A catalyst in founding the Pittsburgh Symphony, Frew also served as a member of the original board of trustees of the Carnegie Institution of Washington, D.C., and the Carnegie Corporation of New York.

Judge James H. Reed (1853–1927), a founder of the international law firm Reed Smith, figured as prominently on Carnegie's list as he did in the industrialist's life. Reed had acted as Carnegie's lawyer in the sale of the Carnegie Company's facilities to U. S. Steel in 1901, and Carnegie had named him one of the original directors of the world's first billion-dollar corporation. An outstanding business counselor, organizer, and manager, he also consolidated Pittsburgh's new natural gas, electricity, and urban transportation companies into one of the first energy giants. Judge Reed (he had served briefly as a judge of the United States District Court for the Western District of Pennsylvania) was "liked by everyone because of his wonderful personality and fairness in all things he did," according to banker Richard B. Mellon. This lean, dry-witted lawyer also served as treasurer of Carnegie Institute, Carnegie Library of Pittsburgh, and Carnegie Institute of Technology.[18]

A pioneer manufacturer of light locomotives, the Hon. Henry Kirke Porter (1840–1921) was serving one term as a member of Congress when Carnegie named him to the Hero Fund Commission. Porter's hardworking machines, said to have been the only locomotives built solely for industrial purposes, helped "win the West" at quarries, logging operations, explosives works, grain processing plants, factories, and mines. Porter and his artist wife, Annie Decamp, owned a significant art collection and had built one of the few private galleries in Pittsburgh to display it.[19]

Carnegie's longtime friend Robert Pitcairn (1836–1909) was of course on the list. The two young Scottish immigrants had worked side by side as telegraph messenger boys, Carnegie liked to remember, "for the then magnificent salary of two and a half dollars per week." Like his friend, Pitcairn had learned how to operate the new technology of telegraphy, and he had succeeded Carnegie as a superintendent and general agent of the powerful Pennsylvania Railroad. Always seeking safer, systematic railroad operation, Pitcairn introduced a number of innovations and "gave to America the basic rules for train running"[20] in "the first modern rule book"[21] of 1874. According to one florid historian, "When Robert Pitcairn began his career, the science and art of railroad work were in their infancy. He was one of the … pioneers who blazed a pathway through the untracked wilderness, ceaselessly marching toward the goal of perfect systematized knowledge."[22] A broad-faced, disciplined man with an enormous mustache, Pitcairn is also credited with introducing a pension for retired Pennsylvania Railroad employees, one of the first pension funds anywhere.

Carnegie's next choice was William J. Holland, DD (1848–1932), who introduced the world's first "celebrity dinosaur."[23] Throughout his life this internationally known "churchman, educator, artist, traveler, scholar, scientist, and public-spirited citizen"[24] managed to find himself at the right place and among the right people. He had come to Pittsburgh as pastor of the fashionable Bellefield Presbyterian Church and soon officiated at the marriage of Henry C. Frick and Adelaide Childs. Once he met Carnegie, the two remained, in his words, friends for life. "We were like two brothers," Holland would tell a reporter in 1931. "No man living knew him like myself."[25]

In 1891, he became chancellor of the Western University of Pennsylvania (University of Pittsburgh) and increased the enrollment eight-fold by starting the schools of law, medicine, and dental surgery, and the departments of electrical and mining engineering. Admitting women for the first time,[26] the university consolidated its campus in Oakland, near Carnegie Institute—of which Holland also became director in 1898.

In 1899, Holland oversaw the Carnegie Institute expedition to Wyoming to excavate a dinosaur skeleton that would be known worldwide as *Diplodocus carnegii*—the first dinosaur to be seen by millions of people. Carnegie and his museum would present casts of this 85-foot fossil to national museums in England, Germany, France, Austria, Italy, Russia, Spain, Argentina, and Mexico, and William Holland personally installed each one. The original went on display in Pittsburgh when Carnegie Institute expanded in 1907. Holland would later serve as the Commission's second president, from 1923 to 1932.

Charles C. Mellor (1836–1909) "was not an ordinary man," claimed Holland of his fellow commissioner and Carnegie Institute trustee. "He was an artist, but he possessed also the instincts and capacity of the man of affairs. He had scientific tastes, and by reading and observation had acquired a large fund of exact scientific knowledge; but he also possessed a poetic imagination, which scientific study did not deaden." An organist and amateur botanist, Mellor ran the music business started in 1831 by his father, a friend of Stephen Foster. The store was the first to sell a piano in Pittsburgh and, in 1877, one of the first to install a telephone.

By no means a steel millionaire, Commissioner Edwin H. Anderson (1861–1947) was the librarian who organized the Carnegie Library of Pittsburgh—and thus accelerated the trend toward an enormous expansion of library services in urban centers throughout the United States. Directing the library from 1895 until 1904, he shaped it into a multifaceted resource to serve the community—a new ideal for libraries at the time. Anderson created the first Department of Technology in any public library in the country, as well as the first Children's Department. He would serve as director of the New York Public Library from 1914 to 1934.[27]

A real-life Horatio Alger, William Wallace Blackburn (1859–1931) began working for Carnegie companies as a bookkeeper in

1880, became a partner, and rose to become vice president and secretary of Carnegie Steel Company, at that time the largest entity in the United States Steel Corporation. He was a graduate of Duff's Business College in Pittsburgh, the first such business accounting school in the United States.[28]

Thomas Lynch (1854–1914) had worked his way from a clerkship in a company store in Broad Ford, Pennsylvania, to the presidency of the H. C. Frick Coke Company by the age of just 42. He thus shared in the spoils after the notorious Frick–Carnegie lawsuit in 1899, coming away with $640,000 in Carnegie Company stock and bonds. Although Frick remained bitterly antagonistic to Carnegie, and Lynch was a friend of Frick, Carnegie wanted him on the Commission, perhaps because of his experience with coal mine safety. He is credited with being "the father of the 'safety first' movement in the coal industry" and with having drafted the first set of rules for minimizing the dangers of mining.

Carnegie considered the next two commissioners, Thomas Morrison and Frederick C. Perkins, "excellent men of our family, and as such I should like to have them on the Commission."[29] Born in Dunfermline and Carnegie's second cousin, Morrison (1861–1946) became general manager and superintendent of Carnegie Steel's Duquesne and Edgar Thomson Works. He and another machinist patented a successful new cooling process for rails, and he was responsible for several other steelmaking inventions.[30]

Perkins (1870–1935), a graduate of Yale University and Harvard Law School, was a lawyer, a banker, and an early investor in automobile sales. He married Florence N. Carnegie, a daughter of Carnegie's brother Thomas and Lucy Coleman Carnegie.

William Lucien Scaife (1853–1924), a mining engineer who had studied at Yale, in Germany, and in Paris, had also worked in a Belgian coal mine to gain practical mining experience. In Pittsburgh, he established the Scaife Foundry & Machine Company, Ltd. A trustee of the Western University of Pennsylvania, Scaife headed the committee that renamed it the University of Pittsburgh. He also edited *John A. Brashear: The Autobiography of a Man Who Loved the Stars* and served as a trustee of Carnegie Institute.[31]

Another commissioner who devoted time to public service was William H. Stevenson (1857–1930), president of George K. Stevenson Company, an importing grocery business, and a close friend of Carnegie. As a reform member of City Council, he brought about the selection and purchase of the site for Carnegie Institute of Technology, and he served on the "Tech" board from 1902 to 1909. He ran for mayor in 1909. An original board member of the Chamber of Commerce of the United States, he served as president (1912–1914) of the Pittsburgh Chamber of Commerce and as a director for 27 years.

"The father of Pittsburgh's parks," Edward M. Bigelow (1850–1916) was a visionary who, far ahead of his times, stemmed the tide of urban sprawl in the 1880s. The development of Highland and Schenley Parks, Bigelow Boulevard and the Boulevard of the Allies, miles of streets and sewers, the improvement of the water system, and plans for Phipps Conservatory and for the Liberty Tunnels all sprang from his vision for a greener, more livable Pittsburgh. In 1889, he helped persuade Mary Schenley to sell 300 acres of land to Pittsburgh for a public park at a discount price of $75,000, considerably below its $200,000 valuation. "It used to be said that Mr. Bigelow made the taxpayers spend money," stated his obituary. "He admitted the charge laughingly, often, but called attention to the fact that he was constantly urging rich men to spend their money for the benefit of the people."[32]

To Thomas N. Miller, a boyhood companion in the neighborhood they called "Barefoot Square," Carnegie owed his start in the iron business. As purchasing agent of the Ohio and Pennsylvania Railroad, Miller (1835–1911) became a partner in the Iron City Forge Company. In 1864, Carnegie purchased a one-sixth interest in this company, and it became the parent of his first iron and steel interests. Miller sold his own shares to Carnegie in 1867. Although some claimed Miller had been forced out, the two remained friends for life.

Carnegie's original list included four more names: Samuel H. Church, a Pennsylvania Railroad vice president who would succeed Frew as chairman of Carnegie Institute; John Caldwell, an officer in Westinghouse companies and a noted art collector; William McConway, president of McConway & Torley Company and a Carnegie Institute trustee; and John W. Beatty, whom Carnegie had personally appointed as Carnegie Institute's first director of Fine Arts.

THOMAS S. ARBUTHNOT

Thomas S. Arbuthnot served the Commission for 44 years, joining it in 1912. His term as president, the Commission's third and its longest, was from December of 1932 to December of 1956. During that time, Arbuthnot was dean of the University of Pittsburgh School of Medicine and president of the Children's Hospital of Pittsburgh. Minutes from the Commission's meeting shortly after his death reflect the affection Arbuthnot had gained from its members: "He was a diligent and effective leader of the Carnegie Hero Fund Commission and will be greatly missed by his fellow members. Tom Arbuthnot certainly lived a fine and useful life."

Unable to serve, they were replaced on the Commission first by William L. Abbott (1852–1930). Starting as a clerk at age 19, he had risen to become chairman of Carnegie, Phipps & Co. by 37. "Abbott's chief contribution to the success of the Carnegie company was the organization of its unequalled system of sales agencies," according to *The Romance of Steel*. Before 1884, the company had relied exclusively on commissioned sales agents. "This was not satisfactory," Abbott would recall, "for the reason that a commission man makes deals with both sides. We decided that it would pay to send out salaried men who would work first and last for the Carnegie company." He had retired in 1892, "before the melon was cut," he joked.

The Hon. Joseph Buffington (1855–1947) had followed James H. Reed as judge of the United States District Court for the Western District of Pennsylvania when he became an original Hero Fund Commissioner. In 1906, President Theodore Roosevelt would name Judge Buffington to the Third Circuit Court of Appeals, and he would retire in 1938 with the distinction of having served longer, at that time, than any other judge in the history of the federal courts. A trustee of Carnegie Institute, he made important rulings in interstate commerce law, and in 1915 he would write the legal opinion denying the government's claim that U. S. Steel was a monopoly within the meaning of the Sherman Antitrust Act.[33] Additionally, he became known for his work in helping aliens to become citizens of the United States.

Ironically, another of the first commissioners was the son of an owner of a cotton mill—ironic in that Carnegie's first job at the age of 13 was as a bobbin boy in such a mill, at a salary of $1.20 a week. John Beard Jackson (1845–1908) was the cultured president of the Fidelity Title and Trust Company and also a stockholder in the Carnegie Company. A philanthropist and original trustee of Carnegie Institute, Jackson became the first Pittsburgher to donate a painting to the permanent collection of the Carnegie Museum of Art and was an original guarantor of the Pittsburgh Symphony. Also intrigued by natural science, he served as president of the Archaeological Institute of America, Pittsburgh Society.[34]

Last was William Scott (1850–1906), a Princeton graduate who had worked as a civil engineer out west before studying law in the firm of Knox & Reed, forerunner of Reed Smith. Serving as president of both the Allegheny County and the Pennsylvania Bar Associations, he joined an elite group of lawyers who represented Carnegie in the "Iron Clad Agreement" suit brought by Frick. Known as "one of the most gentlemanly lawyers at the Bar and of the Bar," Scott also served as general counsel of Fidelity Title and Trust Company.[35]

CHARLES A.
McCLINTOCK

ACTUARIES, POETS, AND THE METHODS OF DOING GOOD

Thus the first Hero Fund Commission consisted of just the sort of people Carnegie most admired and could trust to make decisions about his philanthropy—hardworking, principled, active, multidimensional individuals with wide-ranging interests and experiences. *American Illustrated Magazine* would describe the commissioners in September 1905 as "shrewd" men "in whom [Carnegie] had very complete confidence, successful men of very large affairs and reasonably entitled to a very fair degree of confidence in themselves."[36] In part, this confidence rose from their commitment to the problem-solving scientific pursuits of their times. Thomas S. Arbuthnot, MD, president of the Hero Fund from 1932 to 1956, once described Carnegie's giving as "seasoned with the genius that marks the great scientist; that is, a meticulous zeal for pertinent organization, detail, and the ability to suspend judgment and abide by the slow accumulations of tedious, undramatic facts." This "scientific method" also marks the Hero Fund, which from the first has had to develop systematic, organized approaches for judging some of the most dramatic, uplifting, and selfless acts of which human beings are capable.

When Taylor called the first meeting to order on April 15, 1904, the commissioners' first task was the formal acceptance of Carnegie's Deed of Trust. Next they adopted a resolution prepared by Holland, expressing "to Mr. Carnegie our appreciation of the high honor which he has conferred upon us in inviting us to administer the affairs of the trust which he has created, and thus in some measure to share with him in the pleasure of doing good." Holland knew the value of praise where this patron was concerned.

Then came the serious business of formal organizing. How in fact should this unprecedented entity operate? Carnegie had given the high-minded idea and $5 million of his money in bonds paying $250,000 a year. Now his "employees" had to make

Charles A. McClintock, known to his countless friends and associates as "Spook," joined the Commission in early 1938. Nearly 19 years later, he became its fourth president and served for 10 years. "Spook McClintock was a man of gracious nature, vitality and abundant wit," the minutes of the October 1968 meeting of the Commission note. "His interests were wide and his understanding ran deep. His greeting had the warmth of the morning sun. He was, perhaps above all, a loyal friend who will long be remembered with the greatest respect and deepest affection."

the concept work—with few guidelines and no previous models to follow. "One great difficulty in carrying out Mr. Carnegie's wishes lies in the fact that the enterprise is so new, so lacking in the parentage of precedent," claimed *American Illustrated*. "And when it comes to deciding whether an act is really heroic or not, one is a little in doubt as to whether a poet or an actuary should be called upon to determine it."[37] Thanks to Carnegie's and Taylor's sagacity, the Commission seemed well endowed with both types.

Five commissioners were promptly named to a committee on permanent organization: Judges Buffington and Reed, Messrs. Taylor, Wilmot, and, as chair, Lynch. Within five days, this committee had recommended the name, submitted by-laws, and suggested monthly meetings of an Executive Committee to "consider cases and make its recommendations in respect to all benefits and medals. It shall cause to be made a résumé of each case and present same to the Commission for final action." Taylor appointed the Executive Committee: Holland as chairman, Anderson, Blackburn, Morrison, Wilmot, and himself.

Meanwhile Carnegie was pushing for publicity, firing off hastily handwritten, penciled notes from his castle in Scotland. "It does not do to have such new ideas fall still-born—I regret the delay," he chided Wilmot in April 1904. "The idea being new, to create an interest in it and let all men feel the Heroes are to be taken care of must be widely known."[38] Carnegie had a very modern understanding of the media's power to shape public opinion, and he knew that the daily papers' appetite for news could quickly date a fresh idea.

The Hero Fund did indeed attract widespread attention in the United States and abroad, and most journals praised the new concept. But Carnegie's "robber baronetcy" and memories of the violent labor confrontation at Homestead in 1892 had made him a divisive figure. A number of voices ridiculed his new philanthropy and questioned "the possibility of administering such a trust in a way to benefit mankind," as Holland later put it. Quite a few criticized what they misinterpreted as the "commercialization" of heroism. Another later dismissed it as a branch of Carnegie's "peace propaganda."[39]

The publicity gave the commissioners even more incentive to move with care, intending to prove the skeptics wrong. It also made their job harder, because few outsiders grasped the purpose of the Hero Fund. Within weeks, 244 letters would arrive at the Commission's offices, asking for jobs and soliciting investments (some people thought the Fund supplied venture capital). Many also reported alleged acts of heroism, mostly undertaken by the writers themselves.

The Executive Committee quickly realized that the Commission's toughest job would be defining, evaluating, and codifying the nature of a heroic act, in line with Carnegie's Deed of Trust and their own experience. "Whether or not Mr. Carnegie had any idea that he was giving his Commission a rather large order is a matter of surmise purely, as also whether the Commission undertook its task in fear and trembling," claimed *American Illustrated Magazine* in 1905. "However they regarded it at the beginning of their labors, it is safe to say that by now they have discovered how difficult a task is cut out for them."[40]

Even Carnegie had to do some rethinking. When Taylor sent letters from self-acknowledged heroes, Carnegie replied, "I think the claims of unknown heroes will have to be thoroughly investigated, if considered at all. Men who write urging their claims appear in court under a cloud. I had in view well-proved cases— known to the public—seen and admired by their fellows—heroes who had attracted public attention,—not such as have only admired themselves. As you say much study and thought will be required to arrive at a working basis."[41]

Not until October 19, 1904, did the full Commission define and approve the Hero Fund's limitations and scope. The commissioners had discussed, debated, and resolved the following:

- The Fund was to be limited to "acts, in which conclusive evidence may be obtained showing that the person performing the act, voluntarily risked his own life in saving, or attempting to save, the life of a fellow being." As Holland would write in 1929, "it will be observed that this regulation, while not removing heroic acts from the field of impulsive effort, nevertheless provides that the performer of the deed must at the time have been conscious of the fact that its performance involved peril to himself."

- Such acts must be performed by persons the nature of whose duties in following their regular vocations, does not require them to perform such an act, i.e., the person must go beyond his duty.

STEWART McCLINTIC

Stewart McClintic joined the Commission in 1947 and was a member for 30 years, the last 10 of which he served as president. He was only the fifth in that position through the Commission's first 74 years. His father also was a Commission member, serving for 26 years. "Stew," as his friends called him, was a banker by profession and an engineer by training, which explains his roles during many years as chairman of the finance committee and treasurer, and his consuming interest in the technicalities of the thousands of rescue acts considered in his three decades of service.

- The heroic acts must be performed in the USA, the Dominion of Canada, the Colony of Newfoundland, and the waters thereof.

- Such acts must be performed on or after April 15th, 1904.

- Mr. Carnegie having directed that, in case of death, the widow and children, or other dependents, are to be provided for until the widow remarries and until the children reach a self-supporting age, and, in the event of disability, the disabled to be provided for until again able to work; the maximum death or disablement benefit to be paid in any one year to any one family or dependent, shall not exceed $1,000, the amount and manner of payment in each case to be fixed by the Commission, upon the recommendation of the Executive Committee, provided in no case, however, shall death or disablement benefits be paid unless it shall clearly be shown that the dependents or disabled need such assistance.

- Medals when awarded shall be presented, in death cases, to the widow or next of kin, and in disability and non-disability cases, to the person performing the act.

- Heroic acts may be brought to the attention of the Commission by applications by the friends of the persons performing them, and through the public press. Death and disablement cases shall be certified to by the attending physicians, and the Executive Committee shall have power to employ a traveling investigator to ascertain the facts in any given case.

By now the Carnegie Hero Fund Commission had in place its first official employees: Sara E. Weir, assistant treasurer, at a salary of $20 per month, and Wilmot, secretary, who earned $2,000 per year.

"THE MEDAL QUESTION"

Next the Executive Committee took up "the medal question"—and it seemed to perplex these capable men more than any other. Carnegie had made it clear that he intended a medal to be the hero's reward. He enjoyed presenting and receiving medals. But—what sort of medal should the Commission award? What would be its design? Should there be categories of medals? The commissioners first discussed soliciting the services of leading American sculptors for an appropriate design. Among those suggested were Augustus Saint-Gaudens and Daniel Chester French.

Talks went on. The January 1905 minutes reported that the Executive Committee was working on the design for a medal "illustrative of Mr. Carnegie's idea of a hero, as defined in his deed of trust, and as a motto the scriptural text, 'Greater love hath no man than this, that a man lay down his life for his friends'" (John 15:13). The committee had now visited leading jewelry firms. And in quite a modern way they recognized that the medal should "tell its own story, without explanation, to persons in all walks of life." They wanted the wording to appear in English rather than in Latin, a "dead language."

Even by May, however, the commissioners found the designs for the medal still not satisfactory in portraying Carnegie's idea of a hero. They took it upon themselves to change the design: the obverse side of the medal would contain only a bust of Carnegie encircled by the words, "Carnegie Hero Fund Commission, established April 15th, 1904." The reverse side would contain the coats of arms of the United States, Canada, and Newfoundland, suitably enwreathed, and the tablet for the inscription, with the motto. They awarded the commission to the fashionable J. E. Caldwell & Company of Philadelphia. This firm had shown "the greatest effort and ability of any of the competitors toward the desired object." And they decided to create three categories of medals: gold, silver, and bronze. All would be three inches in diameter, and three-sixteenths of an inch in thickness.

A HUNGER FOR HEROES

In the meantime, the able Wilmot had devised a system for tabulating and organizing the cases to be presented to the Commission. By May 1905, he had reclassified all cases received since the establishment of the Fund. More than 230 cases had been refused, and 174 were pending.

On May 24, 1905, the Carnegie Hero Fund Commission approved and granted its first 12 awards. The awards included death benefits, disablement benefits, and "betterment benefits," bestowed upon the recipients of medals whom the Executive Committee had deemed worthy of financial help. Three widows of heroes received annual awards, and the sole woman hero received scholarship help so she could continue her studies.

ROBERT W. OFF

Robert W. Off, the Commission's sixth president, served in this position for 22 years, the second-longest term of the first six presidents. During his tenure as president, he oversaw the awarding of more than 2,000 Carnegie Medals and affected many changes, including the implementation of computers and the streamlining of investigative procedures, both of which resulted in significant savings; and, the first women were elected to the board. Following a total of 28 years with the Commission, he retired in 2001 but remains an honorary member.

Announcement of these first awards silenced the doubters. The public and the media responded enthusiastically to the Hero Fund. All the awards are for "acts of a fine, fearless sort, worthy of thought and memory," wrote H. K. Webster. "Every time that Mr. Carnegie's Commission can hold up before us, in a way that commands our attention, a man of our own day and our own or a humbler walk of life, who in some great moment has squarely turned his back upon the Main Chance, they have done us a service. The sight may not make heroes of us, but at least it will melt off something of the crust of cynicism and selfishness which has been blinding our eyes."[42]

"In a time when every possible crime, every form of meanness and selfishness, is exploited at great length by the newspapers, it is well that the story of good deeds should be told as often and as completely as possible," wrote *The Outlook* in 1913.[43]

And in 1996: "Local heroes may never have been as important as they are today, an era when there are so few national heroes. Today the national hunger for heroes may be best satisfied on a small scale, where a single man, woman, or child may exemplify the selfless bravery America has long honored."[44]

And so it was that the Carnegie Hero Fund passed "from the experimental stage to the permanent," in Taylor's words, "where the Hero Commission takes its stand firmly among the great benevolences of the age."

Over a century of amazing change, the Carnegie Hero Fund Commission has naturally met and dealt with extraordinary challenges. The commissioners have also wisely managed Carnegie's "princely" gift of $5 million so that at the end of 2003 the Fund totaled $31 million. And they have carried out these responsibilities with respect for the original, founding commissioners who wrote the first "road map" for modern philanthropy.

A hundred years ago, Carnegie hoped to change the world with large-scale, systematically distributed philanthropy. The Hero Fund Commission was one of his very first attempts to do so. And although his later gifts eclipsed it in size, he always cherished the Hero Fund—perhaps because he recognized the unchanging nature of humanity's hunger for heroes. As Carnegie himself wrote with typical optimism to Taylor in 1905, "You have made a start, and there is to be no finish. It goes on forever."

In Andrew Carnegie's Deed of Trust he specified, "A medal shall be given to the hero, or widow, or next of kin, which shall recite the heroic deed it commemorates, that descendants may know and be proud of their descent."

Numerous documents in the Commission's files tracing the history of the development of the medal from this directive to the first one struck, more than two years later, attest that the process was painstakingly thorough. A reference to this process can be found on page 56, as can other details about the medal's early history, including that they were to be struck in gold, silver, and bronze.

Without any evidence of a formal policy, and without a precedent to follow, it is unclear how in its formative years the Commission decided to award the three medals. Beginning in the early 1920s, however, a policy was adopted that stated that the gold medal would be awarded for heroic acts involving several rescuers, the silver for rescuers who repeatedly risked their lives in the persistent performance of their acts, and the bronze for all other rescues. In early 1981, the Commission decided that the bronze medal would be the only one awarded. The last gold medal to an individual was awarded to **CHARLES L. COE** (✝ *C. H.* 1865), posthumously, who died in a fire rescue act on February 6, 1923. An account of Coe's rescue is on page 146. The last silver medals were awarded to **BRIAN MERVYN CLEGG** (*C. H.* 6476) and **ROBERT STEPHEN GRANT** (*C. H.* 6475) for their rescue of three individuals from exposure in a downed airplane in Lake of the Woods, Kenora, Ontario, in March of 1979.

In all, 19 gold, 617 silver, and 8,128 bronze medals were awarded in the Hero Fund's first 100 years.

Carnegie Medals awarded in 2004 include a banner to mark the Commission's centennial year, which replaces "Established April 15, 1904." The word Commission has been added. On the reverse, the biblical verse has been attributed to John 15:13. The seal of Newfoundland has been removed, and the flora detail has been simplified.

Medals struck in 2005 and beyond will revert to the "Established April 15, 1904" embossing.

(ABOVE) LUIGI BADIA, AN ARTIST FROM SOMERS, NEW YORK, WORKS ON THE SCULPTURE OF THE 2004 CARNEGIE MEDAL.

(FACING PAGE) CARNEGIE MEDAL OBVERSE: SEVERAL STRIKES OF A BRONZE BLANK ARE NECESSARY TO GAIN THE FINAL RELIEF. REVERSE: IN LOW RELIEF IS THE GEOGRAPHICAL OUTLINE OF THE UNITED STATES AND CANADA. IN HIGHER RELIEF ARE THE SEALS OF THE UNITED STATES ON THE BOTTOM, CANADA ON THE TOP LEFT, AND NEWFOUNDLAND ON THE TOP RIGHT. WHEN THE MEDAL WAS DESIGNED, NEWFOUND-LAND WAS A SEPARATE COLONY. THE PASSAGE ENCIRCLING THE MARGIN, "GREATER LOVE HATH NO MAN THAN THIS, THAT A MAN LAY DOWN HIS LIFE FOR HIS FRIENDS," IS FROM THE NEW TESTAMENT, JOHN 15:13. ON THE INSCRIPTION PLATE, OR CARTOUCHE, A BRIEF DESCRIPTION OF THE RESCUE IS EMBOSSED, ALONG WITH THE NAME OF THE RESCUER, THE RESCUED, AND WHERE AND WHEN THE ACT OCCURRED. RELIEF WORK UNDER THE PLATE CONTAINS SPRIGS OF LAUREL, TYPIFYING GLORY, AND ABOVE ARE SPRIGS OF IVY, OAK, AND THISTLE, FOR FRIENDSHIP, STRENGTH, AND PERSISTENCE.

Posed as they are—four late-middle-aged men lined along a rusty railing on the north bank of the Potomac River, their gaze fixed by command to the far end of the Fourteenth Street Bridge—the moment transforms them into something of a monument, yet another one on these banks in Washington, D.C. They are common in appearance and no one recognizes them, this Mount Rushmore of American heroes, these men who defied a blizzard and its awful effects to save what would be the only survivors of a downed jetliner. Willing to pit human strengths against the raw forces of nature, the forces that determined that this plane should not clear that span, they listened to a primal stirring that dared them to think they might triumph.

They did. They gave hope, then life itself, back to three women and two men, who, clinging to sinking wreckage, survived the impact only to face sure death in the ice-clogged, fuel-poisoned waters of the Potomac on a winter afternoon in early 1982. Though to a man they shunned the notion, they were immediately and widely deemed heroes, and then they largely went their separate ways, seemingly linked by only 20 minutes and one overwhelming desire to achieve a common goal. A score and two years have passed, and they reunite for the first time. Like buddies from the trenches of a distant war, there is no space between them. They are familiar as they slap backs and give bear hugs, the sun kinder this day, the sky in full view.

C. H. 6581,
6584, 6582,
6583

It had snowed all morning and into the afternoon, and, in the 24-degree air, the accumulation was paralyzing Washington, D.C. By early afternoon, schools, offices, and businesses were closing, and the roadways became choked with the traffic of the storm's refugees.

ROGER OLIAN, 34, a sheet-metal worker, was among those attempting to evacuate the city. His usual route was across the Fourteenth Street Bridge, and on that day it took him two hours just to get there. Traffic was bumper-to-bumper, and Olian had the additional worries of running on a near-empty tank and a low battery. It was around 4 p.m. In another car on the span, MARTIN L. ("LENNY") SKUTNIK III, 28, was making the same trek. With him were his father and other carpool members. They too had been excused for the day from their jobs, Skutnik's as a government office services assistant. Skutnik recalled six to eight inches of snow on the bridge, and then people out of their cars looking over the railing.

A few miles to the east, at the headquarters of the Aviation Section of the U.S. Park Police, Chief Pilot DONALD W. USHER, 31, and Rescue Technician MELVIN E. ("GENE") WINDSOR, 31, were sitting out the storm, Usher having concluded it was "absolutely inconceivable that we would fly. Not in this stuff." Visibility was severely restricted and cloud cover was about 250 feet, conditions that required a craft certified in IFR—Instrument Flight Rules, or, in the vernacular, "I Follow Roads." Indeed, the unit's jet-powered Bell Ranger helicopter was snug and dry inside the hangar.

The storm had disrupted operations at Washington National Airport, hard by the Virginia bank of the Potomac, just south of the bridge. At about 1:40 p.m., the airport was shut down for snow removal, causing delays, including that of Air Florida's Flight 90, which was to depart for Fort Lauderdale at 2:15 p.m. Deicing of the plane was commenced, and by 4 p.m. it was cleared for takeoff. Aboard were 79 passengers and crewmembers, Kelly L. Duncan, Priscilla K. Tirado, Bert D. Hamilton, Joseph Stiley, and Patricia Felch among them.

Witnesses later reported an unusually heavy accumulation of snow or ice on the plane, and that its takeoff was labored and it lifted off too far down the runway. The plane lost altitude immediately and, less than a mile from the runway, it descended to the level of the northbound span of the bridge. It struck seven vehicles there, killing four people and injuring four others, then took out a length of bridge structure and crashed into the ice-covered Potomac and sank. Seventy-four persons aboard the jet died in the accident. Duncan, Tirado, Hamilton, Stiley, and Felch were not among them; miraculously, they and another male passenger surfaced amidst wreckage and ice floe at points about 120 feet from the Virginia bank.

Olian learned of the crash from another motorist and, abandoning his vehicle, ran to the riverbank, en route hearing the survivors' cries and seeing the plane's tail section above the water. *For a small plane, that's a large tail,* he concluded initially, and then a staggering realization: *If it's not a small plane, where is everyone?* Thinking as he ran, Olian knew he had a choice to make: "If I did nothing, I couldn't have lived with myself. But I knew I could live with myself if I tried and failed, even if I died. Figuratively speaking."

Other people had responded to the bank and were assembling a makeshift line from whatever was available—rope, belts, battery cables, even pantyhose. The situation to Olian was as desperate as it could be, but he thought a visible rescue attempt would buy the survivors time by giving them a measure of hope. He was right; Stiley later said that seeing Olian in action gave a "wonderful psychological feeling." Olian descended the steep bank, then entered the "electrifyingly cold" water. Handed one end of the line, he tied it to himself and continued out. He maneuvered between ice slabs and tried to crawl across the larger ones, often falling and submerging. He shouted encouragement to the victims but knew they were "miles and hours" away. Still, strength waning, he stayed focused. When he was halfway to his goal, the line became taut, and he tried to free himself of it. And then there came a welcome sound: a chopper was approaching.

Within minutes of the crash, Usher and Windsor took calls from the airport inquiring of their unit's availability to fly. There were reports of a missing aircraft, the men were told. Usher's no-fly edict rescinded, the men assembled lines and life jackets and had the ramp plowed. Near-whiteout conditions prevailed when they lifted off, Usher looking through the helicopter's floor windows—its "chin bubbles"—to follow highways to the

(LEFT TO RIGHT)
WINDSOR, SKUTNIK,
AND USHER AND
THE HELICOPTER
USED IN THE RESCUE.

scene. The trip took five minutes, a part of which was through freezing rain, which threatened the craft's rotor system and iced its windshield. As they approached the bridge, a letup in the snow enabled the men to view the carnage below, first the wrecked vehicles, then the broken ice of the river, then the debris in the water. There were people everywhere—*were they the passengers?*—but only a few in the water, including Olian, who was being reeled to the bank. At the jet's exposed tail section, they saw the six partially submerged victims.

Although Usher had extensive flying experience both with the Park Police and during four years in Vietnam, conditions this day provided new tests. In the water, the chopper's downdraft raised debris to threaten its rotor system, the river and immediate atmosphere were contaminated by the jetliner's fuel and its fumes, and ice floes clogging the surface could impinge on the skids should the craft be taken low. On land, the bank was choked with people and emergency vehicles, and small trees lining it had to be minded, even as firefighters pushed branches out of the way. In the air, Windsor would work unsecured through an open door. *If he falls out*, Usher thought, *we're really in trouble*. He knew that further help arriving in time was unlikely: *We were it*.

Windsor dropped the end of a line to the victims. Although suffering from a shattered right wrist and broken arm and ribs, Hamilton put the line around himself, and Usher flew him dangling to the bank. The effort was repeated for Duncan, who sustained leg and arm fractures. Windsor had dropped the line to an obviously injured man at the wreckage, but the man passed it to Duncan. Two lines were dropped on the third trip, and again, the injured man passed one of them off. Stiley secured a line to himself, then he grasped Tirado, who had sustained leg-fracture injury. Felch clinging to the second line, Usher started toward shore, dragging the victims through open water and floating ice. Halfway there, Felch lost her grip and settled back into the water, where she was kept afloat by a life vest. Suffering fractures to both legs, Stiley maintained his hold of Tirado until they became separated on the ice, Tirado left behind as Stiley was pulled to the bank. Weakened, dazed, and blinded by jet fuel, Tirado made futile attempts to swim as she mouthed, *Help!* Usher and Windsor returned and dropped the life ring to her, and with great difficulty she maintained the barest of holds as she was dragged ever closer to safety. Her hold gave out again.

Enter Skutnik, literally. Having watched the rescue from its start, he could bear no more—*I was going crazy*. Unlike his father, Skutnik was untrained in water rescue, but that mattered little. Shucking coat and boots, he plunged into the river and swam to Tirado. After working to secure a hold, Skutnik started to swim in with her. They were met by a firefighter, who took Tirado the rest of the way, Skutnik following. Less than two hours later he was world news, and by the end of the month he was at the State of the Union address, where President Ronald Reagan told the nation that he represented "American heroism at its finest."

With Tirado's safety assured, Usher and Windsor turned to Felch, who had sustained a broken leg, arm, and wrist. As Windsor, unsecured, stepped from the cabin to stand on a skid, Usher took the helicopter to the water, so low that both skids were at times submerged and at other times in contact with floating ice. Bracing himself against the craft, Windsor reached down and grasped Felch, using both hands to secure her while warding off the helicopter's flapping door with a shoulder. With both of them delicately perched on the skid, Usher returned to the bank. Felch was the last survivor out of the water, having endured 30 minutes of its numbing effects.

Their final trip to the wreckage, for the remaining passenger, was a heart-rending one for Usher and Windsor. The man had sunk by then, and their search for him was fruitless. Their successes, however, went on to be widely acknowledged. Along with Olian and Skutnik, they received numerous awards for their heroism, including the Carnegie Medal. Although in a profession "charged with the safety of the public," a Hero Fund regulation that might ordinarily have disqualified them, Usher and Windsor were thought by the Commission to have gone clearly above and beyond the line of duty—unfavorable conditions aside, they had acted outside their agency's jurisdiction.

But to ask *them* if they are heroes? Convinced that his was a human reaction, Skutnik shuns the term, believing that if he didn't act, someone else would have. Consequently, he remains puzzled, sometimes annoyed, by all the attention, the media viewing him as a "prop caught on videotape." Olian too sees his reaction as the result of his humanity: *Heroes are no different—we all have the capability, and when people get to see that, that's good.* Still, he does not embrace the designation. "I've been called a hero," he said, "but I don't believe it about myself."

Usher and Windsor are likewise unimpressed by the title. Windsor maintains that training, experience, planning, teamwork, the skills of his pilot, and even participation by a "higher power" all played pivotal roles. "A hero is spontaneous," he says. "A hero is untrained." Similarly, Usher suspects heroes are "not paid, not expected" to act, and that "they are in hiding until they are actually needed. I don't think I fit into the definition." Having long ago concluded that modesty must be innate in the souls of the bravest, the Commission decided that Usher *did* fit in, as did his three corescuers. In the Hero Fund's thinking, the men assumed extraordinary risk while helping to save others when they had no obligation to do so, the Commission's traditional description of a hero.

"Whatever moved these men to challenge death on behalf of their fellows is not peculiar to them," wrote *Time Magazine* essayist Roger Rosenblatt. "Everyone feels the possibility in himself. That is the abiding wonder of the story. That is why we would not let go of it." FILE NOS: 58226, 58143, 58225, 58224

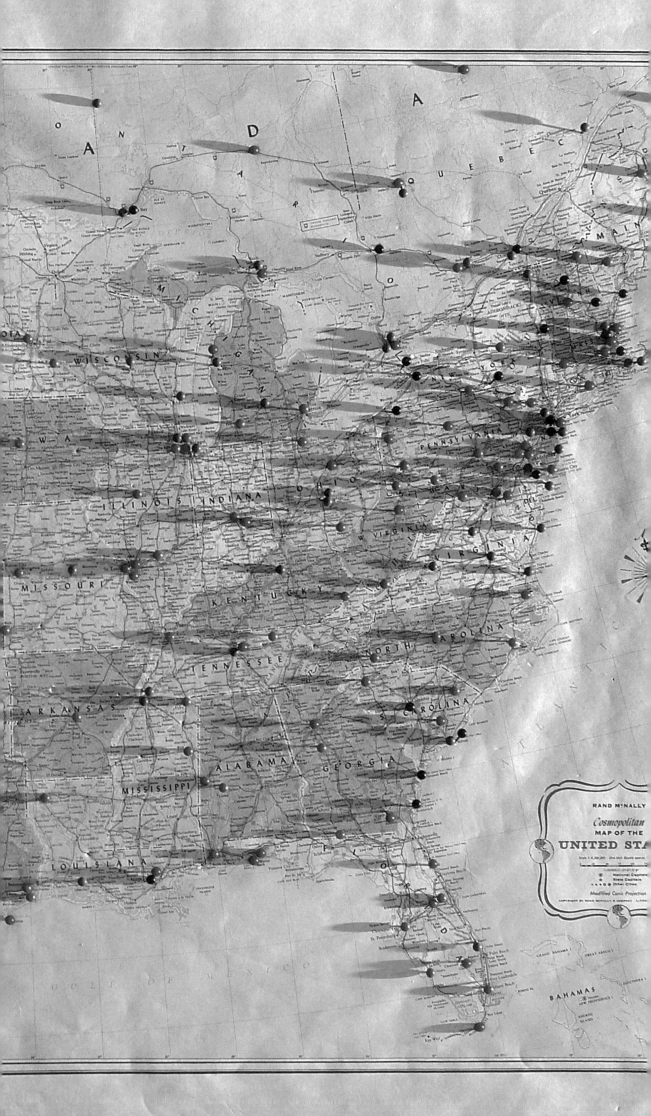

Frank M. Wilmot,
Commission
manager, seated,
center, with special
agents. Photograph
is undated, but is
thought to have
been taken in the
early 1910s.

THE HERO HUNTERS

by MARY BRIGNANO

IV

here is no branch of detective science which is so important and so much neglected as the act of tracing footsteps," announced Sherlock Holmes in 1887. In that year, just 17 years before the creation of the Carnegie Hero Fund, Holmes made his first appearance in detective fiction, and the reading public took to him immediately. Here was a "scientific" detective whose exacting, uncanny observation and deductive reasoning made him a force for justice—a hero who could snare a murderer and right society's wrongs by studying facts and evidence. "There is," Sherlock Holmes says time and again, "nothing like first-hand evidence."

In his insistence on the facts and facts alone, this hero of detective science could be a model for the Carnegie Hero Fund's special agents, later known as field representatives and now case investigators. These men and women have studied and authenticated nearly 9,000 heroic acts since January 1905, and have investigated countless more. For a century, they have worked to fulfill Andrew Carnegie's charge to celebrate the noblest, most unselfish behavior of which human beings may be capable. And the best way they and the Hero Fund's commissioners have found to honor such heroism is through the unwavering, objective search for facts. Rigorously documenting each extraordinary act, case investigators and their dedicated scrutiny give heroism its rightful recognition.

In the words of Herbert W. Eyman, who spent 25 years as an investigator with the Hero Fund, "Essentially field work is a quest for truth. Within the framework of our organization a man … is a hero only if, in our opinion, he risked his life and that fact can be conclusively established." Heroism cannot be proved "through

(PREVIOUS SPREAD) COLORED TACKS ON MAPS IN THE COMMISSION'S OFFICE PINPOINTED THE LOCATION OF RESCUES, RESCUERS, VICTIMS, WITNESSES, AND OTHERS ASSOCIATED WITH CASES BEING INVESTIGATED.

an accumulation of assumptions," Eyman added. "It can only be achieved through thoroughness in the investigation to the point that all doors to speculation are closed." Or, as Holmes put it, "It is a capital mistake to theorize before you have all the evidence. It biases the judgment."

EXTRAORDINARY INVESTIGATORS

Struggling to wrestle Carnegie's philanthropic ideals into a functional, enduring organization, the first commissioners quickly realized that they could not by themselves verify reported acts of heroism taking place over the 7.4 million square miles of the continental United States, Canada, and the then-British colony of Newfoundland. Frank Wilmot, the Fund's manager, announced in October 1904 that, although seven cases had been investigated, 52 more were still pending. How could the commissioners properly judge these cases without trustworthy evidence to guide them? "In all of these cases it is the feeling of the Executive Committee that before reaching a final decision it is desirable that the localities where the alleged acts of heroism were performed should be visited by a representative of the Commission, who may ascertain the facts more clearly," state the minutes for October 1904.

William L. Abbott, who had so successfully launched the Carnegie Company's force of salaried sales agents, moved that the Executive Committee be "empowered to engage the services of such persons as might be necessary to investigate cases for the Commission." Thus in January 1905 the Commission hired its first traveling special agent, George A. Campsey, formerly a reporter for the *Pittsburg Times* newspaper. His salary was $100 a month plus expenses, to be raised to $125 at six months if his services proved satisfactory. His living expenses on the road were not to exceed a thrifty $3.50 per day. A year later, with 195 cases in line for investigation, the commissioners hired a second special agent. He was John P. Cowan, a reporter for the *Pittsburg Gazette*. By 1912, there would be 10 agents, all former journalists.

Why reporters? "Newspaper reporters with college training seemed to be the combination best suited to the work," wrote Commission President Thomas S. Arbuthnot in 1935. Quoting a 1909 magazine article, he claimed that the commissioners found their training and previous experience "conducive to thoroughness of investigation and lucidity of statement."[1] Another writer singled out the educated reporter's ability "to detect fraud and exaggeration."[2]

Again the Carnegie Hero Fund commissioners had demonstrated their innovative approach to problem solving as well as their desire to please their "boss." Carnegie had shown quite a modern ability to shape popular opinion through mass media. He treated reporters well, putting up New York journalists at Pittsburgh's elite Duquesne Club, for instance, when they covered the opening of Carnegie Institute in 1895. He wrote essays for popular magazines. He had shrewdly insisted on publicizing the Hero Fund in order to promote its reach and effectiveness—unlike his rival John D. Rockefeller, who preferred to keep his giving more private.

The commissioners also seemed to understand the trends that had so changed journalism in the late 19th century, when mass communications began to shape popular culture. Technology had dramatically lowered the cost of newspaper publishing, and publishing rivals like Joseph Pulitzer and William Randolph Hearst drove up sales with sensational stories. They also launched journalistic crusades against social injustice and ran exposés of political and economic corruption. Although the targets of these investigations called them "yellow journalism" and "muckraking," reporters like Pittsburgh's Nellie Bly (the pen name of Elizabeth Cochrane) courageously opened readers' eyes to cruelty in mental institutions, sweatshops, and jails, and to bribery in the legislature. The "new" reporters made journalism a profession that appealed to adventurous, idealistic men and women—just the sort of eyes and ears the Carnegie Hero Fund Commission needed.

"The hero hunter must be a good interviewer," stated a *Harper's Weekly* article in 1912. "He must be a keen judge of people. …He must know how to get evidence and how to sift it. Above all, he must have good judgment. He must be young and energetic. And since the job entails months of travel yearly, unmarried men are preferred."[3]

And, by recommending a thorough investigation of each case of reported heroism, the commissioners revealed their own bias for the scientific method. Only by strict documentation of the facts could the elusive nature of heroism be *proved* to a skeptical public. These special investigators also opened yet another new field in American philanthropy. They were in some ways the first scientific program officers. Advocating the case study method to determine a hero's eligibility, they became the experts on whom the commissioners relied to guide their policy.

TO KINGDOM COME WITHOUT A MURMUR

"Facts, and facts only" became the special agent's Holmesian mantra. The Commission outfitted each with the latest equipment: a pocket Kodak camera, instruments for measuring distances, and a typewriter—the camera and the typewriter being fairly new technologies. "With these accoutrements he was ready for the road, wherever it might lead—to the banks of Newfoundland or to the swamps of Georgia," enthused Commissioner Arbuthnot.

The first special agents spent as many as 11 months on the road each year, a routine that changed only in the 1950s. *Harper's Weekly* described a typical travel schedule in 1912:

> The investigator starts from the office in Pittsburgh on a regular itinerary. Perhaps his itinerary will read something like this: Pittsburgh to Steubenville, to Youngstown, to Warren, to Cambridge Springs, to Erie, to Ashtabula, to Cleveland, to Toledo, to Detroit, to Benton Harbor, and thence to Chicago. When the investigator reaches Cleveland, perhaps he finds instructions to go to Louisville, thence to Mansfield, to Indianapolis, and so to Benton Harbor. Arriving at Chicago, he finds orders to go to Milwaukee, then to points in Wisconsin, Minnesota, and North Dakota, and so back to Chicago. From here he is sent through Illinois, down into Missouri and Tennessee, and thence back to Pittsburgh. Thus a trip that was intended to extend from April to June lasts until the end of December. The best hero hunter … will go to kingdom come without a murmur.[4]

Until the 1950s, the investigators traveled just about every mile by rail—and Carnegie steel plants had produced many of these rails. In each town or city, they followed the same routine, registering at a hotel (never revealing the purpose of their visit and always requesting a room at or near the minimum rate), studying the documents relating to the case, interviewing those who had reported the case, interviewing eyewitnesses, studying, measuring, and photographing the site of the act, and finally interviewing the "hero," if he or she had survived. "An experienced investigator quickly scents a case that amounts to nothing, and he as quickly gets to the bottom of it and drops it," *Harper's Weekly* informed its readers. "But on a genuine case he spends anywhere from two to three days to as many months."

"Although the job required you to talk to everybody from millionaires to people who lived in chicken coops, it could get kind of lonely out there," admits retired investigator William A. Dillon. After spending all day in the field and eating a solitary dinner, the investigator used the evening hours to write and type his daily log and detailed report. The report included (and still includes) the time, place, and circumstances of the rescue, along with pertinent facts such as weather conditions or tidal stages. If, for example, the special investigator discovered that the tide had been out at the time of a reported near drowning, he might become suspicious that the "rescue" took place in six feet of water. Each report had to include statements from all those interviewed and information about the witnesses' reputations. Were they honest, reliable people? How old was the rescuer (always listed as RR)? How much did the RR weigh? How much did the rescued (QD) weigh? Exactly how many feet from the approaching train did the QD fall? Exactly how fast was the train traveling? How many seconds did the RR have to save the QD? How far from the riverbank was the QD? How many miles per hour was the current flowing? "When possible," stated an early investigator's manual, "current speeds should be measured by timing a floating object over a measured distance." And, "in runaway cases carefully develop and state clearly *how* the horse was going, i.e., whether running wildly, on a gallop, rearing and plunging, panic-stricken, etc." And, "to determine width of river, etc., from Point A sight object C on a line forming a 60-degree angle (ten minutes on your watch) with the bank. Pace off distance AB, B being opposite C. Distance BC equals AB x 1.7321."

Every question, every measurement, and every judgment led toward one goal: to answer the question, Can it be *conclusively established* that the RR *knowingly risked his or her life* in the attempt to save another human being?

The investigators' single-spaced reports, often accompanied by photos and drawings, are as remarkable today as they were a century ago. In factual, uninflected, even dry language, they recount extraordinary acts of ordinary people. Composed by solitary men in the banal rooms of hotels throughout North America, these disciplined descriptions can bring a reader to tears, and to a new reverence for human nobility.

COLORED TACKS AND CARGO PLANES

Meanwhile, back in the Hero Fund's Pittsburgh office, by 1911 H. A. Pickering had been brought in from the field to "criticize and condense" the special investigators' reports, while a home office manager deployed the travelers from alligator-infested bayous of Louisiana to remote encampments in Alaska. To plot an economical itinerary for each investigation, the manager relied on sectional maps of the United States, Canada, and Newfoundland, each stored in a single shallow drawer of a specially built cabinet. Colored tacks studded each map, blue for the site of the act to be investigated, red and black for the residence of persons who had witnessed the act, green for the residence of persons to be interviewed in regard to acts in another state, and pink for the residence of an original reporter of an act, not living near the scene.

What colored tacks could not reveal were the adventures of the wandering life, a job that would eventually carry investigators by hay wagon, motorcycle, jet plane, "from a roomette in a luxury night train to a dusty seat in a Star Mail Route station wagon, from a deck chair aboard a glittering lake steamer to the bow seat of a small outboard motorboat, from the generally ubiquitous taxicab to self-propelled shoe leather."[5]

Suburban growth, highway construction, and the decline of public transportation led to the use of rental cars in the 1970s. But by the mid-1980s the investigators came in from the field. The Commission's three case investigators now work almost entirely from the Pittsburgh office, relying on telephones and computers and fax machines and the mail to conduct their research and correspondence.

But whether on the road or at a desk, as the *Wall Street Journal* wrote in 1966, "The occupational hazard of working in the field of heroism is an unblinking awareness of the fragility of life and the dangers underlying even mundane activities."

Investigators have at times risked their own lives to uncover acts of heroism, and in the Commission office the memories live on. There was the day Eyman had to take a 17-foot mail boat from Rockland, Maine, across a stormy open sea to Vinal Haven Island—and he made the four-hour trip lashed to the mast. Once he flew on a tiny cargo plane from an island off the Alaska coast to Juneau, lying on crates loaded with fresh salmon. One day he walked a mile-long Florida lane to the home of a reputed moonshiner; wide enough for one car, the road was flanked by deep, water-filled ditches—home, he surmised, to poisonous snakes and alligators. A pack of hounds threatened to tear him apart when he reached the house. But Eyman got his interview—as did Walter Rutkowski when he investigated a "bear case" in the Yukon, traveling on puddle jumper planes from one Inuit town to the next, then chartering a pickup truck and driving into the tundra to track down the peripatetic gold miner who had saved a young woman by taking his ax to the bear that attacked her. The miner received a bronze medal and $2,000 for his valor. Rutkowski received his regular paycheck. But had he not persisted, this heroic act would have gone unrecognized.

RESPECTING THE MISSION

Case investigators are not charged to speculate about or judge *why* some people risk their lives for others. For 100 years, their loyalty has focused on the discovery and distillation of the facts, and they maintain a deep-seated respect for their mission—a respect, even reverence, often missing in today's ironic mood. Agent Eyman believed that a "sacred trust" existed among the Carnegie Hero Fund heroes, the commissioners, and the investigators. As he would write eloquently:

> The establishment of the case, including the environmental features that relate to the risks to which the rescuer exposed himself, must be pursued to the conclusive level. This can be achieved only if the field representative holds conviction that anything less is a betrayal of his responsibilities to the Commission, the individuals recommended for rewards, and just as importantly, himself.

The partly investigated case, like a little knowledge, is a very dangerous thing. It can lead the Commission astray in its evaluation, it can result in unworthy cases receiving awards and worthy acts being rejected.

Attainment of the ideal, which should motivate the field representative in his approach to each case assigned to him, is not easy. Nothing worth doing ever is.

It involves an investigative zeal embracing willingness to go the extra mile to establish the conclusiveness of an important point. It involves unflinching confrontations with all obstacles and barriers to investigative progress. It involves a determination on the part of the field representative to make the case which he currently has under study better covered in all areas than any other he has ever done.

Heroic in its own way, this quest for the truth of each act continues to define the Carnegie Hero Fund Commission's investigators as they begin a new century of "scientific detection." Like Sherlock Holmes's, their work is rooted in justice—the opportunity to reveal and celebrate the greatest altruism a man or woman may achieve. The "hero hunters" offer us hope about our fellow humans and the world we live in—just as Carnegie knew they would.

Hero hunter rescues youth

By GEORGE S. STUTEVILLE

James L. Rethi hunts heroes for a living. After rescuing a drowning 13-year-old boy Monday night he has to look no farther than his mirror.

Rethi, 28, is an investigator for the Carnegie Hero Fund Commission of Pittsburgh. He searches the nation for men and women who have proved their valor by jeopardizing their lives to save another.

The foundation, created by the late industrialist Andrew Carnegie, bestows awards upon worthy heroes. It may have to strike a medallion for Rethi.

THE PITTSBURGH resident had been in Indianapolis three days researching the events around a near-drowning at an apartment complex in 1980.

Rethi left his room at the Sheraton-Meridian to go to the hotel pool for a routine half-mile swim. He sat at the poolside watching two boys play in the water about 9 p.m.

Roy L. Halsell, 13, 653 West 30th Street, pulled himself out and dived back in.

"I ALWAYS notice children, I guess I'm that way," Rethi commented. "After a short amount of time I didn't see the boy surface." Halsell had been underwater about three minutes.

"I looked over the edge and he was laying on his stomach on the bottom."

Rethi, who has a slight paunch pushing at his trunks, plunged to the bottom. He scooped Halsell into his arms.

He lifted the youth to the surface with the aid of Jerry E. Kleber, 28, Pheonix, Ariz., who was attending a conference at the hotel.

RETHI PERFORMED mouth-to-mouth resuscitation. The fourth time he blew into the boy's lungs Halsell began breathing, Rethi said.

Halsell was in serious condition in Methodist Hospital.

The boy sneaked into the pool, his mother, Linda O. Halsell, 31, said. "was somewhere he was not suppo to be."

Doctors said her son was ha respiratory problems, but should cover, she said. Mrs. Halsell also came a hero hunter, saying she w ed to meet Rethi and thank him.

"ME AND Roy's father are thankful," Mrs. Halsell said at Met ist. "God put him (Rethi) there at particular time."

During his three months as investigator, the former newspaper porter learned timing is a crucial gredient to heroism.

"It amounts to being in the r place at the right time and doing right thing."

Rethi said he doubts his life-sa effort would meet the Carnegie fc dation's standard of heroism — ris

"I DON'T feel that I actually ris

HERO HUNTER RESCUES YOUTH

So read the headline on the front page of the Indianapolis Star *on June 15, 1982. The rescuer was James L. Rethi, an investigator for the Hero Fund. Rethi had been in Indianapolis for three days investigating the case of a near drowning. He was staying at a hotel, and at 9 p.m. on June 14 was sitting at the hotel's pool watching two young boys play in the water. One of the boys got out of the water and dived back in, and when Rethi noticed that the youngster did not surface, he went to investigate. The boy was face down on the pool's bottom. Rethi plunged in, scooped the boy in his arms, and with the aid of another man brought him to the surface. Rethi performed mouth-to-mouth resuscitation and the boy soon started breathing, but was then taken to the hospital where his condition was listed as serious. Doctors said at the time that he should recover.*

Rethi told the reporter for the Star *that he doubted his actions would earn him a Carnegie Medal since he didn't think he risked his life. He was right. After giving him a hero's welcome and free lunch back in Pittsburgh, the staff promptly assigned the case a file number—58473— then TD'd it (Turned Down, in Hero Fund parlance).*

(Star photo)

James L. Rethi

my life. I just lifted the boy out of the
water."
    Rethi had dried off, but could not
shake off the excitement from the
danger.
    "My nerves are still on edge, but
I'm all so thankful. Here is a young
life that will continue on."

The Tuscaloosa News

TUSCALOOSA, NORTHPORT, WEST ALABAMA

TUESDAY, SEPTEMBER 25, 2001 50¢

WWW.TUSCALOOSANEWS.COM

4 DEAD, 9 MISSING IN MINE BLASTS

Worst U.S. mining disaster in 17 years

By Johnny Kampis
and Stephanie Taylor
Staff Writers

BROOKWOOD | At least four coal miners are dead and nine more are missing and presumed dead following two explosions in Jim Walter Resources Blue Creek Mine No. 5, North America's deepest mine.

It is believed to be the deadliest U.S. mining disaster since 1984, when 27 people were killed in a Utah mine.

Officials at the mining company said six miners were injured following the initial explosion Sunday at 5:15 p.m., which was caused by a rock falling on a battery charger. Friction from the rock-slide caused methane gas in the mine to ignite.

"I had just gotten a drink of water and walked out into the entry, and the next thing I knew, I felt like I was in a tornado," said Michael Mcle, 42, one of the injured workers. He was in good condition Monday at DCH Regional Medical Center.

'They went in after their brothers'

By Steve Reeves
and Stephanie Taylor
Staff Writers

BROOKWOOD | When the word rang out that six men were down in the Jim Walter Blue Creek No. 5 mine, a 10-person group of volunteers jumped into action.

As they hustled to retrieve their colleagues, a second explosion trapped them, almost certainly killing the rescuers.

"These men are heroes," said Don De-Fossett, chief executive officer of Walter Industries, parent company of Jim Walter Resources.

Men who work in and around mines are no strangers to heroic acts. So also they are no strangers to the Carnegie Hero Fund. Over the 100 years since its founding, the Hero Fund has awarded the Carnegie Medal to more than 150 brave and unselfish men who took part in mine rescues, the first of whom, **DANIEL DAVIS**, 23, died attempting to save a fellow miner from suffocation on July 11, 1904, in Sherodsville, Ohio. The last miner awardees of the Hero Fund's first century were 12 men who died attempting to save a coworker on September 23, 2001, in the wake of a methane explosion at a coal mine near Brookwood, Alabama. It was the worst coal mine accident in the United States since 1984.

✝ *C. H.* 10

23 Sept. 2001
ABOUT 2,140 FEET BELOW GROUND,
BLUE CREEK NO. 5 MINE
BROOKWOOD, ALABAMA

The Sunday afternoon shift in the Blue Creek No. 5 mine was a 32-member crew doing maintenance work in preparation for the resumption of mining on the following shift. Mining machine operator Gaston E. Adams, Jr., and two other men were building wooden cribs to support an area of roof and walls that was showing signs of deterioration. They were in an area designated as Section 4, which was at the east end of the sprawling three-by-two-mile mine. At about 2,140 feet below the surface of the earth, it was the deepest vertical-shaft coal mine on the continent.

✝ *C. H.* 8707, 8708,
8709, 8715,
8711, 8710, 8713,
8714, 8712,
9717, 8716, 8718

Changes in the condition of the roof and walls in the area in which they were working had first been observed two days earlier. Conditions had deteriorated further by the time of the men's afternoon shift. At about 5:17 p.m., a large rock fell from the roof, and then the roof itself fell in that area, releasing about 100 cubic feet of methane. After the fall, Adams and his coworkers walked away from the immediate scene, one of the coworkers saying that he was going to report the situation by telephone to the mine's control room, located at the surface of the mine.

About three minutes after the fall, the released methane exploded. Adams and the two other miners, then about 60 feet away from the site, were knocked over and injured by the blast, Adams perhaps fatally. Critical ventilation controls were damaged in Section 4, disrupting the airflow and allowing additional methane to accumulate. Dust was so thick in the area that it made breathing difficult and greatly hindered visibility.

The effects of the explosion varied in other parts of the mine. About a mile to the west, **JOHN WESLEY KNOX**, working with two other men, felt a small concussion. He took a locomotive toward the scene to investigate. About a half-mile to the east, miners **DENNIS R. MOBLEY** and **CHARLES J. NAIL** also started toward the scene to investigate. They met up with the injured miners at the mouth of Section 4, where Nail was instructed to turn off the electrical power to the section. One of the injured miners, who

A BAND OF BROTHERS
Thirteen miners
died in the Blue
Creek No. 5 mine
in Brookwood,
Alabama, on
September 23, 2001.
Twelve of the miners
were awarded the
Carnegie Medal,
posthumously,
for attempting to
save Gaston E.
Adams, Jr. (facing
page, top).

John Wesley Knox
Dennis R. Mobley
Charles J. Nail
David L. Blevins
Clarence H. Boyd
Nelson Banks, Jr.
Charles E. Smith
Terry Milas Stewart
Joe Riggs
Wendell R. Johnson
Raymond F. Ashworth
Joseph P. Sorah

was a foreman, and Mobley left to find a telephone, meeting Knox while on their way. Knox took them to a telephone, and the foreman contacted the mine's control room, which paged mine personnel and put calls to the outside for help. It was then 5:45 p.m.

Foreman DAVID L. BLEVINS was working at the base of the service shaft in the west end of the mine, about three-and-a-half miles from the mouth of Section 4, when he answered a page. He immediately started toward Section 4, a trip that would take about 45 minutes. Along the way, he met other miners and instructed them to accompany him with fire extinguishers. Knox and Mobley, meanwhile, responded to the mouth of Section 4, where they met up with Nail and learned of Adams' location. The three men's subsequent actions were not witnessed, but it was concluded that they took a locomotive to the end of the track in Section 4, then reached Adams and started back with him.

After finishing a job near the west end of the mine, CLARENCE H. BOYD and NELSON BANKS, JR., traveled east on other chores. Boyd met up with three other miners, CHARLES E. SMITH, TERRY MILAS STEWART, and JOE RIGGS, who had been working in a north extension of the mine. Riggs told Boyd of an ignition in Section 4 and that he was going to help, and Boyd joined the three miners as they left in two conveyances for the scene. At a point about a half-mile from it, they encountered the injured miners, who, leaving the mine, told them that Adams was trapped and hurt, and of his location. Boyd, Smith, Stewart, and Riggs continued east toward Section 4; Banks had been ahead of them and was also on his way to the scene. Their subsequent actions were likewise not witnessed, but it was concluded that they reached the mouth of Section 4 at about 6:10 p.m., then entered it and walked to the end of the track.

WENDELL R. JOHNSON was working in the west end of the mine when he too responded to a page from the control room. He learned of the situation in Section 4, then told two miners working nearby that help was needed there. The three miners traveled easterly to where they met another crew, including RAYMOND F. ASHWORTH and JOSEPH P. SORAH, and alerted them to the situation. Johnson, Ashworth, Sorah, and other miners set out for the scene, ahead of them the conveyance driven by Blevins. At a point about a half-mile from the mouth of Section 4, the two responding parties encountered the injured miners. After the parties shared information, Blevins asked for three volunteers to accompany him. Johnson, Ashworth, and Sorah stepped forward, and the four men continued toward Section 4. They reached its mouth and parked behind the vehicles that had taken Banks and Riggs and his party to the scene. It was concluded that Blevins approached the scene on foot.

A massive explosion of methane occurred in Section 4 at 6:15 p.m., or about 55 minutes after the first explosion. Flames spread through all of Section 4 and to those sections adjoining it. Almost all of the miners remaining in the mine felt or saw effects of the second explosion, which caused widespread destruction of ventilation controls. Other than Adams and the 12 miners who had responded to Section 4, the miners closest to the scene at the time of the explosion were about a mile to the west, and they were blasted by air and knocked down. Nineteen miners evacuated the mine to safety, leaving Adams and the 12 rescuers unaccounted for.

A command center was established on the surface, and rescue teams were assembled. The first team entered the mine through the service shaft at 8:05 p.m. and proceeded through thick dust as they tested for gas, removed debris, and terminated power. As they drew closer to Section 4 two hours later, they found Ashworth, conscious but unable to communicate. The rescuers attempted to stabilize him, and then took him to the service shaft for removal from the mine. He reached the surface at 11:30 p.m. and was taken by helicopter to the hospital, where he died the next day.

Rescue team members continued to search, and at a point about 120 feet from where Ashworth was found, they located the bodies of Sorah, Johnson, and Blevins. Other rescue teams were sent into the mine, and search operations continued throughout the night. By 6:30 the following morning, the teams were evacuated from the mine and debriefed. It was concluded that the missing miners could not have survived the second explosion and that conditions prevented safe re-entry to recover them. A decision was made also to extinguish fire in the mine by flooding the affected sections. Pumping over five days flooded most of the affected sections with 32 million gallons of water from nearby lakes. About three weeks later, water removal began, and six weeks after the explosions, the bodies of Blevins, Johnson, and Sorah were removed. Within days, the bodies of Adams and the remaining eight rescuers were found.

Two years later, on November 17, 2003, in the Old House Chamber of the State Capitol building in Montgomery, Governor Bob Riley and the Carnegie Hero Fund Commission hosted a ceremony in which Carnegie Medals were presented to the families of the 12 men who had acted on behalf of Adams. Mark Laskow, Commission president, told the assembly, "We remember and honor the choice of these miners, in a moment of great peril, to help their brothers, those miners with whom they shared double danger. William Shakespeare wrote in *Henry V* about a bond among men who share danger and that their deeds are remembered. With apologies to Shakespeare, I have modified his words a bit:

> This story shall the good man teach his son;
> And this day shall never go by,
> From this day to the ending of the world,
> But these heroes shall be remembered—
> These few, these happy few, this band of brothers...

"The Brookwood miners were indeed a 'band of brothers,' which they proved not by words, but by their actions."

The Hero Fund's investigation of the case was greatly aided by the exhaustive reports of the Mine Safety and Health Administration and the United Mine Workers of America. FILE NOS: 75904, 75905, 75906, 75902, 75903, 75901, 75909, 75910, 75907, 75646, 75900, 75908

U.S. JOURNAL: LONG ISLAND
HERO INVESTIGATOR

by CALVIN TRILLIN

IV

ON THE ROAD WITH
SPECIAL AGENT HERBERT EYMAN

like many people who travel as part of their daily routine, Herbert Eyman is rarely seen shuffling and reshuffling train schedules or straining for a look out of bus windows to make certain he is going in the right direction. Eyman knows by now that there will always be another train along, and that the bus will probably take him somewhere he eventually has to go. In his territory—the United States and Canada—he is unlikely to become lost, for he has been almost everywhere at least once. Eyman has spent twenty-five years on the road—patiently waiting for trains and sitting unconcernedly in buses that seemed to be going in the wrong direction—looking for heroes. When he arrived at Pennsylvania Station on a Friday morning in late spring and found that it would be an hour before another train left for the South Shore of Long Island—where, three months before, a man was said to have entered a burning rest home and carried a helpless patient to safety—he was undisturbed at the delay. Eyman walked from the ticket window to the coffee shop—a handsome, elderly-looking man with a prominent nose, white hair combed straight back, and a very slight stoop that sometimes makes his movements seem birdlike. He was dressed in a black suit, black tie, and a spotless white shirt. He carried a black notebook.

Eyman ordered coffee, lit a cigarette, and flattened out a sheet of paper on the table in front of him. Carrying a man out of a burning building is what Eyman's employers—the managers of the Carnegie Hero Fund Commission—sometimes refer to as "a simple fire case." Eyman has investigated dozens—perhaps

(FACING PAGE)
HERBERT W. EYMAN

*U.S. JOURNAL:
LONG ISLAND HERO
INVESTIGATOR*—
COPYRIGHT ©1970
BY CALVIN TRILLIN.
ORIGINALLY APPEARED
IN *THE NEW YORKER*.
REPRINTED BY
PERMISSION OF
LESCHER & LESCHER,
LTD. ALL RIGHTS
RESERVED.

hundreds—of fire cases. Except for the water case, they have always constituted the most common act of heroism. Eyman no longer really needs to follow the investigative outline called for by the Commission's Manual of Instructions for Field Representatives—he knows whom he has to talk to and what questions he must ask—but he finds that the outline imposes a discipline that keeps him at the heart of the case. The evening before—in his room at the Bristol Hotel, on Forty-eighth Street, where he stays when he is in New York—he had made an outline, folding a sheet of paper in quarters to provide four miniature pages, as the Manual suggests, and writing in neat longhand the name of the rescuer, Adrian Hoek, and the rescued, John Hughes, with notations under each that the name must be accompanied by address, date of birth, height, weight, and occupation. On the appropriate tiny page, in the required order, he had listed all of the information the Commission would require about the act of heroism—including a description of the scene where the act took place, with relevant measurements, and an indication of what the weather was like, what Hoek was wearing, and how familiar he was with the scene. Eyewitnesses to the act would have to be interviewed if any could be found. It would have to be ascertained, quite specifically, whether or not Hoek had risked his life; as Eyman has explained to those who ask about the standards of the Commission, "a life risk is the minimum for a Carnegie award." He would have to learn the financial circumstances of the rescuer; if Eyman's employers are satisfied that an act of heroism is authentic and that the person who performed it could use money for a worthy cause, they may award the hero not only a medal but up to a thousand dollars in cash. The Commission has an endowment of about twelve million dollars.

In listing people he would have to see, Eyman had used the abbreviations recommended by the Manual: RR for the Rescuer, QD for the Rescued, EW for Eyewitness, and RPR for Reporter, the person who brought the case to the Commission's attention. On the back of the outline he had made a preliminary sketch of the rest home, based on information furnished by the RPR, and as he sipped his coffee he looked it over, studying the route from the back bedroom, where the Rescuer was reported to have found the Rescued, to the back door. Eyman likes to have the scene of the act well in mind before interviewing anybody. The outline he studied had been done on a piece of stationery from the Midtown Motor Lodge in Kinston, North Carolina. Near Kinston, several months before, three passersby had rescued a man who was trapped in the cab of a burning truck.

Field representatives work a five-and-a-half-day week. Assuming that the Hoek case was likely to take up Friday and Monday, Eyman figured he would remain in his room at the Bristol Saturday morning to catch up on paperwork. In addition to case reports, he has to fill out expense statements, requisition forms for office supplies, and a daily report, which must list, among other things, the mail he has received from the Commission's office, in Pittsburgh, the mail he has sent to the office, the people he has interviewed (their names followed by the appropriate abbreviation), and the miles he has travelled by various means of conveyance. He was also thinking of using the half day for one of the calls he had to make on people in the area who are beneficiaries of pensions from the Commission. There was a woman in Yonkers whose daughter, a switchboard operator, had died in a fire while remaining at her post to warn other people in the building. A woman in Babylon was getting a pension because her husband had died while rescuing a man who had been overcome by poison gas while working in a sewer. Eyman also had to visit a woman in Bay Shore whose husband had been killed many years before while performing an act of heroism that Eyman no longer remembered; he had not investigated that case originally himself. He would probably use Saturday afternoon and Sunday to write letters. Eyman gets most of his reading done on trains, and, his health having been imperfect for several years, he has given up some of the pastimes he used to enjoy on the road, such as going to ball-games (he was once a sports reporter) or prospecting for stones to cut and polish on the machinery he keeps at a sister-in-law's house in Pittsburgh. Occasionally, people ask him if he finds the life lonely. Except for three weeks' vacation every year, he moves constantly from hotel room to hotel room. He has not maintained a permanent home since he joined the Commission. "You get a rhythm of life," he says when the question comes up. "You get used to travelling. You have the challenge of the case to spur you on.

If you're interested in meeting new people, your life is full. You work right along."

When the train from New York arrived early that afternoon in Sayville, a town about halfway along the southern shore of Long Island, a dozen people stepped down to the platform. All of them except Eyman seemed to melt away before the train pulled out of the station. He walked to an outdoor telephone booth, where he called Charles Stevenson—John Hughes' son-in-law, the man who had reported Hoek's act of heroism to the Commission—and announced that he had arrived to begin the investigation. As he waited for Stevenson, Eyman glanced at the white stucco waiting room and at the tree-lined streets in front of him. He could not recall investigating any cases in Sayville in recent years, but the ride from New York had brought a number of heroic acts to mind. In New York itself, he has investigated every type of case listed in the Manual: the water case, the fire case, the suffocation case, the moving-vehicle case, the electric-shock case, the high-elevation case, the homicidal-attack case, even the enraged-animal case. At Bay Shore, Eyman had been reminded of an engineer who, having realized that his brakes would not stop the train before it hit a child who was playing on the tracks, had climbed onto a platform on the front of the engine, leaned out as far as he could in front of the train, and scooped up the child. In the investigation, Eyman had decided that a life risk was involved; the engineer could have been knocked to the tracks himself by the impact of meeting the child. The memories jogged into Eyman's mind by the station signs of Long Island towns were of facts brought out in his investigations; like most people, Eyman has never actually seen anybody risk his life in an act of heroism.

Stevenson drove up within three or four minutes. When they shook hands, Eyman called him General Stevenson—a retired attorney, he had been a National Guard major general and, at one time, the adjutant general of the State of New York—but Stevenson did not have a particularly military bearing. He is a short, stocky man with a friendly manner and a slight Brooklyn accent.

"You fellows always just call up that way, without notice?" Stevenson asked as they drove toward the Great South Bay, down a wide residential street with old oaks whose branches nearly met over the center of the road. "I guess that's the way to get the real story."

Eyman smiled and nodded. "How's Mr. Hughes getting along?" he asked.

"Oh, Mr. Hughes is surviving," Stevenson said. "He's in the Suffolk County Infirmary at Yaphank now. My wife will probably be going over to see him later this afternoon. He's not really what you'd call senile, but he's approaching that state. He's living in his childhood a lot." A block before the Bay, Stevenson turned left and drove to a small salmon-colored bungalow. In the living room, he showed Eyman to an easy chair, handed him an account of the case to read, and, explaining that Mrs. Stevenson was at church polishing brass with the Altar Guild, went to the kitchen himself to get some soft drinks. The account—in the alumni bulletin of Stevenson's West Point class, the class of 1924—emphasized the coincidence that Adrian Hoek, the man who had rescued Mrs. Stevenson's father, had a son who was married to the Stevensons' daughter. Eyman studied the newsletter. The Commission considers a man responsible for his own family; no award is given to someone who risks his life saving his children, say, or his wife. In a case where the Rescued and the Rescuer are distantly related, Eyman is responsible for reporting just how close they were, so that those on the Commission can judge whether or not the Rescuer had some personal reason for performing the act. The inscription on a Carnegie Medal reads, "Greater Love Hath No Man Than This, That a Man Lay Down His Life for His Friends." But it is a man's willingness to lay down his life for strangers that is most treasured by the Commission. If a hero has a compelling reason for rescuing a person—that he is obligated to the person, perhaps, or that he values the person's life above his own—he has not really performed what Eyman has called "an act with no thought of self, an act of pure nobility, if you will." The purity of a heroic act would also be mitigated, of course, by the hero's being prudent enough to take special precautions for his own safety. In addition to finding out what special value Adrian Hoek placed on the life of John Hughes, Eyman would have to find out how cautiously Hoek had made his assault on the burning rest home. The clippings sent to the Commission by Stevenson had mentioned Hoek's being a volunteer fireman in West Sayville. A rest home in Bay Shore was clearly outside his area of responsibility—policemen and firemen are almost never given Carnegie awards for heroism in the line of duty—but his fireman's training might have reduced the risk. Eyman would have to find out if Hoek had covered his face with a wet cloth before dashing into the building, and if he had known enough to crouch near the floor, keeping below the smoke.

"I got out the clippings, in case you didn't see them," Stevenson said when he returned to the living room, carrying ginger ale and coffeecake. He handed Eyman a picture spread on the fire from the New York *Daily News*, along with a clipping from a local newspaper detailing Hoek's role, as president of the Great South Bay Baymen's Association, in protesting the Brookhaven Town Board's leasing of clamdigging rights to a man from Huntington. Eyman seemed only casually interested in the clippings. He has never depended on newspaper reports. Stevenson sat opposite Eyman, looking prepared to answer questions. There was an awkward silence. Eyman rearranged the clippings on his lap and drew an ashtray closer to him. Finally, he asked if there had been any witnesses to the act.

"There might have been a bus driver," Stevenson said. "There's a school-bus garage in back of the rest home, and some of the drivers assisted with the rescue. Four people died in the fire, you know, and I think two more ladies died within a week. I don't have to tell you: the primary reason was smoke inhalation. If my father-in-law had one good whiff, that would have been curtains, because he had this difficulty with his lungs."

"Is there a foundation still there that we can look at?" Eyman asked.

"The building is still standing," Stevenson said.

Eyman looked surprised. He felt Hoek's case growing weaker. If the fire had not been serious enough to destroy the building, perhaps the fire department could have brought it under control before it reached the back bedroom. But the smoke might have been sufficiently deadly to constitute great peril even if the flames never reached the back of the house, and, as a man with fire training, Hoek might have known it. The Commission is anxious to know not only whether or not the hero placed his life in peril but also whether or not he *knew* he was placing his life in peril.

Eyman never expects to find an easy answer to the second question. Cases that contain objective evidence that the hero was aware of his peril are so rare that they stand out in Eyman's mind. He often mentions a Florida water case concerning the rescue of an immense fat man who enjoyed floating and dozing in the ocean. The day the fat man neglected to consider tides and was washed out to sea, there were only two people on the beach to hear his cries—a two-hundred-pound college football tackle and a ninety-eight-pound girl. The tackle immediately ran into the water, but when he had gone about chest deep he suddenly realized what he was about to do—he saw the possibility of getting caught in the undertow himself, perhaps, or realized that the fat man might panic and pull both of them under—and he came back to the beach. The girl swam out and brought in the fat man. In his investigation, Eyman had concluded that the girl could not have witnessed the return of the tackle and remained unaware of the peril she would face if she tried to rescue the fat man.

"Perhaps we could go along with your wife if she's planning to visit her father this afternoon," Eyman said.

"I'm not really sure you would find it profitable to go to Yaphank," Stevenson said. "Mr. Hughes probably doesn't remember anything about it. We have trouble getting him to remember what happened yesterday. His childhood in Wales, or South America when he was in business there—that's a different matter."

"If there's any chance at all that he would remember, I ought to talk to him," Eyman said. "He might be the only person who could say for certain that Mr. Hoek was in the room."

Stevenson eventually agreed that they could pick up Mrs. Stevenson at the church, drive to the infirmary at Yaphank, and then drop Eyman at Adrian Hoek's house. Eyman felt pleased with the logistics of the investigation. He usually begins a case by talking to the RPR precisely because the person who took the trouble to report an act of heroism is likely to have enough interest in it to provide some guidance, and perhaps even some transportation. The Commission encourages its field representatives to make their way as frugally as possible.

On the way to pick up Mrs. Stevenson, the General told Eyman some of the facts about St. Ann's Episcopal Church that he had learned in preparing a history of the church on the occasion of its centenary. It is a small country church, built of fieldstone, next to a peaceful meadow. Mrs. Stevenson had just finished her polishing when her husband and Eyman arrived, and she insisted that Eyman come in to see the church interior. Mrs. Stevenson—a nice-looking, talkative lady with gray hair and bright-blue eyes—seemed perfectly willing to have Eyman interview her father. "He really isn't well," she said, in a chatty tone. "He comes and goes. Arteriosclerosis, you know. He's such a sweet old man. Everyone talks about how he coöperates over there. I'm still shocked from the fire. I had just seen those four little old ladies and kissed them goodbye the night before." Eyman nodded, and Mrs. Stevenson switched the subject to brass polishing, saying she was going to get some non-tarnish polish for summer. She picked up her bucket of equipment, and they walked toward the door.

Stevenson drove out through the St. Ann's cemetery so that Eyman could see the graves of some of the founders. "I thought I'd like to be buried here, but I might as well be buried at West Point," Mrs. Stevenson said cheerfully. "It ruined my life—all those Guard meetings—so I might as well end up there." Mrs. Stevenson did most of the talking on the way to Yaphank. She spoke of her father—whom she often called Taid, the Welsh word for "grandfather"—and about the problems of being ill at an advanced age. "I think he's failing, you know," she said. "When he came there, they spoke about physical therapy, but they haven't taken him down to therapy yet. What's the use, with all that's wrong with him? They're able to keep people alive now. They're able to keep these poor little people alive for ten or fifteen years, if you call it being alive. I don't know if it's better or not."

Eyman half nodded. He was concentrating on asking about Hughes' weight and his date of birth.

"This Suffolk County Infirmary is a marvellous place," Mrs. Stevenson said as they drove down the Sunrise Highway. "He gets the finest care. All kinds of drugs. It's been a drain at times. It's certainly changed our retirement. For a while, it was costing fifty dollars a month just for one kind of drug. The place that burned down was expensive, but it was a nice place, too. In the place we had to put him for a few weeks after the fire I had to go over and bathe and shave him every day myself. I took nurse's training years ago. I thought I might as well be doing something while Charlie was at all of those National Guard meetings. With the drugs they have now, they can really keep people alive past—well, their ability to live."

"The Suffolk County Infirmary *is* a fine place," Stevenson put in. "There should be more like it. At *that* place, Taid might live to be a hundred."

"Oh, no, I don't think so, Daddy," Mrs. Stevenson said to her husband. "He's failing."

The Suffolk County Infirmary is a large, well-maintained brick building on spacious grounds. In an auditorium on the first floor, a dozen or so patients, most of them elderly people in wheelchairs, were watching slides of a hospital outing while a volunteer played songs like "School Days" and "Take Me Out to the Ball Game" on an organ. Hughes was reading a Bible when Eyman and Mrs. Stevenson came into the room he shared with another man. Although the left side of Hughes' body was paralyzed—he had to lift his left arm with his right, and his mouth showed signs of a stroke—he did not give the appearance of being old and helpless. A large man who laughed often, he seemed bright and alert, despite his incapacities. "I got out by the skin of my teeth," Hughes said, after confirming that Hoek had rushed into his bedroom and carried him to safety. "I thought he was going to rough me up." Mrs. Stevenson had to shout at her father sometimes to make herself understood, but they seemed to have an easy, joking relationship. Before she left, she said something to him in Spanish and laughed and bent over to hug him. She said she would be back the following day. Hughes' roommate—a large, shambling old man with huge, gnarled hands—had been standing next to his own bed watching the conversation. "My name is Larkin. I'm a clamdigger by trade," he suddenly announced. "I wish my daughter would come that often. I wish I had a daughter like that."

"He's such a gentle little man," Mrs. Stevenson said of her father during the drive back toward Sayville. "Everybody there says how sweet he is. He used to call this the Jack Hughes Turnpike, because we'd come this way when we used to pick him up at the other place on Sundays and bring him to our house for the afternoon. He used to like to sit in the yard and eat ice cream and watch the kids. They still haven't taken him to physical therapy, Charlie. I think they know he's licked."

There was an hour or so before Hoek would be in from clamming, and Stevenson used the time for a ride, occasionally pointing out a church that was founded before or after St. Ann's, or a housing development that was formerly the site of a great estate. Mrs. Stevenson talked of the scene after the fire. Some of the old ladies had been intent on saving their clothing, and hours after the fire had been brought under control there were suitcases on the front yard and clothing flapping from the bushes under the windows. Mrs. Stevenson, who believes she has extrasensory perception, said she had been positive on the afternoon before the fire that something awful was about to happen. "It was Sunday, and I had the strangest feeling when I came home from church," she said. "I knew something was wrong. I called up my son and my two sisters. When the phone rang at seven-twenty that next morning, I said, 'Charlie, there it is. I know that's it.' Oh, look Charlie! Strawberries!"

The car had passed a roadside fruit stand. "It's early," Stevenson said. "They must be Georgia strawberries."

"Florida, I think," Eyman said. "I had occasion to be in Georgia a few weeks ago, and I don't think their strawberries were due for market before the end of this month." Near Atlanta, several months before, a high-school boy had taken a girl in his class on her first horseback ride, and the horse had bolted toward a highway the moment she mounted. The boy gave chase, caught up just as the runaway was about to cross the highway, and managed to turn it onto a bridle path that ran along the road. There was only room for one horse on the path, though, and the boy and his horse continued across the highway, where they were hit by a car and killed. The case had struck Eyman as somewhat old-fashioned. He rarely gets runaway-horse cases anymore.

Stevenson drove past the canal in Islip where Hoek docks his clamming boat. Hoek ordinarily would go nowhere near the rest home in Bay Shore on the way to his boat, Stevenson explained, but that Monday morning the canal was iced in, so Hoek was using a brother's boat, which happened to be docked in Bay Shore.

"It was just one of those flukes," Mrs. Stevenson said.

"There's Mr. Hoek's church," Stevenson said. They were driving through West Sayville and had just passed the First Reformed Church, a neat red brick building with white columns and a white steeple. The houses lining the street looked relatively old, small, and well kept. "Every one of those houses is owned by a Dutchman," Stevenson said. "They've all been here for years."

"They're thrifty, clean people," Mrs. Stevenson said. "They do the right thing."

"They're what you might call hardcore Americans," the General said.

"They do the right thing," Mrs. Stevenson repeated. "They might get killed doing it, but they always do the right thing."

Stevenson turned down Rollstone Avenue, where the signs in front of the houses had names like Van Wyen, Van Essendelft, De Ruiter, and Oeser. The Hoek house was made of weathered shingles and had an old-fashioned porch. The Hoeks were waiting in their living room—a comfortable-looking room that contained such reminders of Hoek's calling as a clock in the shape of a boat's wheel, two or three seascapes, and a bookend in the form of a boatman wearing a yellow slicker. The Stevensons made the introductions, exchanged a few words, and left. Mrs. Hoek—a plump, cheerful woman—offered Eyman the most comfortable chair and took a chair herself on the other side of the room. Hoek sat across from Eyman. A short, powerful-looking man, his face weathered and creased by years on the Bay, he had been in from clamming for a while and had changed into a blue suit for the interview. He sat rather formally, a slight smile on his face, as Eyman asked if he would mind telling the story in his own words first, and then answering questions about it while Eyman took notes.

"When I went into the house, I could feel the oxygen being burned up, and I thought, 'My God! I have to get Taid out!'" Hoek said, after explaining that he had been driving nearby when the fire bell went off.

"And you were trapped once," his wife reminded him.

Hoek didn't seem to hear her. He continued the story, describing to Eyman how he went into Hughes' bedroom, found Hughes eating breakfast, dragged him from the bed, and headed for the kitchen door. "This fellow was there when I got him back to the kitchen, and I said, 'My God! Help me with this man!' I kept him low. The smoke was very bad. I felt filled with smoke up to here." Hoek drew his hand across his thick neck. "I upchucked after I got out."

When Hoek had gone through the story once, Eyman pulled out his notebook and laid it on a table in front of him, with his investigative outline next to it. "I'm going to take some notes now," he announced. "The questions won't be chronological; they follow a report form. Now, your correct name is..."

"Adrian Peter Hoek."

"If you did get a medal, would 'Adrian P.' be the way you would prefer to have it written?"

Hoek smiled and shrugged. He looked at his wife. "I suppose so," he said.

Eyman asked Hoek's address, date of birth, height, weight, and occupation. Mrs. Hoek occasionally offered an opinion about the answers until the questions turned to the actual act of heroism. Then, when she corrected her husband's estimate of when the fire bell went off, Eyman cautioned her formally against consultation.

Hoek answered questions about the construction of the building, about the wind and temperature, about what he and Hughes had been wearing, about how often he had visited Hughes. "When you saw it was the Senior House on fire, was your thought that you'd get anyone, or you'd get him?" Eyman asked.

"Get him. Blood is a little thicker than water, you know," Hoek replied, not realizing that he was affecting the purity of the act.

Hoek answered questions about his service with the West Sayville volunteer fire department, but even before he had outlined his years of experience both he and Eyman seemed aware that they were not in a layman's discussion. They spoke of how the stairwell was acting as a flue, of whether or not the flames were hot enough to pop out the windows, of the progress of the flames along the ceiling, of smoke too thick for anyone who was not wearing a Scott Air-Pak. Hoek seemed to have no doubt that Eyman would understand his description of conditions in the kitchen when he said, "It was a perfect setup for a back draft."

Eyman patiently went through the progress Hoek had made from the back door to the bedroom and back again, ascertaining such facts as which hand Hoek had used to swing Hughes' legs off the bed and precisely how far from the ceiling the smoke had extended. Eyman tends to distrust numerical estimates given by people who have been in a crisis—the Manual for Field Representatives warns that most people overestimate, and it includes a list of American running records, a chart transferring currents from miles per hour to feet per second, and an equation for converting statute miles into knots—but Hoek's estimates sounded authoritative.

Finally, Eyman paused, and with considerable formality said, "This series of questions has to do with your own evaluation of the risk involved in the act."

Mrs. Hoek laughed nervously. Hoek nodded a few times. He was still smiling.

"Do you feel you risked your life?" Eyman asked.

"I sure did," Hoek said. "I broke a promise to my wife, too. She said, 'Ade, don't you ever go into one of those homes.'"

"But I didn't want those poor people to perish," Mrs. Hoek said, half disclaiming her warning.

"A back draft," Hoek said. "A back draft and I'd have been caught and roasted."

Eyman asked the Hoeks a series of questions about their financial position and about what they would do with a cash gift if one happened to be awarded to them; then, his interview complete, he accepted Hoek's offer of a ride to the Sayville station.

On the train back to New York, Eyman decided that he had probably been correct in estimating that he could finish up the Hoek case on Monday. He would have to visit the scene of the fire, and interview the bus drivers and, possibly, some of the Bay Shore firemen. He expected the bus drivers to be rather hostile witnesses. Eyman has found that people who were at the scene of a heroic act themselves are often reluctant to talk about the heroism of someone else. He also expected hostility occasionally from fire departments, jealous of their own responsibilities in removing people from burning buildings. Eyman finds that most people are coöperative, although perhaps not as gracious with their time and coöperation as the Stevensons. Only rarely does he, to his dismay, come across people who "think of 'hero' as a dirty word, who believe that a person who puts his life on the line for somebody else is a sucker." Not long before Eyman went to Sayville, a college boy had refused to coöperate with the investigation of his own act of heroism, believing it would lower him in the eyes of his friends. "He saved three lives, too," Eyman said later. "A boat broke apart and he held them to it. It was a wonderful act, fraught with peril."

Reflecting on the day's investigation, Eyman thought Hoek's case was fairly strong. The relationship between Hoek and Hughes was obviously not close enough to be disqualifying, and Hoek's fire training had actually made his act more heroic, since a layman might have been unaware of the peril that a back draft could bring. Still, there would probably be a lack of eyewitnesses, unless the man who met Hoek at the kitchen door could be found. Eyman would put it all in his report, for the Commission to decide. Three or four times a year, when the Carnegie awards are given out, Eyman is mailed a list of the recipients. He acknowledges receipt of the list in his daily report, and glances through the names. But he is working on another investigation by then, and that one is followed by another, and he has difficulty remembering which of the heroes he investigated were found deserving of a Carnegie medal and which of them were not.*

*Shortly before poor health forced Eyman to give up travelling and take a job at Commission headquarters, Adrian Hoek was given a medal and a cash award for having saved the life of John Hughes. Hoek used the money to repair his clamming boat. John Hughes later died, at the Suffolk County Infirmary.

Over a 20-year period beginning in the late 1940s, a time that might be called the heyday of his career as an investigator, Herb Eyman traveled nearly 375,000 miles, visiting 48 states, including Hawaii, and seven Canadian provinces. His travel records do not show how many times he visited a particular state or province in any one year, but it is reasonable to assume that he touched down in many of them more than once. Florida was on his itinerary every year during this period, including 1955 when he visited 29 other states and five provinces. His travel expenses over the era totaled $71,694.12.

Remarkably, Eyman did not drive.

During those years on the road, Eyman filed 871 case reports and made 651 visits to the homes of beneficiaries to "investigate" their financial circumstances and inquire of their general welfare. A kindly man, he was considered a family member by some of the beneficiaries.

POSTSCRIPT: Eyman's father, Albert, was a posthumous awardee of the Carnegie Medal. He died as the result of attempting to save a woman from drowning in Wildwood, New Jersey, on July 28, 1932. The Commission's monetary grant of $1,000 was used to help pay the tuition of Eyman's younger brother to attend Carnegie Institute of Technology, now Carnegie Mellon University.

An alumnus of Penn State University, Eyman left the editorial staff of the Sharon, Pennsylvania, *Herald* to join the Commission in 1943, taking a 50 percent reduction in salary. His trainer noted that Eyman "has an attitude toward the Commission and our work which his own family experience ... has caused to be most favorable." Declining health made it necessary for Eyman to give up his rigorous travel schedule in 1968, but he assumed an office position and continued his vital role in the Commission's investigative process until the day of his passing in 1978.

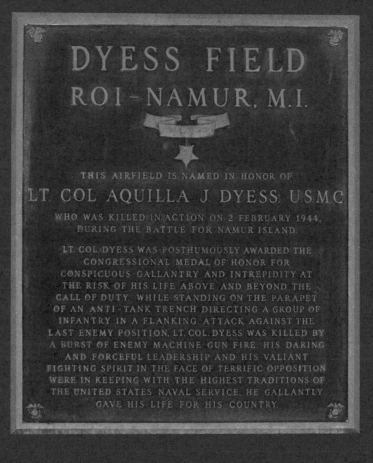

DYESS FIELD
ROI-NAMUR, M.I.

THIS AIRFIELD IS NAMED IN HONOR OF

LT. COL AQUILLA J. DYESS USMC

WHO WAS KILLED IN ACTION ON 2 FEBRUARY 1944,
DURING THE BATTLE FOR NAMUR ISLAND.

LT. COL. DYESS WAS POSTHUMOUSLY AWARDED THE
CONGRESSIONAL MEDAL OF HONOR FOR
CONSPICUOUS GALLANTRY AND INTREPIDITY AT
THE RISK OF HIS LIFE ABOVE AND BEYOND THE
CALL OF DUTY. WHILE STANDING ON THE PARAPET
OF AN ANTI-TANK TRENCH DIRECTING A GROUP OF
INFANTRY IN A FLANKING ATTACK AGAINST THE
LAST ENEMY POSITION, LT. COL. DYESS WAS KILLED BY
A BURST OF ENEMY MACHINE GUN FIRE. HIS DARING
AND FORCEFUL LEADERSHIP AND HIS VALIANT
FIGHTING SPIRIT IN THE FACE OF TERRIFIC OPPOSITION
WERE IN KEEPING WITH THE HIGHEST TRADITIONS OF
THE UNITED STATES NAVAL SERVICE. HE GALLANTLY
GAVE HIS LIFE FOR HIS COUNTRY.

THE REMARKABLE JIMMIE DYESS

by PERRY M. SMITH

A. JAMES "JIMMIE" DYESS is the only person to be awarded both the Carnegie Medal and the Medal of Honor, America's two highest awards for heroism. Dyess was born in Augusta, Georgia, on January 11, 1909, graduated from Clemson College in 1931, joined the United States Marine Corps Reserves in 1936, was placed on active duty in November of 1940, and was killed in action on February 2, 1944. He was 35 years old.

There were many times during his youth in Augusta and North Augusta, South Carolina, when Dyess showed his concern for the welfare of others, but it was an event on July 13, 1928, that first prompted him to demonstrate his willingness to risk his life to assist those in distress. The setting was the beach on Sullivan's Island off the coast of South Carolina, just a few miles north of Charleston. A tall, strong young man with flaming red hair, "Big Red," as his friends called him, had just finished his first year at Clemson, where he was an offensive and defensive end on the undefeated freshman football team. On that hot summer day, a violent storm had blown up unexpectedly. It produced high winds and huge waves. What happened next is best told by the account that appeared a few days later in an Augusta newspaper.

C. H. 2375

"Detailed information has reached Augusta relative to the near drowning of Mrs. Roscoe Holley of this city which occurred at Sullivan's Island last Friday afternoon. Mrs. Holley was in the surf which was exceedingly rough. The tide began to ebb and she was being rapidly taken out to sea. Several attempts at rescue were made and given up because the parties attempting were not expert swimmers and realized the hopelessness of their efforts. There were no surf boats available, no life guards on the spot at the time. Finally when all hope of rescue seemed gone, a young Charleston lady, Miss Barbara Muller, with courage and bravery unsurpassed, started out in a last ditch attempt to save the drowning girl. At this point 'Jimmy' Dyess an Augusta boy who had been bathing further down the beach came upon the scene and realizing the situation went immediately to the rescue without pause to consider the danger involved in such an attempt in such a heavy sea. Both he and Miss Muller reached Mrs. Holley after she had been carried, perhaps, two hundred yards out. While both the rescuers were expert swimmers, it looked for what seemed to be an interminable time to the observers who stood in breathless suspense on the beach, that the trio was doomed to certain destruction. Finally it could be seen as they appeared from time to time at the crest of the huge waves, that they were gaining slowly and after about thirty minutes, they reached the beach and safety, where Jimmy's training in the Boy Scouts was of further service in aiding the resuscitation. When seen by a *Chronicle* reporter, 'Jimmy' said, 'Huh, that's nothing: what else could a man do? If there is any credit it is due Miss Muller, the bravest girl I ever saw. It looked for a time that we were all gone for a long stay but luck was with us.' On lookers give high praise to Miss Muller for a display of bravery and self sacrifice seldom equaled and never surpassed and add that but for the strength and cool headedness of Jimmy Dyess both girls would undoubtedly have been lost."

C. H. 2374

For his heroic act, Dyess was awarded the Carnegie Medal, as was 22-year-old BARBARA H. MULLER. Already, by age 19, Dyess had displayed two of the three most important qualities of a great leader: courage and compassion. Over the next few years, he would develop the third quality, competence. After graduating with a degree in architecture and returning to Augusta, Dyess went to work for the Augusta Lumber Company. In 1934, he married Connor Cleckley of Augusta, and in 1935, a daughter, Connor Cleckley Dyess, was born.

As a reservist with both the Army and Marine Corps during the 1930s, Dyess had so honed his military skills that when he was called to active duty he was ready to command troops. After having been assigned as the executive officer and later as officer in charge of the Marine barrage balloon school in 1941 and 1942, he finally got the leadership job he wanted so badly. In 1943, he was placed in command of the 800 Marines of the First Battalion of the 24th Marine Regiment of the 4th Marine Division. Dyess was one of the very few Marine Corps reserve officers, without previous combat experience, to be given command of a combat battalion.

Dyess led his battalion into combat in January of 1944, when his division attacked the Japanese island of Roi Namur in the Marshall Islands in the Central Pacific. Fighting was heavy the first day of the battle, but it wasn't until dusk approached that Dyess met his first major challenge. A small patrol from another Marine battalion was ordered to move forward on a reconnaissance mission. Led by Corporal Frank Pokrop of Milwaukee, Wisconsin, the patrol initially encountered little resistance. Without realizing it, the Marines had moved through enemy lines and into an area of great danger. A few minutes later, the Japanese spotted them. Pokrop and his buddies were far enough behind the lines that they began to receive fire from three directions. Very soon all but one of the Marines in Pokrop's patrol were wounded and pinned down by the crossfire.

Dyess, who by that time had moved to the extreme right of the front line of troops, heard the heavy fire and realized that the Marines were caught beyond enemy lines and were under heavy pressure. He also realized that, with darkness setting in, there was not much time left if they were to be rescued. The fact that these Marines were not from his own battalion made no difference to Dyess; they were in serious trouble, and he knew instinctively that something had to be done quickly to help them. He organized a small rescue force, which included some infantrymen and a half-track vehicle, and charged forward.

A. James "Jimmie" Dyess and his wife, Connor.

Corporal Pokrop and the other Marines in his patrol were in desperate shape. They were pinned down and couldn't move. There were no medics with the patrol to tend to the wounded. By using fire and maneuver, Dyess and his rescue party were able to fight through the enemy lines, provide suppressing fire, and reach the stranded Marines. Some of his men assisted the wounded Marines back to friendly lines, while Dyess and others continued to provide covering fire. There is no question that Dyess saved the lives of these stranded Marines—the Japanese would take no prisoners in the battle for Roi Namur. The rescue was completed just as darkness engulfed the battered island.

As the battle continued throughout the morning of the 2nd of February, Dyess was in the front leading seven light tanks up Narcissus Road. The tanks were supported by two of his infantry companies, Able and Charlie. Dyess was a dynamo of energy, encouragement, and direction. He was leading men, most of whom were still teenagers, who were experiencing their first days of combat. Most slept very little the night before because of the shift schedule, the rain, and the noise and confusion from the Banzai attacks. They were tired and scared. Dyess was not only giving directions and support, he was firing at Japanese positions. As Dyess moved up and down the line, a number of Marines yelled at him to stay low and to keep his head down. He ignored their pleas. He wanted to direct the fire of his fellow Marines and in order to do so exposed himself to Japanese rifle and machine gun fire. His final words were, "Let's go! Let's get the chestnuts out of the fire."

At about 10:45 a.m., Dyess rose once again to observe the enemy's firing positions, and to direct fire against them. His attention was focused on the last of the Japanese pillboxes. Within seconds, Dyess was hit in the head. He was killed instantly. Willie Turner, Bob Fleishour, and two others grabbed a stretcher and gently placed him on it, and then carried Dyess the half-mile distance to the beach. His body was buried on Roi Namur, but, at the request of his family, it was returned to Augusta after the war had ended and placed in the family mausoleum.

Dyess's extraordinary contributions to his nation and to his fellow man have been recognized in Augusta, in Kansas City, and on the Island of Roi Namur. In Augusta, the Jimmie Dyess Parkway was opened in 1998. In 2003, the Augusta Museum of History completed a permanent exhibit, which highlights Dyess's heroism as well as two ships, the USS *Dyess* that served the Navy from 1945 until 1981, and the USS *Augusta*. The Marine Reserve Center near Kansas City was named in his honor, as was the airfield on Roi Namur. FILE NOS: 29312, 28690

MAJOR GENERAL PERRY M. SMITH USAF (RET.) IS THE AUTHOR OF SIX BOOKS, INCLUDING *RULES AND TOOLS FOR LEADERS, ASSIGNMENT PENTAGON*, AND *A HERO AMONG HEROES: JIMMIE DYESS AND THE 4H MARINE DIVISION*. HE ALSO PRODUCED A VIDEO, *TWICE A HERO: THE JIMMIE DYESS STORY*, AND ASSISTED IN THE EDITING OF *MEDAL OF HONOR* BY PETER COLLIER, WHICH HIGHLIGHTS THE LIFE STORIES OF AMERICA'S LIVING MEDAL OF HONOR RECIPIENTS. HE IS MARRIED TO DYESS'S DAUGHTER, CONNOR DYESS SMITH.

CASTING A SAFETY NET:
THE BENEFICIARIES

by ELIZA S. BROWN

V

The Carnegie Hero Fund has recognized more than 8,700 acts of heroism, all examples of selfless response to immediate need and often reported in heart-wrenching and inspiring accounts. In many cases, the stories go on, played out in the Commission's generous support of the heroes and their dependents over years, sometimes decades. Through the process of supporting these beneficiaries over the past 100 years, the Commission has distributed more than $27 million in outright grants, tuition, funeral expenses, and other support. Yet the beneficiaries' stories are not only about financial aid. Beyond the dollars distributed, countless lives have been touched. Long-term personal relationships have been formed, drawing the Commission and its staff into the major decisions and intimate details of beneficiary families. In some cases, these relationships have been life sustaining, in others life changing.

Andrew Carnegie's original intent was to mitigate the negative financial harm resulting from an awardee's death or disability. To ensure that no heroes or their dependents suffer pecuniarily as a result of heroism, Carnegie empowered the Commission with great resources and flexibility in distributing them:

> For exceptional children exceptional grants shall be made for exceptional education. Grants of sums of money may also be made to heroes and heroines as the Commission thinks advisable, each case to be judged on its own merits.[1]

During an era that provided far less by way of governmental safety nets for the less fortunate than exists today, Carnegie saw an

(FACING PAGE) CAROLYN DELANEY HAS BEEN A BENEFICIARY OF THE COMMISSION FOR SEVERAL YEARS. HER DAUGHTERS, JOANNA AND CRYSTAL, WERE RECIPIENTS OF TUITION ASSISTANCE. HER HUSBAND, **JOE DELANEY** (✠ *C. H.* 6809) WAS AWARDED THE CARNEGIE MEDAL FOR ATTEMPTING TO SAVE TWO BOYS FROM DROWNING IN MONROE, LOUISIANA, ON JUNE 29, 1983. DELANEY, 24, DIED DURING THE ACT. HE WAS A STAR RUNNING BACK FOR THE KANSAS CITY CHIEFS PRO-FESSIONAL FOOTBALL TEAM, AND THE AMERICAN FOOTBALL CONFERENCE'S ROOKIE OF THE YEAR IN 1981.

opportunity to make a difference in the lives of people who were often already disadvantaged even before a selfless act of heroism brought further hardship. At the time the Fund was established, workmen's compensation laws were not yet in existence to help the disabled or killed or their dependents. And, as an article about the newly formed Commission published in *American Illustrated Magazine* in 1905 pointed out, "Carnegie spent most of his life in close association with men who made their livelihood in the extra hazardous trades…and…acts of heroism of a homely sort …were matters of course in his personal experience."[2] Indeed, many of the documented cases portray difficult lives that might have warranted philanthropic intervention even without the addition of heroic sacrifice. They ranged from those who were simply of modest means to those who seemed to navigate from one health or financial disaster to the next.

With the designation of the first heroes on May 24, 1905, the beneficiary story began to unfold. Pensions were granted to widows until they remarried and orphans until they reached the age of 16. Educational awards tended to be made to younger persons to prepare them for usefulness in life. Betterment awards were "bestowed upon the recipients of medals, whom the Executive Committee have decided to be worthy of financial help," for such expenditures as purchase of a home, payment of debts, establishment in business, medical treatment, or any purpose to improve the condition of life. That first year, three widows of heroes were voted annual awards "to relieve them to some extent," and one hero was awarded money to continue her studies.

As it grew in experience during the first 10 years, the Commission crafted more specific guidelines, creating three categories of pecuniary awards: death benefits, disablement benefits, and betterment benefits. Death benefits were designed to assist widows and other dependents of deceased heroes. Disablement benefits offered similar assistance to heroes injured in their acts. Betterment benefits included seven types of support: business establishment, educational expense, health restoration, home purchase, indebtedness liquidation, living expense, and miscellaneous aids. Offered in cases where no losses resulted from the heroic acts, betterment benefits nonetheless sought to "improve the condition in life of the beneficiaries in a permanent way."[3]

DISASTER RELIEF

In the early years, the Commission also responded to large disasters, including the San Francisco Earthquake of 1906 and five coal mine disasters and floods in Ohio and Indiana in 1913. In subsequent years, as Carnegie had predicted, the needs of the beneficiaries grew to the point that such special grants were discontinued. The last 20 years, however, have seen a renewed commitment to making a difference in such situations. The Commission gave $20,000 to the West Virginia Recovery Foundation following catastrophic flooding in 1985, and $25,000 each to the San Francisco Earthquake Relief Fund and the Hurricane Hugo Relief Fund in 1989. Most recently, 2002 giving included two $50,000 grants to foundations established in the wake of the September 11, 2001, terrorist attacks. All in all, the Commission has made 12 disaster grants since 1904.

THOUGHTFUL AND PRUDENT

Regardless of the type or level of support, the benefits have consistently been distributed and monitored in a thoughtful and prudent manner. Driven by Carnegie's original mandate to serve as fiduciary stewards and by the constraints imposed through federal tax law to give "to persons in definite need of charity," the Commission staff has traditionally given each case painstaking scrutiny. A series of forms calls for financial information such as real estate and personal property holdings, income from all sources, debts, and expenses. Renewals are typically made for three- to five-year periods, but beneficiaries are required to provide an annual financial report. The case files reveal a continuum of vigilant support that can carry the beneficiaries through the life passages of childhood, education, marriage, the birth of children and grandchildren, and elderly parent care, and into burial planning. And, while the Commission's early dealings reflected a paternalistic attitude that characterized the era as a whole, it fulfilled a need for wise counsel in the lives of many who had nowhere else to turn. In more recent years, the Commission has adapted to changing times with a less intrusive, though still conservative, approach.

For much of the life of the Commission, any initial award or subsequent support was distributed only upon adequate completion and approval of an "Application by Beneficiary for Use of

Pecuniary Award." This process was taken seriously, and often the award money was commuted for later use. As the Commission advised one beneficiary in 1919, "Before making payments of pecuniary awards, it is our policy to require beneficiaries … to submit propositions for their use which will meet with our approval," and "do not obligate yourself, anticipating the use of the money for the purpose, until your plans are approved by us."[4] In one early case, in which an 8-year-old boy rescued a 6-year-old boy from drowning in 1907, the negotiations lasted for decades. Originally awarded $2,000 in funds set aside for education, the awardee ultimately decided that he would not pursue further education and the grant was commuted to $1,000 for a worthy cause. While the Commission would not approve his proposed house purchase, it nonetheless repeatedly renewed communications and ultimately paid him in monthly installments during his retirement years, concluding in 1959. This resolution was reflective of the Commission's new approach of the late 1950s, aggressively reconnecting with awardees who had unresolved accounts and paying out a number of outstanding pecuniary awards.

SOBER AND PROPER

During its early years, the Commission examined not only the proposed use for the grant awards, but also maintained that it was "our custom always to look into the morals of a beneficiary."[5] Carnegie's Deed of Trust, in fact, clearly stated, "No grant is to be continued unless it be soberly and properly used, and the recipients remain respectable, well-behaved members of the community." To his credit, Carnegie added a forgiving clause to cover those whose morals had perhaps fallen short prior to the heroic act: "The heroes and heroines are to be given a fair trial, no matter what their antecedents. Heroes deserve pardon and a fresh start."[6]

Even as late as the 1930s, the Commission set forth specific expectations regarding behavior, as stated in a 1931 letter to a beneficiary, a widow with three small children:

> We shall expect you to live an upright life and to be circumspect so as to avoid even the appearance of evil; to bring up your children well and send them to school regularly unless they are sick until each has finished a high school course; to keep out of debt; to save something to meet extraordinary expenses … and to

accept in a kindly spirit such suggestions as we may make in the best interests of you and yours and to be guided by them.[7]

At times, the Carnegie Hero Fund support represented nearly all of the widow's income. One of the children would remain on the rolls for 72 years, until her death in 2003.

ENDURING RELATIONSHIPS

Such long-term relationships are not uncommon. In one particularly protracted case dating to 1910, a hero who served as the "leading spirit" of a rescue team that saved a stranded sailor in the raging surf of Lake Superior was granted a pecuniary award of $1,000. It was not collected prior to his death in 1913, when he left a widow and three very young children. Following a thorough investigation of the widow's financial circumstances, the Commission decided to support her. When her second marriage dissolved, the Commission became intimately involved in the disposition of the children, encouraging the mother to send them to "board" with an aunt.

In grappling with this "difficult case," the Commission investigated through third parties how the widow "has been behaving ... and what care she has taken of her children ... ." The case was doggedly pursued over several years through two dozen pieces of correspondence, despite the Commission providing no financial support. As each child came of age, the Commission renewed the contact and attempted to provide educational support. This intimate level of involvement positioned the Commission to be proactive in identifying ways to help the family, corresponding directly with doctors and with schools to help meet the family's needs. By 1968, when the middle child had reached the age of 60, she successfully petitioned the Commission to use the money for dental care. By 1977, the case still had a balance of $302, which, with two siblings agreeing, was paid to the other to assist with "heavy expenses."

Other cases of the same era reveal similarly enduring relationships. One young man, who drowned in 1916 in a Tennessee lake trying to save two women and an infant, left a widow who stayed on the beneficiary rolls for 71 years. At her death in 1987, her son wrote, "Words cannot express what a truly great role the

Commission played in her life, and in mine as well. This is particularly true during my really young years. We shall always be grateful."[8]

ADVICE AND COUNSEL

No subject seemed beyond the Commission's purview during the early years. One beneficiary received a letter in 1919 offering advice on home furnishings. "Our special agent reported that you had no floor coverings for your rooms. We feel that your floor should be covered with matting or carpets.... Please understand that in writing this letter, I have only one object in view and that is to serve the best interests of your children and yourself."[9]

In the case of a woman widowed when her husband attempted to rescue a drowning woman at Atlantic City in 1915, the relationship lasted until the widow's death in 1980. The advice was quite specific, the kind one might expect from a close family member, and ranged from the effective treatment of a goiter to particular bond issues that offered promising returns. In the early 1950s, she was still buying bonds monthly and dutifully reporting on their serial numbers and maturity dates.

Countless beneficiaries have testified to the Commission's life-sustaining influence. Clayton C. Hoskins began his published memoir, *A Jump in the River*, with a description of his father's heroic act in 1927, in which he drowned in the Muskingum River to save a young woman. Hoskins, who witnessed the event just five days short of his third birthday, would later recognize the Commission's support as critical to his upbringing. "The monthly check kept us alive," he wrote. "It made the difference between our living with the assurance that we would have shelter, clothing and food, and the reality that without that money we might have to give up as many as two out of three of those necessities."[10]

C. H. 3969

A current beneficiary, **GEORGE HEMPHILL**, has been on the rolls since 1954, when he assisted in an attempt to rescue a truck driver whose 5,200-gallon tanker of gasoline was struck by a train and exploded into flames. Hemphill's insurance settlement, government compensation, and public donations were not enough to support his family, much less enable him to keep the farm that had been in his family for 100 years. While some doctors gave Hemphill only a few years to live, others said that living on and maintaining the farm would give him the purpose he needed to carry on.

The Carnegie Hero Fund provided the additional support that helped the Hemphills to do just that. When debating construction of a new house on the farm in 1969, Mrs. Hemphill wrote to Manager David Oliver that she had consulted the doctor about the advisability of embarking on such an ambitious project. The doctor had replied, "I have read *The Life of Andrew Carnegie* many many times and I am sure if he could tell you what to do, he would say go home and start to work. That was his purpose," the doctor added, "to help people help themselves." "So I came home," Mrs. Hemphill wrote, "and we started to work."[11] Indeed, the farm has sustained Hemphill, still living there nearly 50 years after his heroic act. "George enjoys the farm," wrote his wife in 2000. "It means so much to him. You make this possible."[12]

MORAL SUPPORT

The relationships forged in the process of supporting beneficiaries often transcend the financial aid. The Commission's role has played out primarily in the form of career guidance, emotional support, or just friendly correspondence. A case in point is **RALPH KELLEY**, paralyzed from the waist down since rescuing two women from a factory fire in Nashua, New Hampshire, as a teenager in 1938. Despite that the initial monthly check ultimately became unnecessary as he succeeded in business, he has corresponded faithfully with the Commission for 65 years, sharing the joys and sorrows of his life: two successful marriages, raising two adopted children, coping with the loss of one wife to cancer and one child in a tragic accident, the closing of his business, and the deteriorating health of advancing age. Through it all, Kelley has viewed the Carnegie Hero Fund Commission as a beacon of support. "I am sure you can appreciate the fact that the Commission has been an important part of my life," he wrote in 1989. "I have appreciated the financial help extended to me for many years as well as the advice and encouragement from your various officers."[13]

One of the most colorful stories in which the relationship far exceeded the financial support involved a Native American youth of 16 who saved a 10-year-old boy from drowning outside a fishery in Douglas, Alaska, in 1953. In 1959, the Commission attempted to alert the hero to a $250 balance in his account available for his use. He proved difficult to find but was finally located, serving four and a half years in a federal prison, from which he was released in 1961. Despite his hopes to use the money for education for himself or his three-year-old son, he soon wound up in prison again, this time for an eight-year sentence. During that time, Commission staff wrote to the man, encouraging him and offering to hold the money until his release. In a poignant letter of 1965, he wrote gratefully, "Would it be possible to give this generous scholarship to a person of my choice?" Soon thereafter, the Commission sent him the balance, and he used the money to subscribe to several periodicals. As it turned out, he was an aspiring writer and poet, and he began an intense four-year correspondence with Oliver, exchanging letters almost monthly. Oliver would send him encouraging words and poetry, and he would respond with poetry of his own. Reaching out beyond Oliver to embrace other members of the staff, he referred to "all of you there at the Commission, my friends," and requested that they add lines to the monthly letters and even send photos for his album. Sadly, the correspondence ended as the hero entered his third stint of incarceration, leaving this story with an undetermined ending.

SCHOLARSHIP ASSISTANCE

Educational support has always been a priority of the Commission, one that it tenaciously pursues. The staff follows the growth of beneficiary children and contacts them when they approach college age, even children who were in their infancy at the time of a parent's death in the performance of a heroic act. Both the scholarship moneys and the accompanying guidance have often proven to make a difference in the lives of beneficiaries. For one daughter of a hero who drowned in a 1954 rescue attempt, the Commission's relationship with her mother lasted 42 years, representing as much as a third of the family income at times. On her mother's death in 1997, the daughter wrote, "Over the years the Carnegie support has meant a great deal to our family. I probably would not have felt I could afford to attend college…if Mom hadn't continued to receive Carnegie support."[14]

Another education grant beneficiary, a 16-year-old boy who saved a girl from drowning off Long Island in 1964, wrote repeated notes of gratitude, including the message, "It just seems impossible that something I did without thinking, or without

taking time to reason why, would result in changing my whole future."[15] Tragically, this young hero died suddenly before he could finish his medical training, which had been supported in part by the Commission.

Other examples reveal the potential of the education grants for long-term, positive results. MARYLAND WILSON SHYTLES rescued a young girl from drowning in a lake in Hendersonville, North Carolina, in 1928, when she was only 12 years old. Five years after the incident, Shytles was informed of her eligibility for scholarship aid, which she eagerly accepted. Reflecting some 50 years later on the support she received, Shytles described the critical role played by C. B. Ebersol during his tenure as manager of the Commission. "He was truly a guardian angel," she wrote, "piloting me through my undergraduate years and continuing to counsel and advise me long after my award was depleted."[16] Shytles in a later letter cited the importance of Ebersol's advice "not to overlook the importance of extra-curricular activities. We want you to become as well-rounded an individual as possible."[17] She went on to earn M.A. and Ph.D. degrees in speech and journalism, and enjoyed a long and distinguished career as an academic, which yielded not only personal satisfaction but also significant influence over countless students. Shytles' gratitude to the Carnegie Hero Fund she summarizes simply: "Whatever success I have experienced professionally I owe to Mr. Ebersol and the Commission."[18] "How very blessed I was to come under its wing."[19]

CONTAGIOUS GENEROSITY

At the time of its 75th anniversary, the Commission instituted a change in its award policy that would trigger even greater positive effects in the lives of others. Beginning in 1979, heroes or their surviving families received initial automatic lump-sum grants, which have increased from $1,500 to the current level of $3,500, and which might still be augmented with other kinds of support. The change to lump-sum grants has been pivotal, prompting a number of altruistic awardees to direct the money to worthy causes that leverage the Carnegie money to touch even more lives.

The catalytic effect of these gifts is a reflection not only of the contagious nature of generosity, but also of the personal values and interests of the heroes and their families. Such was the case of a 19-year-old Pennsylvania boy, JAY PAUL OBERHOLTZER,

C. H. 2532

(FACING PAGE) ROBERT P. STCHUR (C. H. 7463), AN ORTHOPEDIC SURGEON NOW PRACTICING IN PUNTA GORDA, FLORIDA, WAS AWARDED THE CARNEGIE MEDAL FOR SAVING A 13-YEAR-OLD GIRL FROM DROWNING IN SIDNAW, MICHIGAN, ON JULY 5, 1989. STCHUR WAS 17 YEARS OLD AT THE TIME. THE COMMISSION PROVIDED STCHUR WITH TUITION ASSISTANCE FROM HIS SOPHOMORE YEAR AT CENTRAL MICHIGAN UNIVERSITY THROUGH FOUR YEARS AT WAYNE STATE UNIVERSITY SCHOOL OF MEDICINE.

✝ C. H. 8529

who died in 2001 attempting to save his 10-year-old brother from drowning in a frozen pond. His grieving parents chose to apply his $3,500 award to Christian missionary work, writing, "Just as Jay Paul loved to serve, we chose to give the award money to missions for the work of Christ in people's lives."[20]

That same year, a Virginia man rescued a 10-year-old boy from drowning in the James River, and then used his $3,500 grant to establish an educational trust for the boy, considered to be disadvantaged and at risk. A pastor, business consultant, and professor of aeronautical science, **STEVE BINGHAM** explained his motivation: "I believe so strongly in the value of education in shaping the lives of young people. Education is more than just one level of life; it extends through the whole life of the person. God did not save that boy out of the river to die in the street. My hope is to continue building the life that was saved."[21]

Arguably the most compelling case of philanthropic use of the award came in 1993, when **PAUL LESSARD** leveraged a portion of his award as seed money to fund The Lighthouse Project. This character education program pays for nationally recognized inspirational speakers to address high school students in Guilford County in North Carolina. Lessard works closely with the woman he rescued from a submerged car, Ella Mae Bowman, to select speakers who have overcome dramatic obstacles by basing their life decisions on sound values. Among the speakers have been a Vietnam veteran telling of his near-death combat experiences, a Nazi death camp survivor, a former gang member, and a blind man who hiked the entire 2,160-mile Appalachian Trail. During its first 10 years, the project reached more than 500,000 students.

"One of the great blessings and indeed, the great catalyst was your organization and 'the Medal,'" Lessard wrote about the project recently. "You changed my life, you gave me the ability to serve others, and I will always be eternally grateful for this."[22]

Other heroes have chosen to apply their award money to help those who might find themselves in similar dangerous situations in the future. **MANUEL JOSEPH "MANNY" TROMBLEY**, who rescued two elderly neighbors from their burning house in 1998, used his $3,000 award to make donations to civic and municipal organizations. Included among them was the local fire department, kicking off a campaign to buy a pair of thermal imaging glasses that enable rescuers to locate victims in smoke-filled spaces.

C. H. 8651

C. H. 7796

C. H. 8247

Still others, though they might not actually have applied the Commission's support to a charitable purpose, seemed to derive from it something of a generous spirit. Hemphill wrote in 1980 that he wondered if there might not be another beneficiary who needed the $80 per month more than he. Another hero of the early 1980s, in response to an offer of tuition from the Commission for his son, wrote, "Thank you once again for your help, but I was able to get help from my family once again.... Carnegie has been so helpful words cannot describe, so maybe this money can help out another Carnegie recipient...."[23]

A BROAD REACH

The statistics of lives touched through financial and other support are impressive. During the first 25 years, the Commission awarded 19 gold medals, 526 silver medals, and 1,760 bronze medals. Incident to those awards, it provided support to 319 widows, 696 orphans, 31 parents, nine siblings, and 12 heroes in indigent circumstances. Betterment awards to 1,363 heroes included 372 educational awards.

Subsequent reports every 25 years have revealed a similarly broad reach. By 1979, the cumulative total had reached more than $9.2 million for continuous support, $1 million for education, and $3.2 million for all other heroes. For the year 2003, giving totaled $706,000, including monthly support of 74 beneficiaries ranging from $100 to $400, scholarships to 26 students, and funeral assistance.

Not surprisingly, the generosity of the Carnegie Hero Fund Commission has prompted a deluge of grateful letters over the years. "I wish to thank you and the Commission for your financial support and your kindness and friendship. You'll never know how much *all* these things have helped me thru the years and how very much I appreciate the Commission and what it has done and is doing for me."[24] "You have eased the burden of my financial situation in too many ways to tell you."[25] "Mr. Carnegie surely did have a big heart."[26] A number of beneficiaries sought to thank Carnegie while the benefactor was still alive. Among those was a woman who ultimately would receive support for 49 years and who wrote, "It is certainly grand to know that God has put such a thoughtful and liberal man in this world as Mr. Carnegie. It surely must be a blessing to him to know that he has made many a sad heart glad."[27]

TWICE A HERO

Looking n...

at course of Rr...

For nearly all Carnegie Medal awardees, risking their own lives to save another is a once-in-a-lifetime experience. But in the 100-year history of the Commission, there are four men who, remarkably, met the challenge again and became awardees of a second medal.

CASE OF HENRY NAUMANN   FILE No. 24477-A

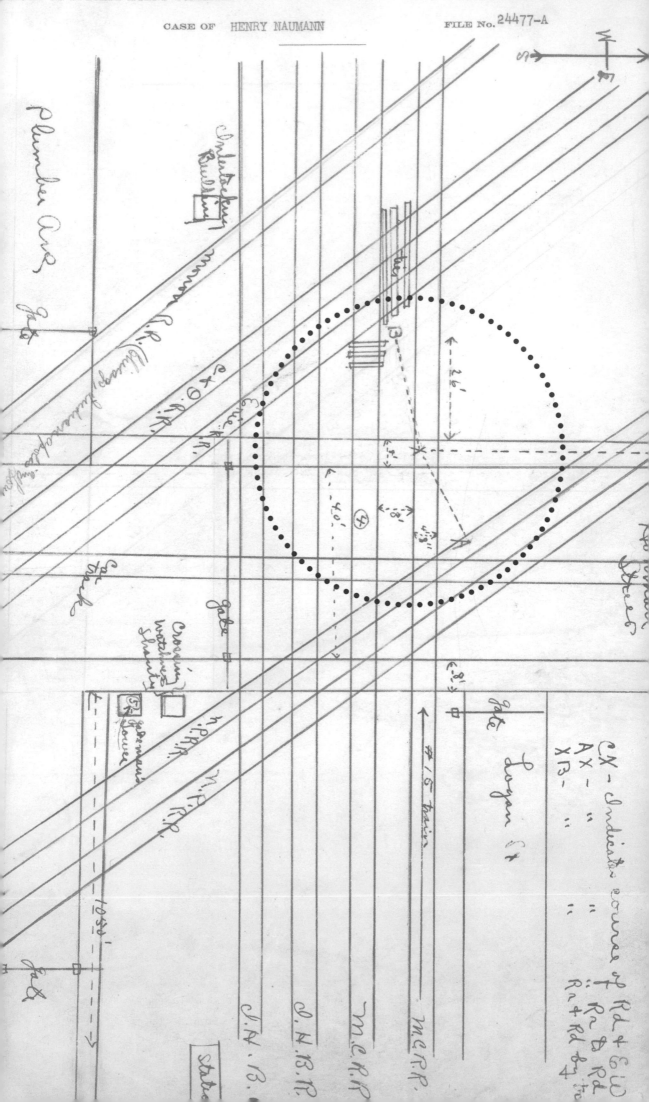

HENRY NAUMANN, 46, was a watchman at the Hohman Street crossing of several railroad tracks in Hammond, Indiana, at midday on June 16, 1924. In addition to Naumann, 10 mechanical gates controlled pedestrian and automobile traffic as an average of 318 trains a day passed through the crossing that summer.

C. H. 1972, 2278

Naumann considered himself quite agile and boasted that he could outrun a man 10 years his junior. His fitness was more than a boast. It proved to be of life-saving quality when he dashed 25 feet in just a few seconds to push a woman, 56, from the track on which a train was quickly bearing down. Naumann's timing was nearly perfect. Only his foot was clipped by the train's engine as both he and the woman fell in a heap at the track's side, largely uninjured.

Just shy of three years later, in late March 1927, and within feet of the same spot, Naumann and another woman were not nearly as fortunate. This woman, 52, who had ducked under a crossing gate and was hurrying to beat an oncoming train, tripped on a rail and fell with her body across the track. When Naumann first saw her there, he was about the same distance away as when he started his first rescue, and the train was traveling at about the same speed as the first. This time, however, he reached the woman when the train was only 10 feet away. He grabbed at her clothing and pulled, but the train hit them both. They were hurled 30 feet. The woman was severely injured and died three hours later.

A fellow worker was the first to reach Naumann, who instructed him, "Look at my leg." His right leg was badly crushed. Naumann was taken to the hospital, where the leg was amputated during a stay that lasted more than two months. Naumann told the Hero Fund's investigator that he thought he and the woman had not much chance of getting out of the way of the train and that he was "all done." Ironically, Naumann, tired from the strain of his job, had recently tendered his resignation, and the day after the rescue attempt was to be his last at work. FILE NOS: 24477, 69361

(PREVIOUS SPREAD AND BELOW) PHOTOGRAPHS OF THE HOHMAN STREET CROSSING IN HAMMOND, INDIANA.

(FACING PAGE) COMMISSION INVESTIGATOR'S SKETCH SHOWING COURSE OF HENRY NAUMANN'S FIRST RESCUE.

SYDNEY

WORLD

ELIMINATION

RUDELL ST

WORLD'S

RALPH DU

WORLD'S

RALPH DUPAS

RINGSIDE TERRACES BLEACHERS

mission Prices: 70/- 30/- 15/- Reserves

MONDAY, MAY

STADIUM

TITLE

...UT — 12 Rounds

...ITCH

...2 WELTERWEIGHT

...s

...PAS

...3 WELTERWEIGHT

...n Kippax & Stadium

RUDELL STITCH

...2. AT 8·00 PM

16 Sept. 1958 and 5 June 1960
DAM, OHIO RIVER
LOUISVILLE, KENTUCKY

C. H. 4230, 4350

RUDELL STITCH was a 26-year-old professional welterweight boxer ranked number three in the nation on September 16, 1958, when he became a hero by rescuing Joseph Schifcar, a workman at a dam on the Ohio River near Louisville, Kentucky.

Schifcar, 37, was standing on the dam's sill, plugging leaks, when he lost his footing and was swept over the eight-foot drop to the water below, where he broke his leg on a rock. He struggled to keep his head out of the swift current but was hampered by his injury and the weight of his boots and wet clothes.

Stitch, fishing on the rocks below the dam, quickly waded into the river to where he could grab Schifcar, who by then was nearly submerged. But Stitch also lost his footing, and both men were pulled into deeper water. Although a strong swimmer, Stitch could not overcome the fast-moving current. Instead, he supported Schifcar while they drifted 68 feet across submerged rocks into shallower water, where another fisherman was able to wade in and help Stitch tow Schifcar to safety.

Less than two years later, in early June of 1960, at the same dam, Stitch would attempt to save another man. Neither survived.

Stitch and Charles Oliver, 25, another boxer, were fishing at the dam. They were walking across the sill when Oliver, who couldn't swim, slipped and was washed into the river, pulling Stitch with him. The two became separated in the 10-foot-deep water, and the current quickly carried Oliver downstream toward a bridge. Stitch, who somehow had removed his boots, raincoat, and pants while submerged, surfaced just in time to see Oliver, now several yards farther downstream, get carried beneath the bridge and then sink near one of its piers. Swimming to where Oliver had disappeared, Stitch dived but came up empty-handed. He dived again, but this time did not surface. Several hours later, both bodies were recovered downstream. Stitch's second Carnegie Medal was awarded posthumously. Stitch's last bout was on May 24, 1960. At the time, he was ranked the number two welterweight in the world. FILE NOS: 44528, 70049

STITCH AND WIFE,
ROSA, WITH SONS
(L. TO R.) RUDELL III,
RODNEY, AND
DONALD CHARLES.

C. H. 4038, 4127

JOHN JAMES O'NEILL, SR., 46, would easily have been excused from helping in the rescue of a woman who had jumped from the Yonkers City Pier into the Hudson River on May 5, 1954. In addition to several other men being present and witnessing the jump, O'Neill had a "long-established medical history of cardiac condition," which was known to the other men.

Not only did O'Neill jump from the pier, 14 feet above the river, he had just run about 500 feet after hearing the commotion over the woman's leap, which was described by police as a suicide attempt. He then swam several feet, submerged, grasped the woman around the waist, surfaced, and made his way to a ladder that was being suspended over the pier's side for him. Removed from the water, the 41-year-old woman was quickly revived. O'Neill was treated for shock and exposure and was hospitalized for a day.

Another woman, 62, reported to be despondent over the death of her husband, caused O'Neill to perform his second heroic act two and a half years later. Although the scene was the same, conditions this time were considerably different. It was late December, 1956, at 8:30 in the evening. The temperature was 27 degrees, ice was forming on the pier's walls, the wind was blowing at or above 40 mph, and waves in the river were striking the pier with "force and severity."

O'Neill, a municipal road worker, would normally not have been working at the time, but due to the foul weather he was asked to return for emergency duty. While waiting for a truck to be loaded with salt, O'Neill and a fellow worker noted the woman walking rapidly past them and out to the pier's edge. Concerned, both started after her, but before they reached her, she jumped into the darkness of the river. O'Neill's companion, a poor swimmer, ran to get a rope and ladder and to summon additional help. He was fearful O'Neill would attempt another rescue.

O'Neill this time did not jump from the pier but from a nearby structure he thought would take him closer to the woman. Swimming an irregular course and hampered by his wet, heavy clothing and the waves, he eventually spotted the woman's coat, which was floating above her head. Growing weary, he reached her with difficulty. Her weight, the heavy wind, a backwash from the pier's walls, and his waning strength all contributed to his taking five minutes to swim only 25 feet with her to a retaining wall. There, men with ropes pulled the woman from the river. O'Neill, ice forming on his face and clothing, was then helped from the water, 30 minutes after beginning the rescue. He was treated for shock and exposure, and a cardiogram revealed "severe effect" on his heart. He convalesced for two months at home before returning to work. FILE NOS: 43682, 69414

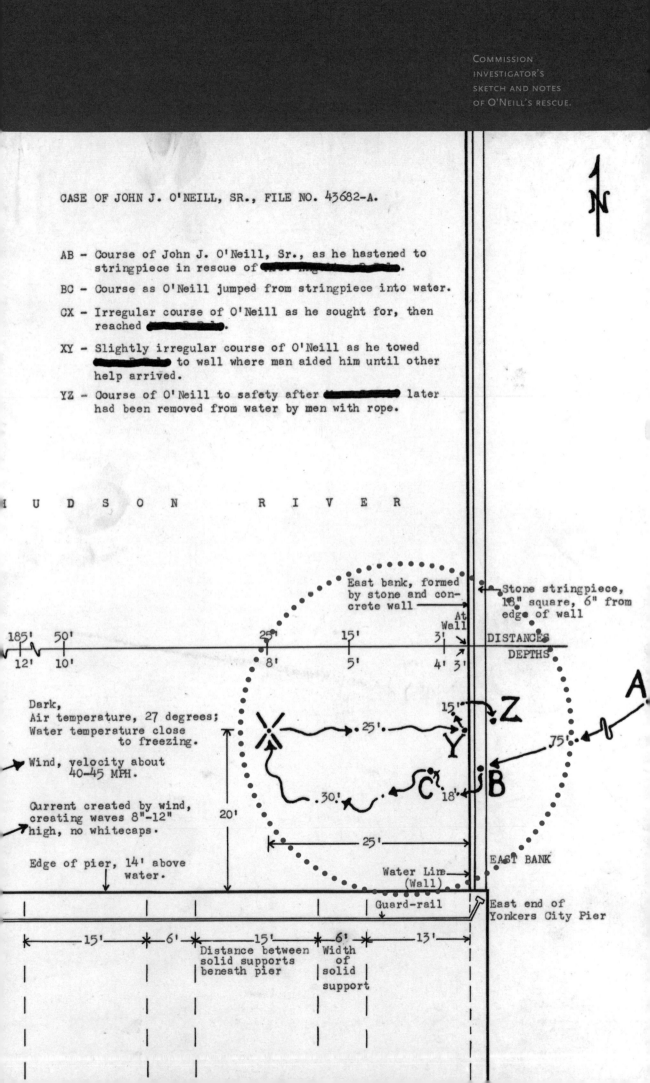

CASE OF JOHN J. O'NEILL, SR., FILE NO. 43682-A.

AB - Course of John J. O'Neill, Sr., as he hastened to stringpiece in rescue of ▓▓▓▓▓▓▓▓▓▓▓.

BC - Course as O'Neill jumped from stringpiece into water.

CX - Irregular course of O'Neill as he sought for, then reached ▓▓▓▓▓▓▓.

XY - Slightly irregular course of O'Neill as he towed ▓▓▓▓▓▓▓ to wall where man aided him until other help arrived.

YZ - Course of O'Neill to safety after ▓▓▓▓▓▓▓ later had been removed from water by men with rope.

H U D S O N   R I V E R

East bank, formed
by stone and con-
crete wall →

Stone stringpiece,
18" square, 6" from
edge of wall

| 185' | 50' | | 25' | 15' | 3' | At Wall | DISTANCES |
| 12' | 10' | | 8' | 5' | 4' | 3' | DEPTHS |

Dark,
Air temperature, 27 degrees;
Water temperature close
              to freezing.

Wind, velocity about
      40-45 MPH.

Current created by wind,
creating waves 8"-12"
high, no whitecaps.

Edge of pier, 14' above
                water.

15"

.25'

Z

Y

.30'

C

18'

B

.75'

A

20'

25'

EAST BANK

Water Line
(Wall)

Guard-rail

East end of
Yonkers City Pier

| | 15' | 6' | 15' | 6' | 13' | |
Distance between   Width
solid supports   of
beneath pier   solid
                      support

12 May 1963 and 15 Oct. 1991
PHIPPSBURG, MAINE
EAST SWANZEY, NEW HAMPSHIRE

C. H. 4723, 7657

C. H. 4722 ✢

Unlike the rescues of the other twice-awarded heroes, DANIEL STOCKWELL'S were as different in type as they were far removed from each other in years and miles. The first, when Stockwell was a 20-year-old college student, took place off the rocky shore of the Atlantic Ocean in Phippsburg, Maine. Steven L. Quattropani, also 20 and a student, was swimming in the ocean in mid-May of 1963 when he was carried seaward by waves four- to six-feet high. From shore, DALE ARNOLD HATCH, 18, another student, attempted to toss Quattropani a lifeline made from articles of clothing, but Hatch was swept into the ocean by a large wave.

Stockwell then ran to a small beach almost directly opposite the two men in the water. He tied a rope around his waist, entered the surf, and swam to Quattropani, who was by then unconscious. With others pulling on the rope, both were towed to shore. The body of Hatch, who had submerged, was later washed ashore. Hatch and Stockwell were each awarded the Carnegie Medal, Hatch posthumously.

Twenty-eight years later, on October 15, 1991, Stockwell, now the principal of a high school in East Swanzey, New Hampshire, learned that a shooting had occurred in the school's cafeteria, which was crowded with 900 students. A 16-year-old boy armed with a .30-caliber rifle had shot and wounded two students there, then ordered 15 others into a classroom. When Stockwell reached the classroom door, he saw through the window that the armed student was reloading the rifle.

Stockwell knocked on the door and entered. The boy pointed the gun at him, but Stockwell calmly talked him into letting the other students leave the classroom in exchange for him becoming the boy's hostage. For nearly 40 minutes, all the time with the gun pointed at him, Stockwell discussed the boy's demands with him. Positioned outside the doorway, the chief of police then entered the classroom and ordered the student to put the rifle down. Stockwell left the room, another officer entering to subdue the student. FILE NOS: 46697, 46551, 66972

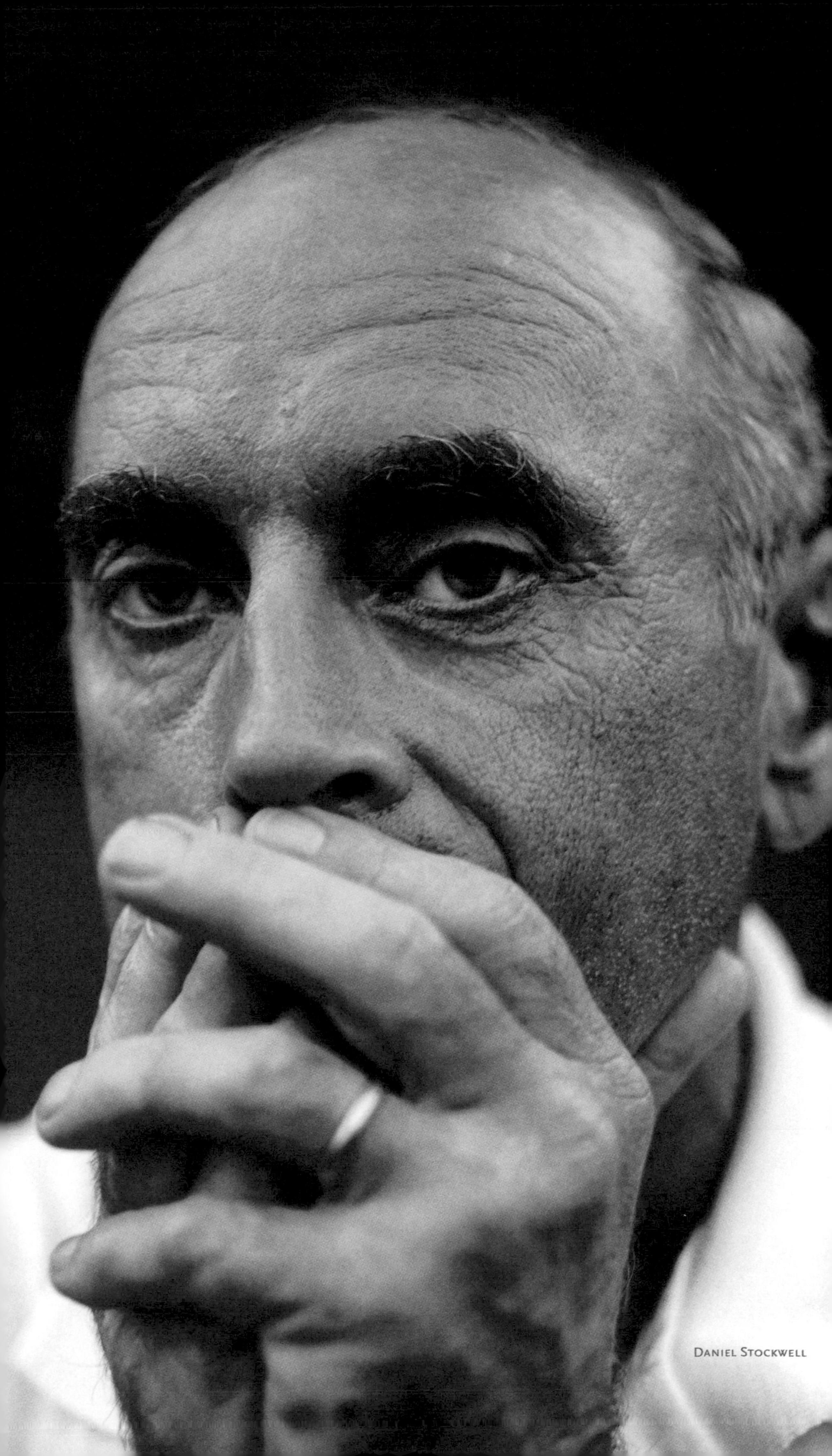

Daniel Stockwell

IN THE HERO FUND'S FIRST 100 YEARS, CARNEGIE
MEDALS WERE AWARDED TO 8,764 INDIVIDUALS. THE
HEROES PROFILED ON THE FOLLOWING PAGES ARE
REPRESENTATIVE OF THIS GROUP AS TO AGE, GENDER,
GEOGRAPHICAL LOCATION, AND DATE AND TYPE OF ACT.
THE FUND'S AWARDEES ALL MET THE COMMISSION'S
PRINCIPAL REQUIREMENT FOR BEING AWARDED THE
MEDAL: THEY VOLUNTARILY RISKED THEIR LIVES TO
AN EXTRAORDINARY DEGREE WHILE SAVING OR
ATTEMPTING TO SAVE THE LIVES OF OTHERS.

C. H. 4240

SHIRLEY F. O'NEILL, an 18-year-old-student, became a hero on May 7, 1959, when she risked her life to rescue the victim of a shark attack.

Albert Kogler, also 18, was swimming in San Francisco Bay near the Golden Gate Bridge about 150 feet from shore when a shark attacked him, tearing off parts of his arm, shoulder, and back, and causing severe bleeding.

O'Neill had gone to the beach with Kogler and, swimming nearby, was the only other person in the water. She heard Kogler's cries, then saw the water churning and reddening around him. O'Neill started to shore but then turned and swam back to Kogler. The attack having ceased, O'Neill put her arm around Kogler's chest and, aided by the current, began paddling them through two-foot swells back toward shore. When they were within 60 feet of the beach, a fisherman cast out a weighted line, which O'Neill wrapped around her wrist and Kogler's uninjured arm. They were then pulled in to where two other bystanders could wade out and get Kogler.

Kogler was rushed to the hospital, but died two hours later in spite of transfusions and emergency surgery. O'Neill was not injured.

News of the attack—termed unprecedented in San Francisco by marine experts—took up almost half of the front page of the following day's *San Francisco Examiner*, and it was reported in *Time* magazine and the *Congressional Record*. The case was called to the attention of the Hero Fund by, among others, the mayor of San Francisco, a former "special agent" of the Hero Fund, and Carnegie Medal awardee **MILEY B. WESSON, M.D.**, of San Francisco, whose own act of heroism 27 years earlier had its special measure of drama *(see below)*.

The Hero Fund's response to O'Neill's act may have been as unprecedented as the shark attack. Three weeks after the rescue, Special Agent Irwin M. Uhrling had a case report filed with the office and in mid-June the Hero Fund announced its award. Executive Committee members had been queried by mail, and the award was decided without the formality of the committee's meeting, its usual procedure. FILE NO: 44705

(FACING PAGE, TOP) SHIRLEY O'NEILL'S RESCUE WAS FRONT-PAGE NEWS THROUGHOUT THE UNITED STATES.

(BOTTOM) COMMISSION INVESTIGATOR'S SKETCH SHOWING COURSE OF O'NEILL'S RESCUE.

C. H. 2805

Wesson, too, knew to respond immediately in a life-threatening situation. While he was operating on a child, an x-ray technician in the room seized a bare wire charged with 30,000 volts and fell unconscious to the floor. Knowing the live line would kill the technician and probably the child if it came into contact with the metal operating table, Wesson, 50, grasped the line to pull it away. He lost consciousness briefly and fell to the floor, his weight pulling the wire free, breaking the circuit. Recovering, although having sustained fractures to vertebra and right clavicle, he regained his footing and completed the operation. FILE NO: 32051

Killed

Shark

Beach

raves Attack
Youth Ashore

San Francisco State College fresh-
angled and all but devoured, ap-
t white shark, while swimming at
the Presidio with a girl companion

aid the
cedented
y or ad-
least in

Kogler
former
nd base-
se, Butte
etterman
rs after
despite

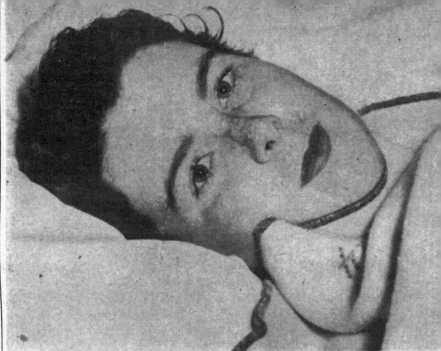

SHIRLEY O'NEILL—CO-ED WAS HEROINE IN SHARK ATTACK
... resting in Letterman Hospital after nightmarish adventure

'Couldn't Leave Him!'
Heroic Girl's Stark Tale
Of Tragedy at Beach

San Francisco, California

Marin County

GOLDEN GATE

Golden Gate Bridge

Mile
Point

San Francisco

Baker's
Beach

1 mile

2 miles

2' swells

PACIFIC
OCEAN

A 90°

20'

150'

27'
deep

Current

B C D

5' 25'
5'
deep
1' high
breaker
5'

X— Point at which shark or other marine
    animal attacked Albert C. Kogler

AX— Course of Shirley Frances O'Neill to
    Kogler, reversing previous
    shoreward flight

XB— Course of Miss O'Neill assisting Kogler

B— Point at which a heavy fishing line
    reached them and was tied by Miss
    O'Neill to Kogler

BC— Course of Kogler and Miss O'Neill drawn
    shoreward by line

C— Point at which two men, wading only,
    met Miss O'Neill and Kogler

CD— Course of two men to beach with Kogler;

CHARLES ZOLNINGER
AND JULIUS B.
GORDON, NOT VISIBLE,
WERE WORKING UNDER
THE DEBRIS, WHILE
WILLIAM H. REED,
BARELY VISIBLE UNDER
THE SHORING PLANKS,
WAS PROVIDING
ASSISTANCE.

On October 28, 1913, **CHARLES ZOLNINGER, JULIUS B. GORDON, WILLIAM H. REED, SR.**, and **JOHN F. STEINBOCK** worked tirelessly in the 16-hour rescue of two men from the collapse of an industrial water well.

C. H. 1065, 1066, 1067, 1068

Seven men were working in the well, a hole that was 45 feet deep and 20 feet in diameter. The circumference of the well was lined with two walls of cemented brick, the inner wall rising just several feet from the well's bottom. Two platforms supporting pumping machinery weighing 4,500 pounds were imbedded in the outer wall 20 and 32 feet below the surface. At about 9:00 a.m. the outer wall began to collapse from the bottom up. Within seconds, a tangled mass of bricks, sand, timbers, and machinery fell in on the workers, killing four of them almost instantly. A fifth man died a few hours after the collapse, but two others survived and remained trapped under tons of unstable debris.

Zolninger, a 30-year-old plumbing contractor, Gordon, a 22-year-old laborer, and Reed, a 39-year-old laborer, arrived on the scene shortly after an alarm was sounded. A ladder was lowered to the top of the debris pile, and Zolninger and Gordon descended into the well, even though others warned them that portions of the wall were likely to collapse. Reed followed the two shortly thereafter. The men cut through the wooden debris to create an 18-inch hole, and then managed to reach one of the victims and help him out of the hole. It was now 10:30 a.m.

Zolninger and Gordon then entered the hole to look for the second victim, Reed taking a position at the mouth of the hole. They began cutting away more timbers to reach the other victim, who had been calling for help and telling the rescuers he was pinned under timbers and unable to move. Meanwhile, men at the top were shoring the well's wall. Zolninger and Gordon took turns working on cutting and removing timbers and debris in the cramped space, aided by Reed who provided tools and other assistance.

Around 2:30 in the afternoon, the men were able to free one of the victim's legs, but his other leg was pinned in the timbers. A doctor was persuaded to enter the hole to determine if amputation were possible, which after viewing the scene he said would mean death for the victim. So all climbed back out and, working with others, they removed sand and other debris from the top of the pile of rubble. After eight hours of work, however, a great quantity of sand caved in to the well. Discouraged, Zolninger said there was no chance now to rescue the victim, and said he was going home. Soon, though, he was encouraged to make another rescue attempt, and Gordon volunteered again to accompany him. Others were asked to assist, but only Steinbock, a 45-year-old farmer, agreed. After three more hours of dangerous work, and nearly 16 hours after the cave-in, the second victim was freed and transported out of the well.

FILE NOS: 11973, 13258, 13260, 13259

C. H. 3125

Thirteen-year-old **Norma Bedell** saved a baby from being killed by an enraged pig on June 12, 1941.

For three years, Bedell had been living on the farm of her foster parents, Mr. and Mrs. Ernest McKenzie, near Salineville in east central Ohio. In the late afternoon, the ninth-grade student was doing chores, tending cows in the barn. A toddler, 22-month-old James Ferguson, whose parents were visiting the McKenzies, had accompanied Bedell into the barn. A 450-pound sow, mother of 10 piglets, attacked young Ferguson, knocking him onto his back, and began biting him on the head.

Bedell immediately ran to the pig and pushed it away far enough to hoist the child onto the top of a box nailed to the wall. The sow charged Bedell, knocking her over and biting her on the side and stomach. The girl fought back, pushed the pig's head away, and struggled back to her feet. She took shelter in a nearby feed bin, but was unable to close the door, because the sow was in the way. Twice then it tried to get at the child, who was slipping off the box. Bedell grabbed a pitchfork and struck at the sow. The pig backed far enough away to allow Bedell to go to Ferguson and protect him until his mother arrived. Bedell fled the barn with them, the sow still menacing.

Though cut badly on his head, Ferguson healed with no ill effects. Bedell sustained four long gashes, but she recovered within a week.

FILE NO: 39131

C. H. 1826

On May 29, 1922, **Harley W. Pullen**, a 12-year-old schoolboy in Big Creek, Mississippi, rescued a young farmer who was being dragged by a runaway mule.

Pullen's neighbor and friend, Max Doolittle, 24, had been returning from the field riding sideways on a plow mule. When the 850-pound animal reared, Doolittle tumbled off its back. One of his feet got caught in a trace chain, and the frightened mule galloped off, dragging the boy 1,500 feet over a plowed field and a road.

When Pullen saw the mule dragging Doolittle, he immediately ran some 500 feet toward the approaching animal. When they met, Pullen tried to grab its bridle, but the mule struck him in the chest hard enough to knock him to the ground. The mule then took several steps past Pullen and stopped. Not injured by the blow, the young boy got up, stepped up to the mule, seized its bridle, and released Doolittle. Although Doolittle was disabled for five days from his injuries, he made a complete recovery.

FILE NO: 23002

At just past midnight on September 26, 1925, **TEODORO O. RIOS**, 30, and **MATILDE ROBLEDO**, 46, put their lives at risk to save a fellow worker from an explosion.

C. H. 2200, 2199

Rios and Robledo were part of a four-man powder gang setting a grid of dynamite charges on large rocks of ore at a copper mine near Santa Rita, New Mexico. Only the light from the men's lanterns illuminated the area. The fuses of 25 to 30 charges had been lit when the foot of a third powderman, 25-year-old Alfonso Sias, was caught under a rock measuring eight feet in diameter. Seeing that Sias was trapped, Rios, Robledo, and an older brother of Sias, who was the crew's foreman, ran to him. After trying unsuccessfully to free Sias, the three men began to throw away the lit charges near Sias. After they had each pitched four to five sticks as far as they could, one of the charges exploded. The last charge Rios threw exploded in the air.

The concussion flung the three men to the ground and extinguished their lanterns, but they were able to crawl 35 feet and take shelter under a steam shovel. Other explosions followed, and one, which Sias said seemed to be just 10 feet from him, shifted the rock holding him, allowing him to also crawl to the steam shovel and safety. None of the men was seriously injured.

FILE NOS: 25675, 25676

YOLANDA FABBRI displayed courage, strength, and determination, and refused to allow a deranged man to drown himself and his two children.

C. H. 3152

On July 2, 1939, the 24-year-old Chicago housewife was walking along the shore of Lake Michigan when she came upon a harrowing scene. A despondent 36-year-old laborer was trying to drown himself, along with his 7-year-old son and 2-year-old daughter. He had already thrown the boy off the concrete wall into deep water and then jumped in with the baby in his arms.

A strong, trained swimmer, Fabbri reacted quickly and got the boy to safety. By then, the man was 20 feet from the wall, still holding his daughter. Fabbri swam out and got a grip on the baby. The man resisted and punched Fabbri in the jaw. When he went under the water, Fabbri wrestled the child away and swam back to the wall.

Then she swam back toward the man. The would-be suicide was now weakened, so Fabbri was able to get her arm around his chest and tow him to shore. Bystanders hauled the pair out, but the man leapt right back in. Fabbri leapt in the water and towed him to safety again. He went back in a third time, but a lifeguard who had arrived got him out and restrained him until police could take him away.

Fabbri risked her life to prevent a triple tragedy. FILE NO: 37845

C. H. 6589

On December 29, 1980, **WILLIAM C. BRISBANE** scaled the side of a burning San Francisco apartment building to save a woman trapped on an eighth-floor balcony.

About 8:00 that morning, a smoky fire broke out in the apartment of 23-year-old Annika Backlund, forcing her to flee to the balcony of a neighboring apartment, where she became trapped and was close to panic.

Brisbane, a 32-year-old transit worker, was in his apartment half a block away when he became aware of the fire and Backlund's plight. Although he did not know the young woman, Brisbane thought he could help. He started climbing the building by standing on the railing of one balcony, then pulling himself up to the next. Repeating that method, he climbed until he was on the balcony immediately below Backlund.

He then reached up to Backlund and guided her down to his side, and the two escaped through the seventh-floor apartment. Both were taken to a hospital, where they were treated for minor injuries and smoke inhalation. FILE NO: 57555

C. H. 8431

On April 19, 2000, **LYLE D. BAADE**, a 66-year-old retired construction worker and heart-transplant recipient, single-handedly tackled a man armed with three pistols and an assault rifle.

That afternoon, Baade and his wife had been attending a homeowner's association meeting of a retirement community near Phoenix, Arizona. At a little after 2:00, the couple was leaving the meeting in the recreation center for Baade's doctor's appointment for his annual heart check-up.

As they were exiting the room, they encountered a man, 66, entering the room. He blocked their way and told them to go back inside. When Baade protested, the man shoved him into the room. Although he did not recognize him as a former resident of the community, Baade did see the .22-caliber pistol in his right hand.

Baade and his wife retreated into the room and to the end of a 25-foot-long partition that separated the foyer from the main space. The man went the other way. As Baade shouted, "He has a gun," the man started firing into the group of more than 40 attendees, shouting, "I'm going to kill you all." Two women and two men were hit in the first volley. The man then put down the empty pistol and picked up a loaded AR-15 assault rifle that he had put in the room several minutes before encountering Baade.

Baade reacted quickly. He later recalled that, despite his age and infirmities, he knew he could get to the assailant before the assailant could turn the gun on him. Crossing the length of the partition, Baade hit the heavier man at full force, knocking the rifle from his hands. Both men fell to the floor, with Baade on top, and then they struggled for control of the rifle.

The assailant managed to pull the trigger and fire off one round, which struck a man in the foot, but Baade was able to prevent him from shooting more. Three other men then pounced on the gunman and, despite discovering that he had two more 9-mm pistols on him, were able to keep him pinned until the police arrived.

The two women died of their injuries, but the men recovered. Baade suffered scratches and contusions, but his heart proved to be up to his courage. FILE NO: 74499

14 Jan. 1938
RELIABLE WOOD HEEL CO.
NASHUA, NEW HAMPSHIRE

RALPH KELLEY was 16 years old on January 14, 1938, when he helped two women escape from a fire at the Reliable Wood Heel Company in Nashua, New Hampshire.

Having graduated from high school the previous June, Kelley was employed as a floor boy at the plant that manufactured celluloid-covered heels for shoes. Near quitting time that cold winter afternoon, Kelley was working on the ground floor of the two-story facility, his third day on the job. A fire broke out among highly flammable materials and waste, and quickly mushroomed out along the ceiling toward the building's only staircase. All the workers on the second floor managed to escape, except for Margaret Dow, 31, and her sister Ethel Carter, 28, who was panicked by the flames.

Without hesitation, Kelley ran to the top of the staircase and took one of the women by the wrist. He turned to lead them back down but saw that flames had reached the staircase. Instead, he, Dow, and Carter ran across the room to a window that overlooked the snow-covered ground 17 feet below, and opened it. With flames reaching the second floor by then and quickly spreading, Carter, Dow, and finally Kelley climbed through the opening and dropped to the ground. The two women sustained minor injuries from their ordeal and quickly recovered. Kelley, however, had fractured two vertebrae in the fall. Hospitalized for five months, the teenager was permanently paralyzed from the waist down.

In addition to receiving a Carnegie Medal for his heroic act, Kelley was awarded a monthly grant from the Fund to help compensate for his injuries. He received that grant for 35 years. Over the decades since the fire, Kelley has also corresponded actively with the Commission and has nominated numerous others for consideration as medal recipients.

FILE NO: 38184

C. H. 3176

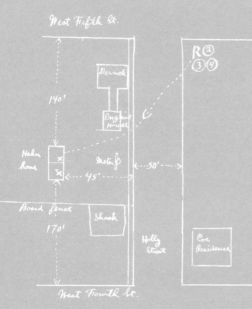

West Fifth St.

140'

Derrick

Engine house

Hahn house

Meter

45'

50'

Board fence

170'

Shack

Holly Street

West Fourth St.

R ⓐ
③ ④

Coe Residence

6 Feb. 1923
HAHN RESIDENCE
BURKBURNETT, TEXAS

C. H. 1865 ⇕

On February 6, 1923, 30-year-old CHARLES L. COE died while trying to rescue two small children from their burning home in Burkburnett, Texas.

Three-year-old Arnold Hahn and his 1-year-old brother, David, were sleeping in the bedroom of their parents' small, single-story dwelling when a fire broke out. The flames spread rapidly through the flimsily constructed structure, its walls lined with heavy paper.

Coe, a neighbor and a father of three daughters, was among several men who responded to the fire. Even though smoke and flames were already leaking from cracks in the building's outer walls, Coe and one of the other men raced in. Making their way through the dense smoke, they checked the bedroom but were unable to find the two children.

Seeing flames starting to sheet over the partition walls, the other man realized they would soon be engulfed and grabbed Coe to warn him. Refusing to leave, Coe jerked away and turned back toward the bed. The other man ran from the house, but, even though his hands and face were scorched, he punched a hole through a panel of a door that led into the bedroom. Almost immediately, the older Hahn child was thrust through the opening, followed by an intense burst of flame.

Unfortunately, before the fire could be extinguished, sections of the house's roof and walls collapsed. Coe and the baby, who was in his arms, were later found burned to death just inside the doorway through which the hero had entered the house. He was posthumously awarded a Carnegie Medal, and his widow received a monthly grant from the Hero Fund for many years. Although badly burned, Arnold eventually recovered. Coe was the last individual to be awarded a gold Carnegie Medal.

FILE NO: 23074

Upper sketch-- General view of Hahn house and surroundings
Lower sketch-- Hahn house in detail.
RX'X--Course of Coe to the children and with them
M--Point at which Donaho deserted Coe
X'-Point at which Coe delivered Arnold to safety
X--Point at which Coe's body was found with David's.

CHARLES L. COE,
DRILLER, AND DAUGHTER
FRANCES. THIS PHOTO
WAS TAKEN ABOUT 1920.

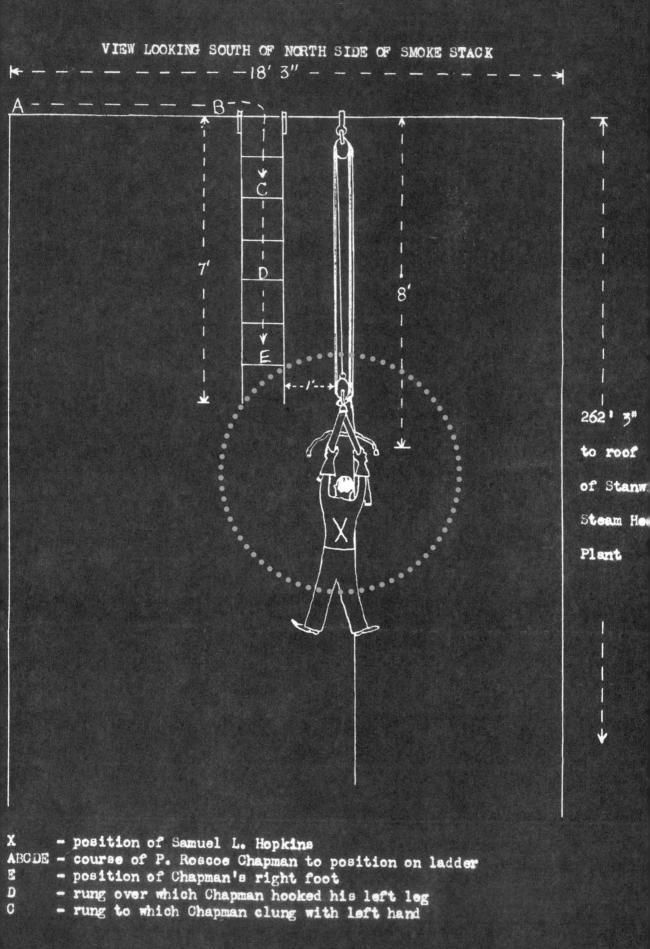

CASE OF P. ROSCOE CHAPMAN, FILE NO. 41037

VIEW LOOKING SOUTH OF NORTH SIDE OF SMOKE STACK

X   - position of Samuel L. Hopkins
ABCDE - course of P. Roscoe Chapman to position on ladder
E   - position of Chapman's right foot
D   - rung over which Chapman hooked his left leg
C   - rung to which Chapman clung with left hand

Forty-nine-year-old **ROSCO CHAPMAN** earned his Carnegie Medal on May 15, 1947, when he saved a co-worker from a fatal fall.

C. H. 3533

Chapman and Samuel Hopkins were painting a smoke stack that rose 260 feet from the roof of the Stanwix Steam Heating Plant in downtown Pittsburgh. The two men had just climbed to the top of the 18-foot-diameter, steel-clad, brick-lined stack following their lunch break. They normally worked from boatswain's chairs hanging from a block and tackle attached to the top of the stack, but when Hopkins climbed down the short, temporary ladder from the chimney's top and swung into his chair, a strap snapped and his seat dropped away. Even though one of his work gloves had wet paint on it, Hopkins managed to grab the ends of the broken strap and hang on, dangling eight feet below the top of the stack.

(FACING PAGE)
COMMISSION
INVESTIGATOR'S
SKETCH SHOWING
COURSE OF ROSCO
CHAPMAN'S RESCUE.

Chapman, who had been straddling the top of the stack, immediately circled around to the work ladder and climbed down. Bracing one foot on its lowest rung, he hooked his other leg over a higher rung, and, hanging on to a third rung with his left hand, managed to reach down with his right hand and grab Hopkins' left wrist. Chapman then let go of the ladder and managed to remove Hopkins' work glove, enabling the dangling man to get a better grip on the strap end. Then, by shifting and lifting, Chapman was able to haul Hopkins up so he could get a grip on the ladder and climb to safety.

Though he suffered from shock and a strained back, Hopkins eventually recovered completely, thankful that Rosco Chapman had what it takes to be a hero. FILE NO: 41037

On March 31, 1977, **DAVID G. JACKSON**, 19, stepped into the path of danger to save a co-worker from a falling piece of steel.

C. H. 6290

Jackson and Jerry Duncan, 26, were working on a new vertical shaft of a zinc mine in Gordonsville, Tennessee. The partially constructed, 1,470-foot-deep shaft was 16 feet in diameter.

Both men were working on a platform at a level over a thousand feet below the top of the shaft, when a sheet of corrugated steel suspended at the shaft's opening broke from its supporting cable. Jackson, a driller, heard the metal plummeting down the shaft just as Duncan stepped into its path. The young man reacted instantly and lunged toward Duncan to push him out of the way, but just as he reached his co-worker, the falling sheet of metal hit both men.

While Jackson's push probably saved his life, Duncan's right arm was severed at the shoulder. Both of Jackson's arms were severed near the elbows, but they were able to be surgically replaced. FILE NO: 55716

C. H. 5093

On October 6, 1965, MICHAEL V. ULRICH, 15, crawled into a tight cave crevice three times to extricate a trapped schoolboy.

The previous morning, Morris Baetzold was exploring a side fissure off the main passage of Wild Cat Cave, near Hinckley, Ohio. The 15-year-old boy had wriggled about 25 feet into the narrow slit when he toppled over and became wedged between the cave walls, which at that point were about nine inches apart and four and a half feet high.

Stuck and unable to move, Baetzold called for help. A number of attempts were made to reach him, but all were unsuccessful because no one could fit into the tight opening. News of the boy's predicament was made public, and Ulrich's father thought one of his sons might be able to help. Baetzold had been trapped for 24 hours when the Ulrichs arrived on the scene.

After being briefed about the situation, Ulrich's 12-year-old brother tried first to reach Baetzold but was unable to go very far. Ulrich, an Eagle Scout, then volunteered. With two ropes tied around him and taking the ends of two others, he squirmed into the tight opening.

At about two-thirds of the distance to the trapped boy, the passage became so narrow that Ulrich had to turn on his side and wriggle along parallel to the downward sloping floor, supporting himself on his right arm, until he reached Baetzold's feet. Then, working with only his left hand extended over his head, Ulrich managed to knot a rope to a strap he had maneuvered around one of the boy's legs. Then he backed out to where he could stand.

When rescuers pulling on the rope were still unable to budge Baetzold, Ulrich crawled back in and rearranged the strap so that it was around both the boy's legs. Then, looping the second rope around a clamp that he strapped to a small outcropping above Baetzold and attaching the end to the boy's legs, Ulrich backed out again. This time, rescuers managed to lift and free Baetzold's hips and right arm, but his chest remained tightly wedged.

Ulrich wormed back in a third time and, working with Baetzold, was able to get another rope around his upper body. Then Ulrich backed out again. Baetzold was covered with a slippery solution, and greased boards were slid in under him. Then, lifted slightly by the rope around his chest, he was slowly drawn out of the crevice to a place where he could stand. Though debilitated by his ordeal, Baetzold recovered without consequence. Ulrich, although exhausted and sore from his three forays into the crevasse, each of which had taken half an hour, suffered no serious injuries.

FILE NO: 48334

On November 7, 1960, two employees at an H. J. Heinz Company food plant in Pittsburgh, Pennsylvania, **STEPHAN JAGUSCZAK** and **PETER P. SMOLEY**, died attempting to save a co-worker from suffocation inside a railroad tank car.

✝ *C. H.* 4373, 4374

Joseph Buttice, a 34-year-old factory hand, had climbed down through the small, circular hatch of the tank, in which tomato paste had been shipped. Although the 19,880-gallon tank had been emptied of most of its contents, several inches of paste remained in the bottom, along with nitrogen used as a preservative during shipping. Just after Buttice reached the bottom of the ladder, he was overcome and collapsed backwards into the soupy paste. His supervisor, at the top of the ladder, immediately climbed off the car and ran to a nearby building to report the accident. Jagusczak, a 34-year-old cook's helper, was among several men in the building, and he ran back to the accident scene with the supervisor.

While the supervisor got an air hose, Jagusczak climbed up on the tank car, squeezed through the hatch, and started down the ladder. The supervisor called out a warning, but though Jagusczak hesitated an instant, he continued climbing down. The supervisor scrambled to the top of the tank car and looked into the hatch in time to see Jagusczak also slump, face forward, into the paste.

The supervisor inserted the hose into the tank and began feeding in fresh air. Other men arrived. One supervisor put on an air mask, but was unable to squeeze through the hatch, which was only 20 inches in diameter. Then Smoley, a 25-year-old preparation helper, put on a mask and, after being instructed to leave if he felt affected by the gas, climbed down the ladder. At the bottom, he was only able to turn Jagusczak's head so it was out of the paste before he himself was overcome, collapsing across Buttice.

A man from the plant's safety department arrived and, donning an air mask, climbed down, secured by a rope around his waist and carrying a second. He was able to get the second rope around Smoley and Buttice, and each was hauled out of the tank. A fireman entered the tank for the rescue of Jagusczak.

Although Buttice had been in the tank car the longest, he was resuscitated and, though hospitalized for a time, eventually recovered. However, neither Smoley nor Jagusczak could be revived. In addition to accepting a posthumously awarded Carnegie Medal for their son's heroic act, Smoley's parents were granted money to help defray his funeral expenses. The Commission also awarded Jagusczak's widow a monthly grant, which she continues to receive 44 years later. FILE NOS: 45288, 45287

C. H. 2403

On February 12, 1927, **WINFERD L. HATHAWAY** braved the frigid waters of Lake Champlain to rescue five fishermen stranded on an ice floe.

That cold Saturday morning, Albert Reynolds, 61, Henry Mero, 56, Leslie Mero, 20, John Pedro, 27, Clarence Sayword, 12, and James Moore, 15, were fishing in three sheds built several hundred feet out on the frozen lake near Essex, New York. A stiff wind of 40 mph was blowing, and even though the air temperature was 10 degrees Fahrenheit, it caused the ice field to heave and break. The five, sensing danger, started for shore by jumping from one ice floe to another, but soon were stranded on a slab 400 feet square, which began to heave in the wind-driven waves.

Hathaway, a 19-year-old farm boy who had recently been laid off from a local paper mill, was at his parents' home by the lake. He saw the ice breaking up and noticed the five small forms in the distance. Realizing the trouble they were in, he dragged a light canoe out across the shore ice and paddled across a 300-foot stretch of choppy water that had opened in the broad floe. Alternating paddling the canoe and pulling it across ice, and twice slipping into the water to his waist, Hathaway took 45 minutes to reach the men, huddled on the dwindling slab.

Then, since the ice conditions on the opposite shore were better, Hathaway and the others used the canoe to ferry themselves from floe to floe for two miles to safety. They then walked several miles along the lake's east shore where they found solid ice, and then crossed to the west shore. None of the five was seriously injured, saved by Hathaway's quick thinking and skillful courage. FILE NO: 28961

C. H. 1451,
1452, 1453,
1454, 1455

On April 4, 1917, five men braved pack ice in the Atlantic Ocean to save seal hunters stranded on a drifting ice field off the northeast tip of Newfoundland.

At 4 a.m. that day, John Marsh, Philip Way, 57, and Way's 42-year-old nephew Robert started a hike of several miles out on the field of packed ice along the Atlantic coast to hunt seals. The wind shifted, causing the sea to heave and break up the ice. The three men became stranded on separate ice cakes that were tossed in waves up to six feet high as the field drifted from shore. Before long, Marsh fell from his cake and drowned. The two Ways clung to separate cakes, which threatened to break apart. When they were spotted, they were a half-mile apart and more than two miles from shore, drifting across the mouth of Bonavista Bay.

Sixty-three-year-old **HEZEKIAH ABBOTT**, a local fisherman, was the first to respond. He organized a boat to go out and try to find a way through the ice to rescue the two stranded men. Four local fishermen, including two brothers, **David Abbott**, 58, and **Henry J. Abbott**, 42 (who were not related to Hezekiah), along with **Daniel Butler**, 57, and his nephew, **Isaac J. Butler**, 38, joined him. All volunteered even though none of them could swim and several other men had refused to go.

The five of them loaded a day's rations into a 20-foot-long work skiff and entered the mist-bound ice field. They made slow, arduous progress through the slurry of slushy ice, using oars where they could and pushing larger cakes aside with gaffs where the field was more tightly packed. At times, the men climbed out of the boat onto larger cakes and pulled the boat along.

After more than an hour, the rescue party finally reached the older Way and took him aboard. A half-hour later, they got to his nephew. Then the boat was turned back toward shore, but they made slower progress because the ice had now become more tightly packed. Two hours later, they emerged from the ice field about three miles from where they had entered, all hands safe. A motorboat towed them to shore, where a crowd of hundreds greeted them. Other than being tired by their efforts and stress, none of the men was injured. FILE NOS: 18029, 18030, 18031, 18032, 18033

25 Dec. 1906
NEW LAKE
OLATHE, KANSAS

On December 25, 1906, two young men went to the aid of a skating companion who had fallen through weak ice, and then another young man went to their rescue when they fell in.

Three of the men, all deaf and mute, were students at the Kansas State School for the Deaf who had gone skating that sunny Christmas afternoon on nearby New Lake. About 2:30 in the afternoon, one of them, Ernest Albright, 21, was about 100 feet from shore when he broke through the ice and began floundering in eight-foot-deep water.

Another student, **Rollo Eastman**, 19, immediately went to Albright's aid. He tried to pull him out by hand, but the ice crumbled under Eastman and he tumbled into the water as well. The same thing happened when **Thomas Herrman**, 21, tried to extend a short board toward Albright.

Earl A. Ames, 20, was standing on the bank when he saw what had happened. Borrowing a pair of skates and grabbing the reins from a horse standing nearby and tying them into a strap about 20 feet long, Ames skated some 600 feet to the floundering trio. He tossed one end of the strap to Albright and, after several attempts, managed to pull him out of the water and then dragged him to shore, even though his feet broke through the weak crust. Ames skated back to the hole and threw the strap toward Eastman and then Herrman, but they were already exhausted. Neither could grab hold of the rope, and both sank into the icy water and drowned.

FILE NOS: 1524, 1525, 1475

C. H. 207, 206

C. H. 205

C. H. 4059

On January 19, 1956, **DOROTHY KOCHS**, an exotic dancer who performed under the name of Tina Lamont, saved two policemen from being shot by a robber in the Gay Nineties, a Cleveland nightclub.

The 32-year-old single mother of a 3-year-old daughter was sitting at the bar after the club had closed when a patron, also at the bar, pulled out a gun and demanded money from the club's two managers. Unknown to the gunman, however, the club's porter had slipped out and found two officers who were on duty nearby.

(FACING PAGE)
PHOTOGRAPH OF
DOROTHY KOCHS IN
AN ARTICLE SHE
WROTE ABOUT HER
HEROIC ACT FOR
THE JULY 1956 ISSUE
OF *FRONT PAGE
DETECTIVE.*

Their pistols drawn, the policemen entered the club, but the gunman turned and took direct aim at them. Kochs reacted instantly. Taking several steps toward the gunman, she grabbed his arm and pulled down, just as both he and the officers fired. The gunman's bullet went into the floor. Four shots fired by the policemen struck and killed the gunman instantly, but a fifth hit Kochs in the spine. She survived, but was paralyzed for life from the waist down. "In a split second," Kochs said some months later, "fate handed me a lifelong challenge. I may not win, but I like challenges."

In addition to being awarded a Carnegie Medal for her bravery, Kochs received a cash award, which she used to purchase a small boarding house. That and a monthly grant from the Commission helped Kochs to support herself until she died in 1981. FILE NO: 43838

C. H. 2690

On December 13, 1932, **MELVIN J. MAAS**, 35, a U.S. House of Representatives member from Minnesota, confronted a distraught man brandishing a loaded pistol in the Capitol Building in Washington, D.C.

Shortly after 4 p.m. that afternoon, the House was in session, with Maas and some 125 other members present. Another 75 people in the gallery watched the proceedings. Suddenly, a 25-year-old department store clerk appeared at the gallery rail, waving a pistol and demanding to speak.

Many of those present ran for the exit doors; others took cover behind furniture. But Maas, who at first started to exit the chamber with the possible intent of going to the gallery to disarm the man, walked with his arms slightly raised to a point below the balcony where the man stood. Then, despite the fact that the assailant pointed the revolver at him, Maas quietly reasoned with the man until he dropped the weapon into his hands. At that point, two armed policemen arrested the man and led him away. FILE NO: 32730

ELSIE H. McEVOY, a 28-year-old housewife in the town of Hinton, Alberta, saved a young neighbor boy from being mauled by a cougar.

C. H. 4553

On the afternoon of March 16, 1962, 6-year-old Brian Kilbreath was playing with other children in a sparsely wooded area near their homes in Hinton on the eastern slopes of Canada's Rocky Mountains when a young cougar attacked. Knocking Kilbreath to the ground, the cat began biting him on the face and neck. Two of the other boys ran to the nearest house for help. Despite the fact that she was recovering from recent surgery, the slightly built McEvoy, herself the mother of two, responded to the boys and ran into the woods.

Although winded, McEvoy grabbed a dead branch and began striking the cougar on the head until the branch broke. Then she stooped and grabbed the cougar's head by the scruff and smacked it on the snout with the stub that remained. The cat rose and turned, but when McEvoy pushed, it slumped to the ground. Picking up Kilbreath, she carried him toward an armed party of neighbors looking for them.

(FACING PAGE) ELSIE H. McEVOY WITH THE PELT OF THE COUGAR THAT ATTACKED BRIAN KILBREATH (ALSO PICTURED).

While the injured boy was taken to the hospital, McEvoy led the neighbors back to the scene of the attack. They found the cougar nearby, its skull fractured by McEvoy's blows and, to be sure, shot it three times.

Though critically injured and requiring more than 100 stitches on his face and neck, Kilbreath survived. McEvoy suffered no serious wounds and had recovered the following morning. In addition to being honored with a Carnegie Medal, her act earned letters of acclamation from both the Prime Minister of Canada and former vice president of the United States Richard Nixon. FILE NO: 45957

On October 3, 1927, **LEWIS A. KEE**, 56, prevented a quick-tempered husband from murdering his wife and her aunt.

C. H. 2314

Leona Cordrey, 24, and her 36-year-old husband had been having marital difficulties. She had filed for divorce four days before, and her husband was under an order to remove his belongings from the couple's farmhouse within the next week. Fearing her husband's wrath, Mrs. Cordrey had asked her aunt to stay with her. She had also asked Kee, a neighbor, to stay at the farm and help with the chores until her husband left. Kee and Cordrey, who were friends, were sharing a bedroom in the farmhouse.

At about 4:30 in the morning, Kee was awakened by screams and hurried through the farmhouse, fearing that Cordrey was striking his wife. Cordrey, meanwhile, had just attacked his wife with a hatchet, fracturing her skull, and had struck the aunt, also on the head. Kee found Mrs. Cordrey outside the screened door of a sleeping porch, her husband nearby, hatchet raised, about to strike again.

Kee opened the door between them, preventing Cordrey from taking another swing at his wife, but the younger man stepped around the open door and hit Kee with the hammer edge of the hatchet, knocking him to his hands and knees. Mrs. Cordrey escaped through the porch and out of the house. Cordrey continued to hit Kee with the hatchet, now with the sharp edge, but Kee finally managed to grab hold of the hatchet's handle.

Cordrey wrestled free, grabbed a shotgun, and ran out of the house in pursuit of his fleeing wife and the aunt. He took a shot and hit the aunt, but she and Mrs. Cordrey continued running for a half a mile to a neighbor's home. Cordrey, who at some time had set fire to the house, fled to a garage, where a short time later he killed himself with a revolver.

Though seriously injured, both women eventually recovered. Kee, who had difficulty escaping from the burning house, suffered five fractures to his skull, and sustained several other severe injuries, including a deep cut on his right shoulder. FILE NO: 27810

28 June 2001
LAKE DELTA SPILLWAY
ROME, NEW YORK

C. H. 8601, 8602

On June 28, 2001, **ROBERT B. KEANE** and **DAVID M. CIRASUOLO** came to the aid of five people in a boat about to be swept over a 60-foot-high spillway.

Late that warm summer afternoon, three adults and two children were on a 17-foot boat, cruising on Lake Delta, near Rome, New York. At 6:38, they were in the vicinity of the spillway over which the lake flowed into the Mohawk River when the boat's motor failed. Despite repeated attempts to restart the engine and efforts to paddle the boat, it drifted toward the precipice.

Cirasuolo, 34, was fishing with Keane, 27, in the latter's 18-foot boat about a quarter of a mile away when he noticed what was happening. The two men responded immediately, but by the time they reached the stricken vessel, it was dangerously close to the lip of the spillway.

The boat's occupants slipped into the water, from which Cirasuolo plucked the children. Keane maneuvered his craft close enough to rescue two of the adults who had remained near the stalled boat, which now was pinned against the lip of the spillway. Twice they bumped the helpless vessel, but it did not dislodge. They managed to get two victims aboard, but then their boat also lodged against the spillway. Fortunately, by then another boat had arrived. The remaining adult in the water swam a line to it from Keane's boat, and it was towed away from the dam, where its engine was started. Everyone was taken to safety. FILE NOS: 75449, 75450

On August 6, 1919, **HERBERT A. FRIEDLICH** saved a young climber from a fatal fall in Glacier Park, Montana.

C. H. 1726

Friedlich, a 26-year-old, Harvard-trained lawyer was among a group of horse riders enjoying park trails at the base of a mountain known as Pinnacle Wall.

Earlier that day, Raymond Kraft, a 21-year-old clerk, had set out on a risky adventure, a solo climb of the mountain. He had made his way 350 feet up along the edge of a glacial seam on its flank. When he tried to traverse the 30-foot-wide strip of ice, Kraft slipped, sliding 75 feet and breaking three bones in his ankle. Painfully, he had lowered himself down along narrow ledges until he reached a point from which he could go no farther. Below him was a nearly vertical slope of bare rock that plunged for 150 feet.

Although he had never met Kraft, Friedlich responded to the call for a rescuer. With great care, he slowly made his way some 250 feet up Pinnacle Wall toward Kraft. At two places, he had to lean back for handholds on the steep slope and swing his feet out to climb higher. Finally, Friedlich reached the stricken climber and slowly helped him down to safety. Kraft recovered, and, other than being shaken by the two-and-a-half-hour rescue, Friedlich suffered no injuries. FILE NO: 19833

On January 16, 1907, **ALEXANDER FRASER**, 46, entered the engine room of a powerhouse soon after the steam chest of an engine exploded, releasing a torrent of scalding steam at 85 pounds of pressure, to search for a co-worker he thought remained inside.

✝ *C. H.* 541

The accident occurred at 4:30 that afternoon at the Allston, Massachusetts, facility of the Boston Elevated Railway Company.

People on the scene feared that a stationary engineer, Frank Stenberg, was trapped inside, but he had escaped unseen out another exit. When Fraser, who tended the boiler in the plant, was told of Stenberg's perceived plight, he immediately entered the steam-saturated room, with no regard for his own safety, to search for the missing man. Badly scalded when he finally emerged about five minutes later, Fraser was later taken to a hospital, where he died the next morning of external and internal burns.

In addition to accepting a posthumous Carnegie Medal for her husband's bravery, Fraser's widow received a monthly death benefit for both herself and her daughter for many years. FILE NO: 6318

C. H. 7080

It was the night of February 19, 1986, when **ANDREW WRAY MATHIESON** of suburban Pittsburgh acted heroically to save a woman's life.

The Pittsburgh Penguins had just finished a National Hockey League game with the Winnipeg Jets. Mathieson, 57, and his wife were among the 12,558 fans in attendance, as were Mathieson's secretary, Jane Celender, 39, and another woman in their party. The foursome was standing at the Mathiesons' car in the hockey arena's parking lot when they were approached by Celender's estranged husband, a large man at more than six feet tall and 250 pounds.

After Celender refused her husband's order to get into his nearby car, the man produced a loaded .38-caliber handgun and, from a distance of 10 feet, fired at her. She was not struck, but the round hit her purse and remained lodged there. She started to run for refuge behind a van parked 50 feet away.

Mathieson recognized the assailant and pleaded with him: "Jim, don't do this." He then approached the gunman, but the gunman turned toward Mathieson and shot him at point-blank range. Although the bullet struck Mathieson in the upper right chest, he continued toward the assailant and took him to the pavement, where he struggled to hold him by the legs. The gunman fired again, striking Mathieson a second time, then stood.

Mrs. Mathieson, meanwhile, had secured the other woman's safety and began to approach her wounded husband. The gunman fired twice more, striking her once, also in the right chest, and Mathieson, for the third time. Mrs. Mathieson continued toward her husband as the assailant returned to his car, got inside, and inflicted a fatal gunshot wound. Both Mathieson and his wife required hospitalization for their wounds, Mathieson's treatment including surgery to remove a part of his right lung.

Mathieson's obituary in the *Pittsburgh Post-Gazette* 15 years later was a lengthy one. It had to be, to cover the list of accomplishments and affiliations represented in the 72-year life of this quiet, industrious powerhouse, who was widely known and universally respected as financial advisor, corporate director, and foundation executive. His "confidence in himself was no greater than the trust others could place in him," the obituary read. Never was that more evident than on the night of his heroic act.

Celender paid tribute to her late boss: "He always tried to do what he could to make a difference and make someone's life better." She is living proof of that. FILE NO: 60937

On January 22, 1926, **GROVER C. BREWER**, a 41-year-old clergyman in Sherman, Texas, saved three children from a rabid dog.

After leaving his office late in the morning, Sherman happened to see a dog with foamy saliva at its mouth snap at a child. Thinking the dog might be rabid, he got out of his car and followed it several blocks when he encountered a policeman, also in pursuit of the animal. Brewer returned to his office.

An hour later, Brewer went out again. While driving, he spotted the same dog, this time in an alley approaching a street where three children were. When Brewer got out of his car and motioned for the children to stay back, the dog turned toward them. Brewer then started to remove his overcoat to try to capture the dog, but the animal jumped up and struck him on the breast with both paws. As Brewer grabbed it by the throat, the dog snapped and bit him on the left wrist.

Brewer struggled with the writhing, 50-pound animal, at one point banging its head against the wall of a garage. Another man then arrived and both held the dog for several minutes until the dog catcher arrived with a rope. The dog catcher then left to get his gun, returned in a few minutes, and shot and killed the dog. Brewer removed the dog's head and sent it for tests, which confirmed that it had been rabid. Subsequently, Brewer underwent a series of shots for rabies, but he suffered no other ill effects from the encounter. FILE NO: 26339

On September 14, 1908, **G. JAMES SHAW**, 40, foreman at an elevator manufacturing company in Goderich, Ontario, risked his life and limbs to save a fellow worker.

A few minutes before noon that day, Harry Videan, a 36-year-old plant laborer, was working at a car-pulling machine when his left wrist became caught in the winding rope and drum of the machine. In response to Videan's cries for help, Shaw ran to the machine's leather power belt and, with his hands, tried to pull it off the pulley around which it turned at a speed of 4,000 feet per minute. Unsuccessful on his first attempt, Shaw grabbed the belt again, and held on as it pulled him toward the pulley. Just as his arm reached the pulley, the belt slipped off.

Although Videan was badly mangled, he eventually recovered. Shaw suffered no serious injury from the rescue. FILE NO: 3652

(ABOVE)
CAPTAIN CASTO

(FACING PAGE) THE
RESCUE BY CAPTAIN
MARK CASTO AND THE
CREW OF THE *ALBERTA*
WAS WIDELY REPORTED,
PARTICULARLY ALONG
THE EAST COAST. THE
MEDAL WAS PRESENTED
TO CASTO BY THE
CLOVER CLUB OF
PHILADELPHIA.

14 Jan. 1906
FREIGHTER S.S. CHEROKEE
BRIGANTINE SHOALS

On Sunday morning, January 14, 1906, seven volunteer sailors braved an Atlantic storm to save 54 people stranded on a storm-tossed freighter.

Two afternoons earlier, the *S.S. Cherokee* had become disoriented in foggy weather and gone aground on the Brigantine Shoals, a shelf of submerged sandbanks five miles offshore northeast of Atlantic City, New Jersey. The 2,556-ton, 264-foot-long *Cherokee* had been steaming north from San Domingo with a crew of 46, 10 passengers, and a mixed cargo. Though a rescue boat offered to evacuate the ship, everyone chose to stay aboard, assuming the *Cherokee* would be pulled into open water. That attempt had to be abandoned when gale force winds blew in. By Sunday morning, after two sea-battered days on the shoals, the ship was starting to take on water, and concern grew for the safety of her passengers and crew.

Captain **MARK CASTO**, 36, was skipper of the *Alberta*, a local 58-foot, 10-ton, two-masted fishing smack. Aware of the *Cherokee*'s plight since it first went aground, Casto decided to act at 9:00 that Sunday morning when he heard a message that 11 feet of water was in the *Cherokee*'s hold. He contacted his crew, fishermen **NELS GREGERSEN**, 26, **FREDERICK BOUCHIE**, 47, **MARIUS NELSEN**, 25, **JOSEPH M. SHUTE**, 30, and **AXAL HOLMQUIST**, 26, and the ship cook **LEWIS J. JOHNSON**, 25, and proposed attempting a rescue. Despite the apparent risks, all six men volunteered to come along.

They provisioned the *Alberta* and cast off under dark clouds at about 10:00 a.m. After maneuvering to within 200 feet of the *Cherokee*, one of the *Alberta*'s dories was smashed during a launch attempt, and a second dory, with Casto, Gregersen, and Bouchie in it, was broken apart when it hit the side of the *Cherokee*. The three men, with two others, then rowed back to the *Alberta* in one of the *Cherokee*'s lifeboats, which had to be abandoned once the men reached the *Alberta*, leaving them with no lifeboats. Casto, though, had brought a line with him from the *Cherokee*, and tied it to the *Alberta*.

By means of the line, the two boats were pulled closer to each other, and another line was then attached to a small lifeboat on the *Cherokee*. It took 12 trips of the lifeboat to take everyone off the foundering freighter. Casto then raised anchor and sailed to shore without the aid of power since the ship's engine had been disabled.

Captain Casto was awarded a gold Carnegie Medal, the first awarded by the Commission. A silver medal was awarded to each member of the crew.

FILE NOS: 796, 797, 798, 799, 800, 801, 802

L HANDS SAVED FROM STRANDED
EAMER WRECKED ON TREACHEROUS
IGANTINE SHOALS

ve Commander of Little Fishing Schooner
rought Into the Inlet at Atlantic City
Passengers, Seamen and Life-Saving
Crews Who Were in Danger of
Being Swept Into the Ocean

of the fishing schooner. The passengers landed were United States Consul William Handy, of Trinidad, who was forced to abandon his papers in which there were records of the revolution on the island, and his clothing; Ensign H. MacL. Walker, of the United States Navy, who has been detached from service with the Yankee and is to do special duty at Washington; Robert H. Pearson. N. Train and Joseph Schwartz York, and Edward Lapor merchant; Elias Amaras their two small daughters.

Exhausted from their sleep every moment of which they expect

ht hours, and she has filled through
the water breaking from deck crevices and
cain doorways. Her hatches remained
m. She however, has been driven in
mile and a half within 24 hours on the
shoals where a wrecking tug cannot reach
er. She is doomed to remain a new
victim of the treacherous shoals.

CAPTAIN CASTO AND CREW
OF SCHOONER "ALBERTA"
WHO RESCUED PASSENGERS AND CREW
STEAMSHIP CHEROKEE

C. H. 5756

On October 14, 1970, **JOSEPH C. WIEST**, 35, crossed a pit of hot slag to help a fallen co-worker.

At about 4 a.m. that day, Frank Simmer was on a small platform over a three-sided concrete pit where molten slag was gathered. Suddenly, the platform gave way, tumbling the 57-year-old man 27 feet into a corner of the pit. Although that corner of the pit was free of slag, Simmer was seriously injured by the fall.

Wiest, a floor helper on duty that morning, ran to the pit's open end, which was blocked by a thick layer of slag. Although its interior was at least 500 degrees, the cooling slag had already crusted over, but its surface temperature was still about 212 degrees. Trusting that the crust would support him and that his thick-soled shoes would protect him, Wiest stepped onto the slag and quickly covered the 25 feet to where Simmer lay.

Despite the pit's intense heat, Wiest hoisted the fallen man to his shoulders and started back. He was almost safely across when he slipped and fell on the hot slag crust, still holding Simmer. Then another workman stepped onto the slag and helped Wiest back to his feet so he could carry Simmer the rest of the way. Both men were taken to the hospital, where Simmer died three days later of shock and burns. Although also treated for burns, Wiest recovered without permanent injury.

This rescue provided the title to a book on the Commission, A Walk on the Crust of Hell, *by Jack Markowitz. (Stephen Greene Press, Brattleboro, Vt.; 1973)* FILE NO: 51759

C. H. 1213

C. H. 1214

C. H. 1215

On March 27, 1916, **JAMES E. DOUGHERTY**, **EDWARD DAVIS**, and **ROGER W. WELLS** all entered an industrial kettle to aid stricken co-workers.

The accident occurred at a chemical company plant in Heidelberg, Pennsylvania. At 2:30 that morning, Charles Galbreath, 18, climbed into an empty benzene kettle that had to be cleaned before work at the plant could proceed. Normally, he would have worn a protective helmet, but the man who was in charge of the helmets had failed to show up on time for work that morning, according to local news coverage. Shortly after Galbreath got to the bottom of the ladder in the eight-foot-deep tank, he was overcome by the fumes and collapsed.

Without taking any precautions, Dougherty, a 21-year-old worker, climbed through the manhole in the top of the kettle and was able to lift Galbreath up within reach of other men, who lifted him out. He revived. By that time, however, Dougherty himself was overcome by the fumes and collapsed back into the kettle.

Then Davis, a 32-year-old pump man, climbed in, a wet handkerchief tied over his mouth and nose. The fumes affected him before he could do anything and he climbed out. Then Wells, a 40-year-old guard in poor physical condition, made an attempt to reach Dougherty. With a rope around his waist and wearing a makeshift facemask, Wells descended the ladder. However, he was unable to do anything to help before he started choking from the fumes and climbed out.

With the rope tied around his waist, Davis made a second attempt. He managed to tie a second rope around Dougherty and then hurried out of the kettle. As he emerged, however, he gasped and fell unconscious. Using the rope, other men hoisted Dougherty out through the manhole.

Dougherty was revived with a pulmotor, although he suffered acid burns and was disabled for a month and a half. Wells, who did not lose consciousness during the incident, was disabled for two weeks with lung congestion. Attempts to revive Davis were unsuccessful, and he was pronounced dead.

Davis left behind his wife, a five-year-old son, and a three-year-old daughter. The Commission provided a monthly grant for his widow for nearly 50 years until her death in 1965. FILE NOS: 16293, 16291, 16474

On January 10, 1918, 13-year-old **R. VERNON CALLAWAY** stood for more than an hour in shoulder-deep, freezing water trying to keep a fellow student from drowning.

C. H. 1614

During noon recess on that 20-degree day, a group of four boys were skating on the ice that covered flooded lowlands near their school in St. Joe, Idaho. Three of them had so much fun that they decided not to return to school. Some time afterward, one of them, 12-year-old Roland Cyr, fell through a weak spot in the ice into four feet of water. He paddled to keep his head above water while the other boy who was nearby tried unsuccessfully several times to haul him out.

Although a non-swimmer himself, Callaway skated over to help. Lying on the ice with the other boy holding onto his hands, he stretched his leg toward Cyr. The younger boy managed to grab Callaway's foot, but when the third boy tried to pull them out, the ice kept crumbling under them until both Cyr and Callaway slid back into the frigid water.

Although the water was up to his shoulders, Callaway was able to support Cyr while the other boy ran to get help. Several times, Callaway tried to lift Cyr out of the water, but each time the weak ice thwarted his effort. Even after Cyr lost consciousness, Callaway kept his head above the surface of the water. When several men finally arrived and pulled both boys from the water, Callaway was at the point of passing out himself, the sleeve of his coat frozen to the surface of the ice.

Unfortunately, Cyr, who had a weak heart, never regained consciousness. Though treated for three weeks for exposure, Callaway made a complete recovery. FILE NO: 18732

C. H. 8590, 8591

C. H. 8592, 8593

On March 25, 2000, three 17-year-old high school students went to the aid of a chaperone of their hiking trip who had been swept by a wave into dangerous surf. Two of them drowned. A local fisherman also risked his life in the rescue attempt.

Barbara Clement, 45, was a parent chaperoning a group of Canadian high school students hiking a remote ocean-side trail near Shelter Cove, California. Around 12:40 that afternoon, as the group was crossing a surge channel on Black Sands Beach, Clement was surprised by a wave and was knocked off her feet. While struggling with her backpack, she was pulled down the beach by the rush of the backwash.

DAVID M. ELTON and BRODIE MACDONALD immediately dropped their packs and ran to help Clement, who was struggling to regain her footing. The two boys reached the woman and were helping her to her feet when a large wave broke over them. Its backwash sucked all three deeper into the roiling surf.

The third student, JORDAN D. NIXON, and the 37-year-old leader of the expedition both dropped their packs and ran to help, but they too were sucked up by the surging, 48-degree water and dragged seaward by the strong current.

A call was made to the Coast Guard, which sent out a distress call, and several local fishermen responded in their boats. One spotted Nixon floundering in the water beyond the breakers and was able to rescue him. Meanwhile, another fisherman, DONALD J. SACK, 46, had piloted his 18-foot boat more than six miles to reach the area. Sack came across Clement, also floating outside the breakers. He pulled out her limp body and passed it to another boat. Then Sack saw the group's leader still struggling some 60 feet from shore, but well inside the 12-foot breakers. At considerable risk, Sack maneuvered his boat into the turbulent waters to a point where he could get the man's attention. Throwing him a line, Sack towed the nearly unconscious man through the breakers. Then holding him against the boat's side, he carefully steered it to calmer waters where another fisherman boarded his boat and they pulled the man aboard.

Nixon and the leader were evacuated to a hospital and were treated for near drowning and hypothermia, but both were released the following day. Sack twisted his right knee but also recovered. Along with Clement, Elton and MacDonald drowned. Despite an intensive search, the two students' bodies were not discovered until several days had passed.

FILE NOS: 74353, 74354, 74917, 75085

CHARLES N. WRIGHT, assisted by **WILLIAM L. DILLARD**, saved a fallen climber from the edge of a 2,000-foot precipice.   *C. H. 840, 841*

It was warm and dry on Sunday afternoon, May 14, 1911. R. Augustus Baty had walked with some friends to the top of Whiteside Mountain, near Highlands, North Carolina. At a point known as Fool's Rock, he either slipped or intentionally stepped over the edge and tumbled 150 feet down a nearly vertical slope. He would have plummeted to certain death over the sheer cliff at the bottom of the slope, but he became entangled in a small rhododendron bush growing just two inches from the edge. Battered by the fall and unconscious, Baty lay lodged there with an arm and a leg dangling over the edge of the cliff.

Wright, a 38-year-old storeowner in Highlands, and Dillard, a 33-year-old liveryman, had also been hiking, with their wives, on Whiteside. Alerted to Baty's predicament, the two men descended an embankment 15 feet to the top of the slope. Then they slowly zigzagged down and across its rocky face, using inch-long indentations and protrusions for hand and foot holds, attempting to reach an intermittent line of rhododendrons growing along the slope's lower lip.

Partway down, Dillard lost his nerve, but Wright coaxed him several steps to a place of relative safety. When Wright's wife saw what he was doing, she began screaming, which nearly unnerved him as well. After a moment, however, he regained his composure and continued down until he reached a bush just above where Baty lay. Then Wright slowly lowered his feet to the narrow ledge just 24 inches from the brink, reached down, and grabbed the collar of Baty's jacket.

Feeling a hand on his collar, Baty jerked suddenly, which so alarmed Wright that he nearly lost his grip. Ordering Baty to be still, Wright was able to pull the stricken man back a bit from the brink. He then reached up, grabbed a bush, and wrapped his legs around its base, which allowed him to drag the now delirious Baty farther up. Dillard, meanwhile, had shed his shoes for more secure footing and, in stocking feet, had inched to Wright and Baty. Then the three men crept 15 feet along the ledge to where another man had descended with a bucket of water with which Wright and Dillard applied crude first-aid treatment to Baty. The rescuers, now numbering three, took Baty back up and across the slope to within 15 feet of the top, and he was hoisted by rope to safety, the rescuers following. The rescue had taken two and a half hours, but all three men recovered without serious injury. FILE NOS: 7327, 7328

C. H. 7440

Over six days in 1989, **DAVID M. NYMAN**, a 31-year-old civil engineer, braved Alaskan snowstorms to save his stricken climbing partner.

On the sunny morning of April 19, Nyman and James Sweeney, 33, were climbing a deep vertical gorge on Mt. Johnson near Ruth's Glacier in Denali National Park when Sweeney was swept away by an avalanche, fracturing and dislocating a hip.

With great difficulty, Nyman managed to lower his partner to a place where they could spend the night in the avalanche-prone area. The next morning, Nyman left Sweeney and skied more than seven miles to a lodge down the glacier. Two of the people staying at the lodge went out to rescue Sweeney, but they were unable to find him and were not equipped to continue searching in the dark.

The following day, when Nyman learned that his friend had not been found, he skied back to Sweeney, knowing that help had been or would be alerted. But another avalanche struck, trapping the men on the mountain. For two days, the climbers remained stranded. Nyman kept moving Sweeney and their camp to dodge avalanches, several of which partially buried them.

On the 25th, with their supplies nearly gone, Nyman decided he had to get Sweeney to safety by himself and began tracking a path through fresh snow that drifted up to four feet deep. Covering several hundred yards at a time, he would then go back to Sweeney and drag him forward. In that way, they progressed almost a mile, descending some 1,200 feet down the mountain, braving several more avalanches, one of which carried them into a deep crevasse. Finally, on April 26, they were spotted by a helicopter and were rescued.

It took Sweeney twelve weeks to recover from his ordeal. Nyman was treated for frostbite and dehydration. FILE NO: 64291

(FACING PAGE, TOP) MT. JOHNSON AND "ELEVATOR SHAFT" WHERE ACCIDENT OCCURRED. (BOTTOM) ROUTE OF DAVID M. NYMAN AND JAMES SWEENEY.

(RIGHT) SWEENEY, IN BED, AND NYMAN AT PROVIDENCE HOSPITAL, ANCHORAGE, ALASKA

1 Sweeney fall/avalanche
2 Sweeney Nyman bivy on April 19
2 Sweeney bivy night of April 20
3 Nyman and Sweeney tent of April 21 and 22
4 Nyman and Sweeny bivy of April 23
5 Nyman and Sweeney snow cave of April 24
6 Sweeney and Nyman bivy of April 25
7 Crevasse fall of April 26

Mt. JOHNSON

tor Shaft

he could handle the cats. He went into the pits to
the audience—none of us knew about it. The mi...
he stepped inside the door, one of the females jum...

Here is author Joe Arcaris at work. At the time this ...
took place, Joe worked at Clyde Beatty's Jungle in Flo...

JOE ARCARIS
PERFORMING AT
CLYDE BEATTY'S
JUNGLE ZOO.

JOSEPH ARCARIS saved a man by facing down five lions on February 9, 1940.

Arcaris, age 31, had been hired to be an animal trainer at Clyde Beatty's Jungle Zoo in Fort Lauderdale, Florida. He was dressing after a show when he heard shouting. Chester Czaja, a 24-year-old circus animal caregiver, had entered an enclosure not knowing it held five untrained lions. The big cats attacked Czaja, knocked him down, and dragged him across the enclosure.

Arcaris arrived shortly afterward. Although an animal trainer, he had never been inside the enclosure nor worked with these particular lions. Nonetheless, the slightly built Arcaris grabbed a six-foot length of 2-by-2-inch lumber left by construction workers and went to help the blood-covered victim, who, unconscious, was now being bitten by three of the carnivores.

Arcaris drove off two of them but broke his wooden weapon while violently beating the third. That lion then dragged Czaja into a niche, where it was joined by one of the others. Arcaris followed the beast to the niche and beat it until it ran off. Then the brave man moved several steps into the niche and confronted the final attacker, striking it on the head with what was left of his stick until the beast finally dropped Czaja and moved a few feet away. To prevent the animal from attacking again, Arcaris walked toward it and struck a final blow, then flourished his club until the lion backed away. Then other workers outside the enclosure drove the five lions into holding cages by firing blank cartridges.

Though seriously wounded, Czaja eventually recovered. The uninjured Arcaris felt that he had done nothing extraordinary. "A man can hardly be considered a hero," he later explained, "if he does something without thinking. If I had been thinking that day, I might never have done what I did." FILE NO: 38229

C. H. 3165

Early in the morning of July 27, 2001, ERIC FORTIER, a 32-year-old orthodontist, rescued two friends who were being mauled by a polar bear.

Fortier was on a six-day canoe trip with his longtime friend Alain Parenteau, 31, and their girlfriends, Anne Dumouchel, 33, and Patricia Doyon, 25. The four were camping along the Soper River in a remote region on the southern tip of Baffin Island in the Canadian territory of Nunavut. The two couples were sleeping in separate tents about 30 feet apart. It was daylight at 3:30 a.m. when Fortier was awakened by something pushing against his foot. Dumouchel then saw the outline of a bear against the roof of the tent, and both began to shout to scare the bear away and warn their friends.

C. H. 8753

The bear, estimated to weigh about 350 pounds, then moved to the other tent and slashed open its top with a paw. When Parenteau and Doyon scrambled out through the door flap, the bear swatted Parenteau on the left hip, and then moved off after Doyon. Parenteau gave chase and tried to distract the bear, but it turned on him, and knocked him to the ground with its paws, cutting him on the head, neck, shoulder, trunk, and leg.

Fortier and Dumouchel climbed out of their tent and saw Parenteau on his back kicking at the bear, with Doyon several feet away throwing stones at the animal. Fortier's only weapon was a folding pocketknife with a three-and-a-half-inch blade. He used it to cut a tent line that was tied to a rock measuring about 18 inches by six inches.

Picking up the rock, Fortier ran to within six feet of the bear and threw it, hitting the animal on the shoulder. The bear turned toward Doyon, who tried to run but slipped and fell. The bear quickly caught up with the young woman and began to maul her. Fortier and Dumouchel threw more rocks at the bear and distracted it long enough to allow Doyon to flee. But as the bear followed her, she fell, and again the bear began to paw her, slashing her clothing and skin. Armed with only the knife, Fortier ran to the bear and stabbed three times up under its neck, the final thrust drawing blood. The animal ceased its attack on Doyon, rambled away behind some large rocks by the water's edge, and disappeared. The attack had lasted less than five minutes.

The party, however, was still many miles from safety, with both Parenteau and Doyon bleeding from multiple wounds. After assessing the injuries, they quickly threw their gear into the canoes to paddle to the planned take-out point. After a short distance, it became clear that Parenteau and Doyon were too weak to paddle, so the two canoes were lashed together, and Fortier and Dumouchel did the work.

When they reached the landing place two hours later, Fortier ran and walked for another hour to a small village, where he was able to get help. Parenteau and Doyon were eventually taken by helicopter to a hospital, where both were treated and released, Doyon the next day, and Parenteau two days later. Neither Fortier nor Dumouchel suffered any injuries.

FILE NO: 76426

27 June 1954
LEAF RIVER
MERRILL, MISSISSIPPI

C. H. 3973

On June 27, 1954, **CHARLES B. VINES**, a 22-year-old former Marine who had been blinded by a bursting mortar shell two years earlier in the Korean War, saved two women from drowning in a Mississippi river.

Anne Ball, 18, and her cousin Barbara Wood, 15, were wading with Vines and his friend, James Peacock, on a submerged sandbar in the Leaf River near Merrill, when both women stepped into deep water and went under. They surfaced 10 feet away, struggling for air. Ball grabbed for

Peacock, who was swimming nearby, but submerged him. When one of his legs cramped, he swam to the sandbar alone.

Vines, the only other person around, heard Wood's screams and immediately swam to her. Holding onto his shoulder, the young girl directed him to Ball, who by now was struggling wildly to keep her head above water. Vines towed both women back across the current toward the sandbar, but when they got near, Wood let go, intending to swim the rest of the way herself. Instead, she was caught by the current and carried downstream.

Vines got Ball to the sandbar and then started swimming after Wood, who was then 200 feet away and being carried into the Pascagoula River. Because he was unable to see, Vines had to change his course repeatedly while he swam, following Wood's screams and directions shouted by Peacock on the sandbar. Swimming 350 feet, he caught up with Wood and towed her back to the bank, where she lost consciousness.

Both women were briefly hospitalized, but they recovered completely. Although Vines was exhausted from his efforts and nauseated from the river water he had swallowed, the blind ex-Marine was fine when he had a chance to rest. FILE NO: 43200

20 Aug. 1928
LONG ISLAND SOUND
FISHERS ISLAND, NEW YORK

On August 20, 1928, **ERNEST F. DAVIS**, a 64-year-old fisherman, saved his grandnephew from being pulled down into the 200-foot-deep water of Long Island Sound.

C. H. 2331

About 3:00 that afternoon, Davis and the 17-year-old boy, Robert Lane, were working together on a slow-moving motorboat setting lobster pots into the choppy sound near Fishers Island, New York. When Lane was casting the pots on one line, he swung a coil of rope over his head. Stooping then to grab another coil, the line dropped, looped around his neck, and was pulled tight instantly by the weight of three 50-pound already-sinking pots. He screamed just as he was jerked off his feet and dragged to the boat's stern. In an instant, he was hauled overboard.

Davis, hearing the boy's yell and thinking the line was around Lane's ankle, started to wrap it around a cleat, but quickly realized it was around his neck. He let go of the line and immediately grabbed a double-edged knife and jumped into the water. He reached Lane just below the surface and was able to slash the line between him and the boat. Then, reaching around Lane's neck, again Davis with one slash cut the length of rope from which the three pots hung. Both men surfaced, and, after catching his breath, Lane was able to reboard the circling boat. Though nearly exhausted by his effort and burdened by the weight of oilskin overalls and high, rubber boots, Davis managed to tread water until Lane brought the boat about and helped him aboard. FILE NO: 28714

C. H. 4466

JOSEPH J. GRANAHAN, a 30-year-old waiter, entered a collapsing New York City tenement to save an elderly woman who was calling for help from the fourth floor.

It was just after 11 p.m. on November 17, 1960. Granahan was relaxing in a nearby bar when he saw clouds of plaster dust outside and thought there was a fire. A nearby building had been recently demolished, but the foundation of the adjacent apartment building hadn't been shored up. Now the five-story brick building was caving into the excavation. It was already separating from the building next to it when Granahan arrived. All residents were accounted for except 83-year-old Helen Giles, who had been asleep in her fourth-floor apartment and was awakened by plaster falling onto her head.

Although Granahan had never been in the building and did not know anyone who lived there, he kicked out the glass panel of the now jammed front door, climbed through the opening, and started up the stairway through a cloud of crumbling plaster and dust. On the second floor, he had to kick through another glass door panel. He proceeded to the third floor, shouting a warning at each apartment he passed.

When Granahan reached the fourth floor, the lights went out, the entire structure groaned and creaked, and visibility was less than a foot. Still, he was able to locate Giles in the hallway and lead her to the stairs. Picking up the frail woman, he carried her down the three flights, the final one as the staircase was pulling away from the wall. He had to lift Giles through the two blocked doorways. Less than four minutes after he brought her out, the building collapsed into a 20-foot-high pile of rubble. Though dazed and bruised, neither was seriously injured.

Granahan received a Silver Medal, the highest award made to an individual in 35 years. He was later able to recount his story for a national television audience, when he appeared as a guest on *To Tell The Truth*.

FILE NO: 45298

C. H. 2411, 2412

On September 4, 1927, two fishermen, **CARL SEIDNER**, 28, and **JAMES W. BROOKS**, 25, rowed through pounding surf of the Pacific Ocean to rescue a family whose fishing boat had capsized.

The Peters family, Kirby, 36, Maude, 45, and Floyd, 13, had been among several groups net fishing that evening from small boats in the mouth of the Klamath River near Requa, California. However, when the tide shifted, creating a strong outflow, they were unable to reel in their net or cut the line that attached it to the boat. The tide dragged their boat toward the ocean. Unbalanced by the net, the craft capsized in the breakers, flinging all three into the water. The father and son managed to find their way back to the boat and hang on, but Mrs. Peters, crying for help, was carried away and drowned.

Witnessing the situation from shore, Seidner and Brooks launched a small fishing boat into the surf. After being twice flung back by breakers cresting at seven feet, the two men managed to row into open water. Searching in the darkness, they finally reached the capsized boat about a quarter of a mile from shore. After hauling in the two, and while waiting for a signal from shore that conditions were favorable for a run through the breakers, they searched the roiling waves unsuccessfully for Mrs. Peters. Then Seidner and Brooks rowed the boat stern-first back toward shore, maneuvering it skillfully through the breakers and riding in on a large wave.

FILE NOS: 27992, 27991

10 Sept. 1942

INTERNATIONAL FIBRE BOARD, LTD.

GATINEAU, QUEBEC

An accident on September 10, 1942, at International Fibre Board, Ltd.'s, wood processing plant in Gatineau, Quebec, gave rise to eight acts of heroism.

C. H. 3294, 3295, 3296, 3297, 3298, 3299, 3300, 3301

Arthur Nerbonne and **DOUGLAS READ** were working in an underground concrete tank where the sludge from wood pulping operations was collected when both men were engulfed in a noxious buildup of hydrogen sulfide, an irritating and highly poisonous gas. Read managed to get to the exit ladder and climb out, but Nerbonne collapsed face forward into the 18 inches of foul broth. Read called for help and immediately re-entered the tank. He managed to drag Nerbonne to the ladder and cradle his head above the pulp before he also passed out, only 30 seconds after re-entering.

MAURICE DORION was the next volunteer to enter the gas-filled tank. After repositioning the men, he felt himself beginning to faint and climbed out. **WILFRED RACINE** took a deep breath and went down the ladder. He managed to raise Read's head out of the liquid, and get Nerbonne into a seated position. **JOSEPH JACKSON** then descended and tied a rope around Read's chest. Succumbing to the effects of the gas, Racine released Nerbonne and ascended the ladder, at midpoint passing **LUCIEN CHARRON**, who had decided to enter the pit. Charron got Nerbonne's head up but, feeling dizzy, sat against the wall of the tank, where he became semiconscious. Men at the top tried to pull Read out, but he slipped out of the rope and dropped limply back into the sludge. After Jackson left the tank, **PHILLIPE TURCOTTE** went in, retied the rope around Read, and helped hoist him out, escaping himself. **LUCIEN VERREAULT** was able to go down and get a rope around Nerbonne before collapsing himself, despite the use of an air hose that had been lowered by then. **DAVID MOREAU** managed to go into the tank, get ropes around Charron and Verreault, and help lift them out.

All of the men who had been overcome were revived with no long-term ill effects. FILE NOS: 39737, 39777, 39774, 39772, 39775, 39773, 39778, 39776

C. H. 7935

(FACING PAGE)
COMMISSION
INVESTIGATOR'S
SKETCH SHOWING
COURSE OF JOHN
ESPADA'S RESCUE
OF TWO CHILDREN.
(INSERT) FERRIS
WHEEL AT THE
BOWCRAFT AMUSE-
MENT PARK IN
SCOTCH PLAINS,
NEW JERSEY.

On August 30, 1994, **JOHN ESPADA**, a 35-year-old carpenter, climbed to the top of a Ferris wheel to save two trapped children.

Shortly after noon that summer day, the amusement park in Scotch Plains was bustling. All 16 benches on the 53-foot-high Ferris wheel were occupied. When the wheel jerked to a stop to allow one group to get off, the restraining bar on the highest seat popped open, tumbling the three children in it forward. Six-year-old Evan Manganiello fell out and dropped to the pavement below. His brother Tyler, 7, and 6-year-old Brittany Pezzillo managed to catch hold of structural members and hold on.

Espada was visiting the park with his wife and 2-year-old son. When he heard about the two stranded children, he ran to the Ferris wheel and soon realized that none of the young park employees would be able to get up quickly enough to rescue them. A good climber and not afraid of heights, Espada spidered his way up the structure to the two children. First he grabbed Pezzillo, then Manganiello and, pulling them on to a supporting beam, hugged both of them close until a park employee arrived with a safety harness.

The two children were lifted back into their seat, and the wheel turned so they could be removed at ground level uninjured but for minor cuts and bruises. Espada also came down safe but sore. Though he suffered a fractured skull, the younger Manganiello did survive his fall. FILE NO: 69068

C. H. 723

On January 18, 1908, 12-year-old **W. ROY STOKES** died attempting to save three young girls who had fallen through thin ice.

At about 9:00 that morning, the Kenly sisters, Sarah, 13, Lorena, 12, and Charlotte, 8, were walking on one end of a frozen reservoir between two coke yards near their home in the village of Coral, Indiana County, Pennsylvania, when the two-inch-thick ice collapsed under them, and the three girls, all non-swimmers, fell into nine-foot-deep freezing water.

Stokes, who was skating near the other end of the reservoir some 400 feet away, became aware of what had happened. Immediately he sped toward where the girls had gone in, even though he was aware the ice in that area was not safe. Lying face down on the surface, he managed to pull Lorena from the water. However, when they tried to reach the other girls, both slipped back into the water. All four bodies were discovered a half hour later. They all had drowned.

In addition to accepting a Carnegie Medal in honor of his son's brave act, Stokes' father received a $1000 death benefit, a portion of which was used to buy a house for his family. FILE NO: 8981

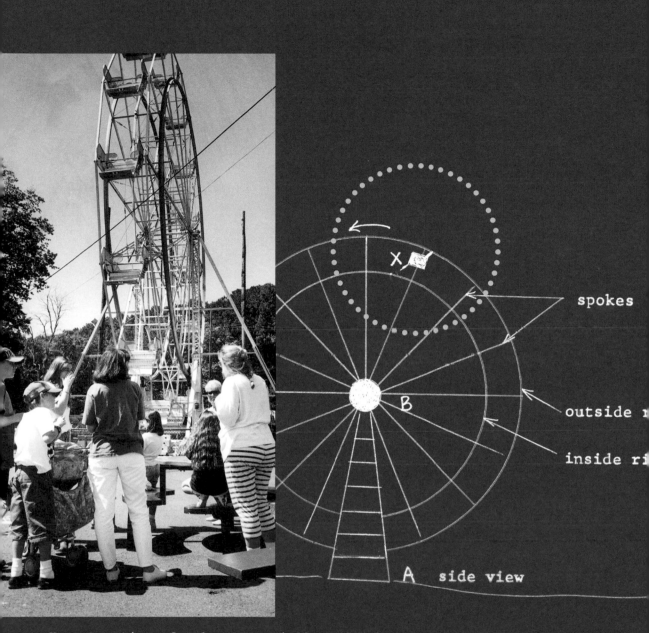

X - Location of Tyler Manganiello and Brittany A. Pezzillo as
     they clung to a Ferris wheel after being thrown from their
     seat

ABX- Course John Espada climbed to the children

X - Point where Espada grasped children and secured them to the
     wheel for several minutes

X - Point at which Espada and another man positioned children
     back into their seat

XA - Course of Espada and children to ground as wheel was turned

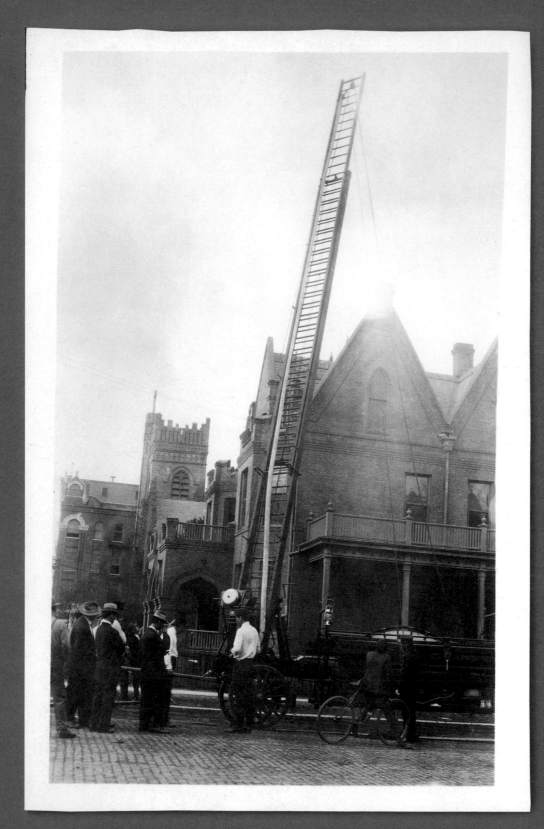

The extension
ladder Forest W.
McNeir climbed.

On February 12, 1910, **FOREST W. MCNEIR**, a 34-year-old contractor and architect, saved a city fireman from death.

C. H. 637

It was about 7:15 that cool, fair Texas evening, but things were hot for Charles Rogers, a Houston fireman. A fire was burning in a three-story brick building that housed a hardware company, in which it was suspected that a quantity of explosives was stored.

Rogers was fighting the blaze from an aerial ladder, when the cable supporting the ladder extension came in contact with a live electrical wire and was burned into two. The extension plunged, catching Rogers' foot between it and the top rung of the stationary ladder. The stricken fireman dangled 35 feet above the ground near a window from which smoke and flames erupted, which frequently engulfed him. Even worse, the live wire was still in contact with the truck, and the current was shocking Rogers.

As soon as the accident occurred, two firemen tried to climb to rescue Rogers, but were knocked away from the truck by an electrical jolt. McNeir arrived on the scene and, even though the firemen had been warned away, jumped up on the ladder and, carefully grasping only its wooden rungs, climbed up toward Rogers, planning to cut off his trapped leg at the knee. However, when McNeir reached up and touched the snagged fireman, he received a shock that sent him flying backwards. As he fell to the ground, he hit the ladder, jarring it enough to allow Rogers to release his foot and slide to the ground.

McNeir was knocked unconscious when he fell, and was taken to the hospital where he was treated for scalp wounds and burns on his hands and face, but he eventually recovered. FILE NO: 5019

On July 30, 1996, **MARIE-EVE RENAUD**, a 22-year-old college student, rescued a motorist from being killed by falling debris.

C. H. 8196

About 2:25 that afternoon, Gerard Gravel, 50, was the driver of a car stopped at a traffic light beneath a railroad overpass that was being rebuilt in downtown Montreal. Above Gravel, a dump-truck driver backed onto the walkway portion of the overpass, which was not intended for vehicular traffic. The loaded truck weighed more than 25 tons, and its rear wheels crushed through the deck, sending large slabs of concrete down onto Gravel's car and trapping him inside. The truck's load of stone and sand spilled partially out and through the hole in the overpass and onto the car.

Renaud was driving close by and witnessed what happened. She jumped from her car and ran to help. Despite the continuing flow of debris, she eventually managed to pull open the driver's door and help Gravel crawl out. Both were able to flee to safety without suffering serious injury.

FILE NO: 72218

C. H. 4853 ✠

ADDIE S. McCORMICK, a hotel switchboard operator, lost her life on July 30, 1964, when she remained at her post to warn guests about a fire.

McCormick had worked the switchboard at the Beacon Arms Hotel in Ottawa, Ontario, for six years, but had been a telephone operator on and off for 48 of her 64 years. She was in the switchboard room at the back of the 12-story hotel's first-floor office when a fire broke out in a storage closet and spread into the foyer. As dense smoke billowed into the main floor, the fire alarm was sounded. The hotel's accountant was in the office and instructed employees to get out, but McCormick stayed at the switchboard.

The first call she placed was to report the fire and summon help. Next she answered calls from at least two of the employees and approximately 60 guests believed to be in the hotel at the time. Then McCormick began phoning guest rooms to notify people of the fire and instruct them to use the stairs rather than the elevator. At least one guest reported getting a call from McCormick, and a maid heard phones ringing in rooms on two floors as she fled down the steps.

Before he left the office, the accountant looked into the phone room and saw McCormick still at her post. Again he told her to leave, and she answered, "I'm coming." By then, flames had nearly engulfed the foyer. The accountant ran out of the building, but, two minutes later, when McCormick didn't appear, he tried to get back in, only to discover the foyer filled with flames, blocking McCormick's only escape route.

Ten minutes after McCormick phoned in the alarm, firefighters arrived and quickly extinguished the flames. McCormick's body was discovered on the floor in front of the switchboard. FILE NO: 47405

C. H. 6713

On June 13, 1982, 14-year-old **CAROLYN B. HARTSOCK** braved a flame-filled hallway three times to save a younger sister and brother.

At 4:30 that morning, the seven members of the Hartsock family were asleep in their two-story home in the town of Castlewood in Virginia's southwest corner, when a lightning strike is believed to have started a fire. Mr. and Mrs. Hartsock were in the downstairs bedroom, 16-year-old David was in one upstairs bedroom, while Carolyn, Loretta, 13, Norma, 12, and Johnny, 9, were in the other upstairs bedroom. David woke to the smell of smoke in the hallway and escaped out a window and alerted his parents. The other children awoke to discover flames filling the upstairs hallway. Loretta dashed down the stairs, while Carolyn roused Norma and pushed her through the flames to the top of the stairway.

Then, with her nightclothes on fire, Carolyn went back to the bedroom to get Johnny, who suffered from cerebral palsy. Wrapping her brother in a blanket, she carried him through the flaming hallway to the stairs, where Norma still stood, too frightened to move. Urging Norma to flee, Carolyn went partway down the stairway to hold back flaming strips of wallpaper so her sister could run down past her and out of the house.

Carolyn then went back up to Johnny and pushed him through the flames before going down the stairs herself. Her father met her at the bottom of the stairway and took her outside, where her mother fell on her to extinguish her burning clothing.

Norma and Johnny were burned badly, but both recovered. Carolyn also survived, but the third-degree burns she received over 85 percent of her body have left her permanently scarred. FILE NO: 58548

On March 9, 1917, 14-year-old **LILY BLANKS CLARKE** saved her 9-year-old sister and two other children from drowning in Lake Beulah in Monroe, Louisiana.

Clarke's sister was with Emma Biedenharn and Leland Petagna, both 14, in a small boat about 260 feet from shore. When the boat took on a little water, Clarke's sister became frightened and jumped into the eight-foot-deep lake. When she did, the boat capsized, tumbling the other two children into the water. Poor swimmers, all three began paddling to shore, but after a short distance Petagna stopped, having found something on the bottom that allowed him to stand and keep his head above water.

Clarke, who had been watching from the shore, happened to be a good swimmer. Realizing she was the only other person in the immediate area, she pulled off her sweater and shoes, waded in, and swam toward the tiring girls, meeting them about 125 feet from shore. With one holding on to each of her shoulders, she started towing them toward safety, but covered only 15 feet in this fashion. After taking her sister 10 feet farther, Clarke returned to Biedenharn and, with difficulty, towed her to wadable water while the sister swam ashore on her own.

Then without stopping for a rest, Clarke swam 240 feet back to the upturned boat and shoved it toward Petagna, who was about 10 feet away. With him clinging to the boat, she propelled it to wadable water, where men assisted them to the bank, Clarke semi-conscious by then. The three children had been saved, and, although exhausted, Clarke recovered quickly.

FILE NO: 17765

C. H. 1438, 1439

On February 5, 1915, two men from Wadsworth, Ohio, risked their lives to save a 5-year-old girl who had dashed into the path of an approaching train.

Though he had only one arm, 29-year-old **PETER J. BACSO** was the crossing watchman where railroad tracks ran through the small town just west of Akron. Bacso was already stopping pedestrians from crossing ahead of the train that was rolling through at 40 mph, but young Lois Shelly was in a hurry. She darted past Bacso and onto the tracks, but she stumbled to her knees between the rails of the track. The engineer of the train, which was then 260 feet away, immediately applied the brakes.

Bacso reacted quickly. He turned and dashed to the girl, the train then only 30 feet away, grabbed her skirts with his hand, and snatched her to safety just as the train thundered past. **CHARLES KUNKLER**, who had been standing a few feet closer to the train than Bacso when Shelly fell, also responded. The 45-year-old Kunkler dashed in front of the train and reached Shelly an instant after Bacso. None of the three was injured.

FILE NOS: 16399, 16133

C. H. 1060, 1062
C. H. 1061, 1063

On March 7, 1913, four mariners from Baltimore returned to a burning freighter containing a cargo of dynamite to rescue two stranded seamen.

WILLIAM E. VAN DYKE, 35, was captain of the *Atlantic*, a tugboat that worked in and around Baltimore harbor with a crew of three, **HENRY M. DIGGS**, 35, **WILLIAM W. MARSHALL**, 39, and **LOUIS H. COMEGYS**, 33. That day the tug was moored in the Patapsco River tending a barge from which several dozen stevedores were transferring 300 tons of dynamite into the hold of the steamer *Alum Chine*. The dynamite was to be used for blasting work at the Panama Canal.

When a fire broke out in the ship's hold, and with everyone aware of the explosive nature of the cargo, a general panic ensued. A number of stevedores crowded into a launch and fled. More than 20 others climbed onto the *Atlantic*, and Van Dyke quickly steered the tug away. However, when the tug had gone about 450 feet, two men were seen on the bow of the *Alum Chine* signaling for help.

After conferring briefly with Marshall, his engineer, Van Dyke concluded that they had to rescue the trapped men. Ignoring the pleas of several stevedores who begged him not to return, the captain turned his tug and headed full speed back to the burning vessel.

Dense black smoke billowed from the *Alum Chine*'s open hatchways, and flames rose from its deck. The two men had climbed down the ship's anchor chain, and when Van Dyke brought the *Atlantic*'s bow underneath them, they dropped onto its deck. Van Dyke backed the tug away as quickly as possible, but when it had gone only 75 feet the dynamite exploded. The detonation completely destroyed the *Alum Chine*. Flying debris killed people on shore two miles away.

The cataclysmic force leveled the *Atlantic*'s pilothouse, instantly killing Van Dyke and Diggs, six stevedores, and one of the two rescued men. Though badly injured, Marshall and Comegys, the other rescued man, and all the other stevedores survived. FILE NOS: 10333, 10334, 10335, 10336

19 Oct. 1964
ANCHORAGE HARBOR
ANCHORAGE, ALASKA

A collision between two fuel tankers near the harbor of Anchorage, Alaska, on October 19, 1964, gave tugboat captain **JACK C. ANDERSON, JR.**, his wife, **LOIS**, and their 17-year-old son, **JOHN**, a chance to demonstrate skill and bravery.

The *Sirrah* and *Santa Maria* were each loaded with millions of gallons of liquid fuels when they collided in an ocean inlet about one mile from the Anchorage city docks. Aviation fuel gushing from a hole torn in the *Santa Maria* quickly ignited and engulfed her stern in flames, along with the bow of the *Sirrah* and one of the two tugboats that had been accompanying the second ship.

Anderson, 41, was owner and pilot of the stricken tug. Lois, 39, was helping him. John was piloting the other tugboat. The elder Anderson radioed his son to stand by the *Sirrah* while they went to help those on the *Santa Maria*. While Jack extinguished the flames on the tug, Lois steered the craft toward the *Santa Maria*, which was drifting on the tide, leaving a wide trail of fire 30 feet high in her wake.

The younger Anderson positioned his tug against the *Sirrah* on the side opposite the flames. Crewmen, fearing an explosion, climbed down an emergency ladder to the tug's deck. But when the *Sirrah*'s captain announced that the fire was under control, the crew re-boarded the stricken tanker. John then steered his tug to help his parents at the *Santa Maria*, which, by then, was engulfed for 175 feet along one side by flames that reached 80 feet above the water.

The older Anderson brought his vessel alongside the *Santa Maria*, manipulating its propellers to keep water-borne flames from igniting the tugboat. When the captain of the burning tanker gave the order to abandon ship, 31 crewmen jumped down onto the tug's deck. The captain and seven other crewmembers launched a lifeboat from the *Santa Maria*'s opposite side and were in short order met and rescued by John, who had arrived with his tug. When it was discovered that one crewmember was unaccounted for, John piloted the tug in a circle around the burning tanker, but to no avail.

The tugboats conveyed all the rescued crewmembers to shore. The fire on the *Santa Maria* was not extinguished until the following day.

FILE NOS: 47535, 47847, 47557

C. H. 4994, 4995, 4996

26 Mar. 1912
ABANDONED WELL
DOTHAN, ALABAMA

C. H. 1020

On March 26, 1912, **HENRY T. MATHEWS**, a 12-year-old delivery boy, volunteered to be lowered 28 feet into an abandoned well to rescue a young boy.

Three-year-old Benjamin Grant was with his nursemaid at the house his uncle rented in Dothan, Alabama, waiting for his father to pick him up after work. Playing in the backyard, the boy crawled under the porch and fell feet first into an abandoned well there. The woman heard his cries and ran for help. Men came and quickly located the young boy, but because the pipe casing was only 13 inches in diameter, none of the men could fit into the hole.

A call went out for someone small enough to help, including a special message to one boy who had a reputation as being particularly daring. All of them refused.

However, when Mathews, who was working in a store that afternoon, heard about the situation, he went immediately to the Grant house and offered his help. At that point, the child had been in the hole for more than an hour, and rescuers feared he could not survive much longer. A rope was tied securely around Mathews, and he was lowered head first into the tight casing. He grabbed Grant's upraised hands and was hoisted with him for a few feet, but then the child slipped from his grasp.

Mathews was pulled up to get a breath of fresh air and then lowered back into the hole, this time with a looped rope. Unfortunately, Grant was still wearing a broad-brimmed hat, which made it impossible for Mathews to get the rope around him. So he removed the hat from the young boy's head and asked to be raised to the surface again. When he was lowered a third time, Mathews managed to get the rope under Grant's shoulders. Both boys were then hoisted to the surface. Neither was injured during the ordeal.

Mathews was modest about what he had done. When a collection was taken up for him at the scene, he tried to run away. In addition to a Carnegie Medal, the Commission awarded Mathews $2,000 to be used for his future education. FILE NO: 8301

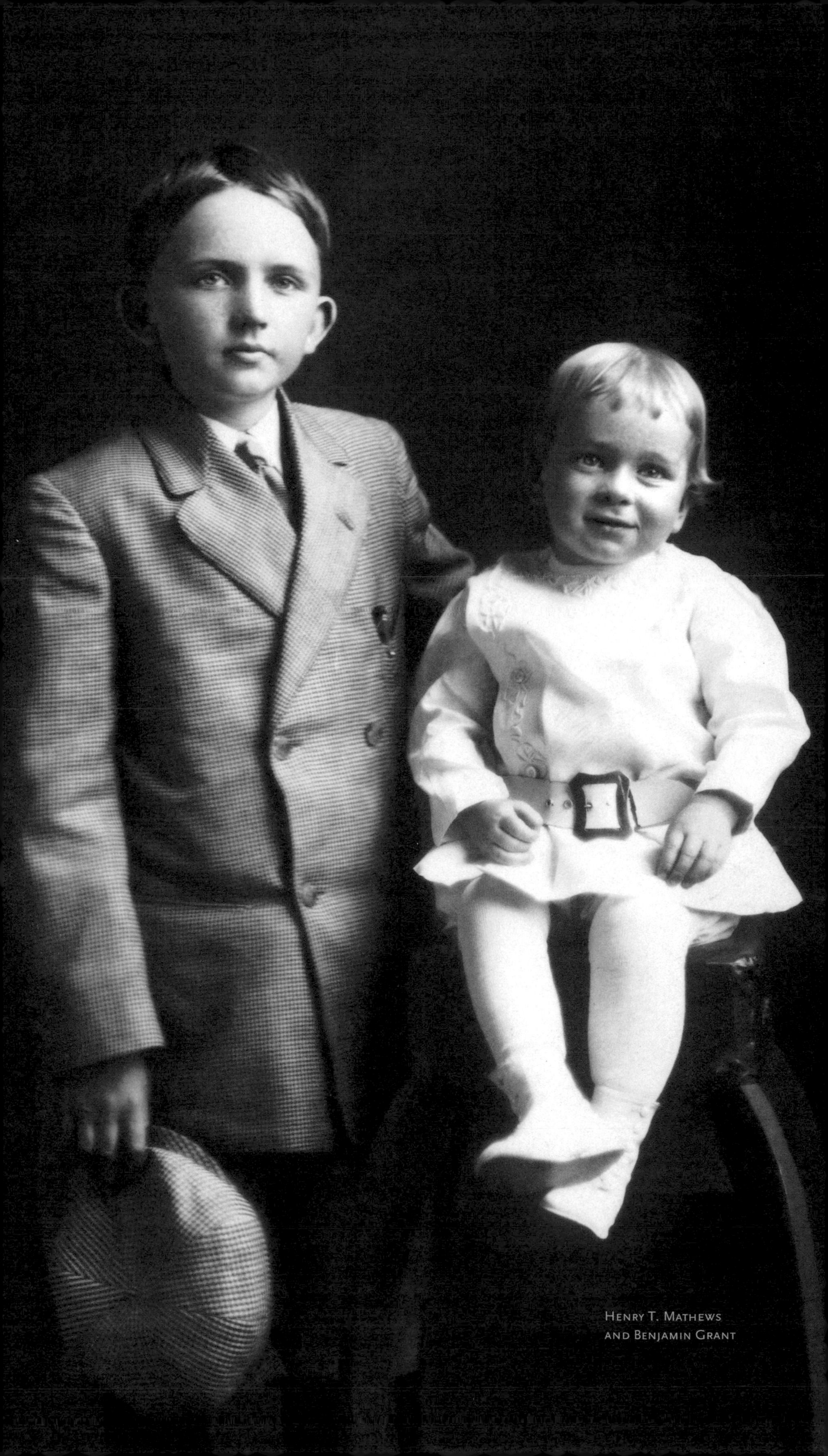

Henry T. Mathews
and Benjamin Grant

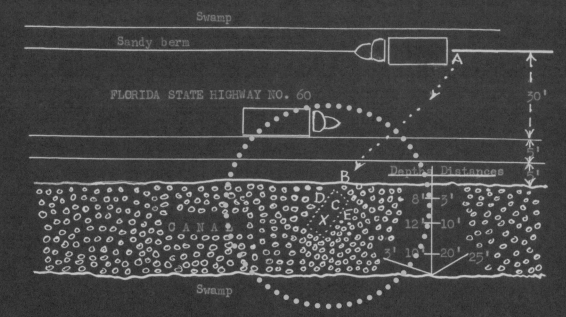

Swamp

Sandy berm

FLORIDA STATE HIGHWAY NO. 60

30'
5'
5'

Depths Distances

8' — 3'
12' — 10'
3' 10' — 20' — 25'

C A N A L

Swamp

AUTOMOBILE THAT FIGURED

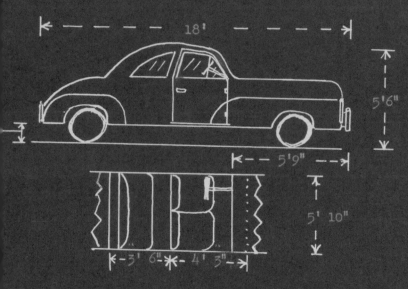

18'

5'6"

5'9"

5' 10"

3' 6" — 4' 3"

X – position in submerged coa
of Carol Baisden

AB – course of Theodore Hender
Sr., to bottom of N bank
of canal

ENLARGEMENT SHOWING ACTION
AT SUNKEN AUTOMOBILE

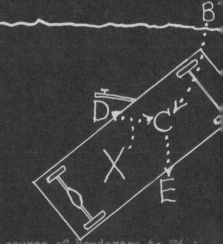

BC – course Henderson waded and swam to C where he
stood briefly on sinking vehicle
CD – course Henderson lowered himself at NW side of car
D – where Henderson's left hand became caught between
door and frame
DCB – course of Henderson to bank after freeing himself
BC – course Henderson returned to sunken vehicle with
tire-iron
C – position of Henderson standing on car as alligator
surfaced about 10' W of him
CE – course Henderson lowered himself to rear SE window
and broke it with tire-iron
E – where Henderson probed through broken window butdid
not touch Miss Baisden
EC – course of Henderson to point at C for air.   CD – course of Henderson to NW door
XD – course Henderson pulled Miss Baisden from auto. DCB – course Henderson towed her to

THEODORE HENDERSON, SR., braved alligators and water snakes to save a young girl trapped in her car at the bottom of a muddy, 12-foot-deep canal near Yeehaw, Florida, a few miles from Vero Beach.

C. H. 3942

The sky was overcast at mid-afternoon on August 17, 1953. Henderson, a 39-year-old truck driver and father of five, was standing with his 10-year-old son and three other men, fixing a flat tire by the side of the highway, when Carol Baisden, 19, drove by. She lost control of her two-door sedan, which skidded on the damp road, plunged over the bank of the roadside canal, and landed on its roof in the dank water, which was inhabited by alligators and poisonous snakes.

Henderson ran to the canal in time to see the car's tires slip beneath the hyacinth leaves on the water's surface. Aware of an eight-foot-long alligator swimming in the canal, he immediately plunged in fully clothed and swam to where the car had sunk. Taking a breath, he groped down to one of the doors and pulled it open a few inches. But the sinking vehicle shifted and the door slammed shut, catching two of Henderson's fingers and dragging him to the bottom. Bracing his feet against the side of the vehicle, he pulled free, but one finger was broken and the nail and tip of the other was torn off. Despite his injuries, he surfaced and swam to the bank.

Even then, Henderson didn't give up. Grabbing a tire-iron, he swam back to the car. The alligator appeared at the surface of the water about 10 feet from one side of the car, so Henderson dove down on the other side and smashed the vehicle's left rear window. Reaching inside, he could not find Baisden, who was unconscious. He surfaced, crossed over the upturned vehicle, took a deep breath of air, and again submerged. This time he was able to open the door of the car, whose interior was now filled with water. Wriggling inside to his waist, he found Baisden and pulled her out. Rising to the surface, he called for help, but since the three bystanders were not willing to enter the canal, Henderson towed the woman to the bank himself. Both required medical attention but recovered within a few weeks without complications.

FILE NO: 42943

Early in the morning of January 16, 2000, **GERALD BOWLES** got out of his car on Interstate 20 in Jackson, Mississippi, to try to help an accident victim.

C. H. 8541

At about 12:30 a.m., a 35-year-old man lost control of his sport utility vehicle, and it flipped over, ejecting him onto the outside lane of the highway, where he was then struck by at least two other cars.

Bowles, a 67-year-old clothing store salesman, was driving toward the accident scene when he saw the man lying on the highway. Bowles pulled his car toward the left shoulder and parked across the highway's outside lane about 35 feet before the man, in an attempt to shield him from traffic. Putting on his car's emergency flashers, Bowles climbed out to get a flashlight from his trunk. He had just opened the trunk when an approaching car hit him.

Thrown into the air by the impact, he landed on the windshield of his car, which was pushed into the median strip. Shortly afterward, a local police officer arrived on the scene and called for an ambulance. The man was pronounced dead at the accident scene.

Bowles sustained multiple fractures and other injuries that required extensive hospitalization, during which he underwent amputation of both lower legs. Bowles later wrote to the Commission, "I have no remorse, I don't look back, I keep my eyes forward." FILE NO: 74697

22 June 2001
HILL CLIMB, MOUNT WASHINGTON
NEW HAMPSHIRE

C. H. 8648

On June 22, 2001, **CHRISTOPHER DUPLESSIS**, a 14-year-old student from Maine, pulled an unconscious race car driver from his burning vehicle.

For several years, Duplessis and his father, Richard, 51, had been volunteer "corner workers" at the Mount Washington Hill Climb, an annual event where drivers race their vehicles on an eight-mile course up New Hampshire's most famous mountain.

About 8:00 a.m. that day, during a practice run, they were positioned about a mile and a half up the course from the start. Edward Romney, 37, was driving his 130-horsepower Legend race car at 70 mph when he lost control, ran off the road, and struck a tree about 200 yards short of where Christopher and his father stood.

Hearing the crash and an explosion, the older Duplessis told his son to grab a fire extinguisher, and the two of them ran to the site and found the car almost totally covered in flames. While the father tried unsuccessfully to extinguish the flames, the son went to the driver-side door of the windowless vehicle, which had popped open from the impact.

Afraid that Romney might burn to death, the young man reached in and, despite the intense heat and threat of explosion, started to pull him from the burning vehicle. However, although Romney had released part of a safety belt restraining his torso, one of his arms was still held by a wrist restraint. Duplessis continued tugging, bracing his feet against the car's frame, until the melting restraint finally gave way and he was able to pull the stricken man free. Then, with his father's help, Duplessis dragged Romney away to safety.

Romney was treated for second-degree burns, several broken bones, and a concussion, but he eventually recovered. Duplessis was not injured.
FILE NO: 75651

On May 4, 1933, **DAVID H. JONES**, 39, and **BENJAMIN F. MAJOR**, 45, risked their lives to save a fellow worker from an explosion.

C. H. 2866, 2867

Jones and Major were part of a 10-man crew igniting fuses of dynamite sticks set to blast apart huge boulders of ore spread across a flat area on the side of a copper pit in Jerome, Arizona. One charge exploded prematurely, throwing one of the miners, 44-year-old John Stout, to the ground. A three-feet-in-diameter slab of a boulder broke off, fell on his legs, and pinned him.

Six of the men fled, taking with them another man who was seriously injured by a flying rock, but Jones and Major responded to Stout's call for help. They briefly tried to free the trapped miner, but when that proved impossible, both men began to frantically pull fuses from nearby sticks of dynamite. Thirty-five sticks had been set within a 30-foot radius, and they each managed to pull 10 fuses. Realizing time was running out, Jones ran to get a pry bar, and Major flung himself down next to Stout to protect him from flying debris.

The dynamite started exploding, and within 30 seconds 15 explosions occurred. The concussion threw Jones to the ground, and rock shards rained down. The other men in the crew then returned and quickly freed Stout. Jones sustained slight burns on his hands while pulling the fuses, but otherwise none of the three suffered serious injury. FILE NOS: 33702, 33703

On March 15, 1928, **SEMKO SAWCZYUK**, a 36-year-old boiler washer in a Sydney, Nova Scotia, steel plant, died attempting to save a co-worker.

✝ C. H. 2300

Sawczyuk was working with Alexander McNeil, 24. The two men were cleaning a boiler, near to which there was a shaft revolving at a speed of 50 to 60 revolutions per minute. There were no witnesses to the accident, but it was the opinion of plant officials that the three-foot-long wrench McNeil was using to tighten bolts slipped, causing him to lose his balance and fall back on the shaft. The first person on the scene, McNeil's brother, saw McNeil being whirled around the shaft. Sawczyuk was lying several feet away, seriously injured. He had grabbed for McNeil, and the shaft crushed his arm and tore off his hand.

Several minutes later, after the machine had been turned off, McNeil was pulled from it, but he was dead. Sawczyuk died four days later of his injuries, leaving behind a wife and four children. His widow received monthly benefits from the Hero Fund for more than 45 years.

FILE NO: 28126

C. H. 3796

DAVID ANDREWS, a 67-year-old farmer in Snow Hill, Alabama, kept a man from being buried alive on January 24, 1952.

John Bell, 34, was cleaning out a water well by hand. He was at the bottom of the 42-foot shaft when the wooden cribbing collapsed, burying him in sand. A fellow worker lowered on a rope was able to uncover Bell's head, but couldn't do any more. A crowd of 30 onlookers had gathered at the top, but the unstable walls dissuaded anyone else from trying to help.

Andrews, who had arrived 90 minutes after the collapse, volunteered to be lowered into the hole. Standing in a loop of rope so as not to touch the sandy walls, Andrews repeatedly filled a bucket with sand that was then hauled out. After half an hour, he had uncovered Bell's shoulders, but then further collapses buried his head under six inches of fresh sand. Andrews labored another hour, uncovering Bell to his waist, when another collapse covered him with four feet of sand.

Metal tubing was lowered, and Andrews was able to push it through the sand and position it close to Bell's head. Oxygen was pumped into the tubing, possibly saving Bell's life. Andrews labored past dark. Finally, six hours after he had started, Andrews was able to tie a rope around Bell's waist so he could be hauled out of the collapsing well. Bell was hospitalized for six days. Andrews was exhausted but recovered after resting.

FILE NO: 42490

C. H. 2679

On February 4, 1932, 29-year-old **EDWARD J. CARTAIN** saved a woman trapped in a ship heavily damaged by explosion.

At just past midnight, Viola Rivers, 33, was sleeping in her berth aboard the tank-ship *Bidwell*, which was docked at a refinery pier in the Delaware River near Marcus Hook, Pennsylvania, when a violent explosion in one of the ship's oil bunkers tore through the vessel. The ship was rammed against the dock, and its superstructure, much of which was constructed from wooden beams, began to burn. The dock, and a warehouse also caught fire. Several of the 20 to 22 people on board the ship were killed immediately.

Rivers, blown from her berth and stunned, tried to escape. Placing a life preserver on each arm, she lowered herself 20 feet down a line, then dropped another several feet into the water in one of the ship's tanks. Patches of oil burned intensely on the tank's ceiling and side beams.

Cartain, who worked at the refinery, was at home that night, but curiosity over the explosion brought him to the dockside. When someone heard Rivers' cries from under the superstructure, and her predicament was realized, Cartain decided to help.

He stripped off his pants and shirt and lowered himself down the sloping side of the ship into the oily water. Then, despite the darkness and chance of further explosions, he swam 60 feet until he reached Rivers, part of his route taking him directly under the ship's burning superstructure. Rivers had been in the water for an hour by this time and was semiconscious. Supporting the woman with one arm, Cartain was able to swim to the side of the wrecked ship by the dock, where a line was lowered and Rivers was then pulled up to safety.

Rivers suffered severe burns from the ordeal and was hospitalized for two months. A gash that he received on his right foot kept Cartain from work for six days. A month later, he developed pneumonia and was unable to work for another three weeks. FILE NO: 31919

18 Apr. 1969

LEAD AND ZINC MINE

SALMO, BRITISH COLUMBIA

On April 18, 1969, twelve men risked their lives to rescue a co-worker from an accident in a lead and zinc mine in Salmo, British Columbia.

C. H. 5863, 5864, 5865, 5866, 5867, 5873, 5868, 5869, 5870, 5871, 5872, 5874

At 5:30 that afternoon, the mine mucker boss, Gilbert Mosses, 53, was at the top of a loading chute when he was caught by an unexpected fall of ore and knocked into the bottom of the chute. Covered except for his head and one arm by rocks of various sizes, Mosses was severely injured but conscious.

A dozen men employed at the mine gathered at the holding bin and worked for the next several hours to reach Mosses and get him out alive. They included shift bosses **ANDREW BURGESS**, 63, and **CARL A. SHELRUD**, 38; mine manager **EDWARD A. LAWRENCE**, 33, warehouse accountant and first-aid man **JOSEPH L. HEROUX**, 33, physician **IAN F. STEWART**, 46, loader operator **DALE R. BURGESS**, 24; and miners **EDWARD M. GLADU**, 36, **BRIAN D. MARTIN**, 21, **ALPHONCE P. GROTKOWSKI**, 33, **JOHN J. VOYKIN**, 37, **WAYNE R. RITTER**, 32, and **GRAHAM D. BINGHAM**, 30.

After an opening was cut in the chute's metal bulkhead, a clearing was made in the rocks piled against it. Andrew Burgess and Shelrud then crawled inside the chute and began fitting in wooden shoring to prevent further collapses. At various times during the rescue effort, Lawrence inspected the situation inside the chute, and Heroux and Stewart crawled in to minister to Mosses. Dale Burgess, Gladu, Martin, Grotkowski, Voykin, Ritter, and Bingham took turns working inside the chute to remove the rocks from around Mosses. When rocks had to be chipped away, a drill was used. If the work loosened the shoring, it was carefully reset.

Three and a half hours after the accident, Mosses was freed. He subsequently recovered from his injuries. None of the other men was hurt during the rescue. FILE NOS: 51810, 51811, 51812, 52348, 52349, 52355, 52350, 52351, 52352, 52353, 52354, 52356

C. H. 421, 417, ✠
487, 422, 419,
416, 420, 418,
424, 415, 414, 423

C. H. 426, 425

Early in the afternoon of November 13, 1909, fire erupted in the escape shaft of a coal mine in Cherry, Illinois, about 100 miles west of Chicago. Four hundred eighty-four men and boys were inside the mine, and 259 of them would die as a result of the fire. Twelve of the dead and two survivors met the qualifications for the Carnegie Medal.

In operation for about four years, the mine was considered to be a model of safety. Two weeks earlier, the electrical system had malfunctioned, and kerosene torches were being used for illumination. Unfortunately, a load of hay inside a mine car, meant for the mules that worked inside the mine, caught fire from one of the torches. Although the car and its burning contents were pushed into a sump, smoke, and then flames, rose inside the escape shaft. The air ventilation flow was stopped and then reversed so as not to feed the flames, but that resulted in smoke being pulled into the main shaft.

An evacuation was ordered; by then, only the hoisting cages in the main shaft offered a possibility of escape. Four miners at work at the time, JOHN BUNDY, 53, mine manager, J. ALEXANDER NORBERG, 38, JOSEPH ROBEZA, JR., 22, and JOHN SZABRINSKI, 29, were joined by four colleagues who responded from their homes, ROBERT CLARK, 28, ANDREW McLUCKIE, 31, JAMES SPEIR, 34, and HENRY STEWART, 28, and three other residents of the village, JOHN FLOOD, 49, DOMINICK FORMENTO, 32, and ISAAC LEWIS, JR., 34, in organizing and carrying out the evacuation from inside the mine. After others were taken to the surface in a hoisting cage, the 11 boarded it, but, because of confusion caused by two different signals sent to the hoisting cage operator, the cage remained below ground for about 10 minutes. Fire reached the main shaft. When the hoisting cage was brought to the surface, the 11 men were dead of burns.

(FACING PAGE, TOP)
A GROUP OF MEN
AND WOMEN ON
THE GROUNDS OF
THE ST. PAUL COAL
COMPANY MINE IN
CHERRY, ILLINOIS.
(BOTTOM) A CROWD
GATHERS UNDER
THE SCAFFOLDING
SURROUNDING THE
MINE'S MAIN SHAFT.

Another man, a mine examiner and boss, CHARLES WAITE, 43, remained inside the mine to help evacuate miners; he was found dead five days later. A second mine examiner and boss, GEORGE EDDY, 48, and an assistant mine manager, WALTER WAITE, 41, joined a group of 19 miners whose escape was blocked. Eddy and Walter Waite directed the miners to construct barriers against the flames and smoke. For seven days, the group remained imprisoned inside the mine until rescuers reached them.

The 14 Carnegie Medals awarded are the most for rescues at a single site.

FILE NOS: 5133, 5126, 5609, 5543, 5128, 4812, 5129, 5127, 5134, 4605, 4556, 5123, 5124, 5125

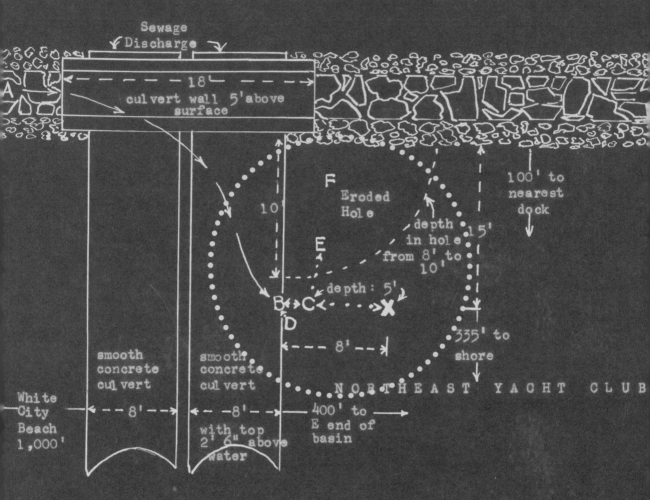

LAKE ERIE

X - where Ronald J. Azzardi struggled at surface after
    falling into basin attempting to get dog at D
AB - course James A. Williams ran
BC - course Williams jumped into basin
CX - course Williams waded to Ronald
XC - course Williams waded carrying Ronald
CB - course Williams lifted Ronald to boys on culvert
DB - course Williams lifted dog to boys on culvert
CE - course Williams strode toward breakwater
 E - where Williams was submerged and remained submerged
 F - where body of Williams was recovered

JAMES A. WILLIAMS, a 41-year-old truck driver from Cleveland, Ohio, lost   ✠ *C. H.* 4445
his life after saving a young boy from drowning in Lake Erie.

On May 21, 1961, Williams was fishing near a concrete culvert that
protruded from a stone breakwater in the lake between White City Beach
and the Northeast Yacht Club. Nine-year-old Ronald Azzardi had been on
the culvert, trying to rescue a dog that had fallen into water five feet deep
and was unable to get back out. Unfortunately, the boy also fell into the
lake and could not climb back up onto the culvert, which rose 30 inches
out of the water. Flailing to keep his head above water, Azzardi only moved
away from the culvert.

Alerted to the boy's distress, Williams, himself a father of two grown
children, ran to the culvert and, even though fully dressed and a poor swimmer,
jumped in. He waded to the boy and lifted him onto his back. Then, with
Azzardi clinging to his shoulders, Williams waded back to the culvert and lifted
both the boy and the dog up to another youth who had arrived on the scene.

When both were safe, Williams began wading back toward the
breakwater 15 feet away, not knowing that a hole 10 feet deep had eroded
along its base. When he stepped into the hole, Williams submerged and
became wedged under the culvert. Other men arrived and, using long poles,
located Williams and pulled him out, but he could not be revived.

Williams was posthumously awarded a Carnegie Medal, and his
widow received a monthly grant to help with living expenses from the
Commission for 35 years.

"I'm not surprised he jumped in after that child," Mrs. Williams
later said of her husband. "He loved children and was sorry when ours grew
up. I know that if he were alive today, he'd explain jumping in by saying
'I saw a child in trouble.'" FILE NO: 45492

Eleven-year-old **KENNETH P. MAGALLANES** volunteered to be lowered   *C. H.* 4653
15 feet into an abandoned cesspool to save a 2-year-old boy.

On February 21, 1963, young Leslie Masutani was with his father in
the yard of a neighbor's house amid the sugar cane fields near Pearl City,
Hawaii, when the child fell into an underground cesspool filled with three
feet of muck and noxious gases but little oxygen. Masutani landed in the
mat of sanitary waste and decaying vegetation and sank up to his chest.

Masutani's father ran to the cesspool's lid, but he was unable to fit
through the 12-by-18-inch opening. Firemen were summoned and responded
quickly, but none of them could fit through the opening either. Two air
tanks were lowered into the hole to provide some ventilation.

Then Magallanes stepped forward. The schoolboy and his mother were bystanders who had come from their home nearby. With his mother's permission, Magallanes volunteered to help. Despite his initial hesitance, the fire captain agreed, fearing that further delay might be fatal to Masutani. A rope sling was tied around the young boy, and he was lowered through the tight opening.

Overcoming his nausea and fear of centipedes and scorpions, Magallanes located the child, pulled him from the muck, and wrapped his arms around him. Unfortunately, when the firemen pulled the boys up, both could not fit through the opening together. Then Masutani slipped from Magallanes' arms and fell back into the pit. After being pulled partially out to get a breath of air, Magallanes was given a second looped rope and again lowered to the bottom. This time, he got the rope around Masutani and held the child in his arms as the firemen pulled them up through the opening one at a time.

Masutani, who had spent 50 minutes in the cesspool, was badly dazed but recovered in several days. Magallanes, having been in the cesspool for nearly four minutes, was nauseated but otherwise uninjured. FILE NO: 46402

12 May 1995
GARRIGAN RESIDENCE
MANITOWOC, WISCONSIN

C. H. 8026 ‡

On May 12, 1995, seven-year-old **KAYLA J. GARRIGAN** died after saving her half-brother from a fire in the family's home in Manitowoc, Wisconsin.

Her father, Todd Garrigan, was at work that evening. His wife, Robin, and son Todd Jr., 6, slept in a first-floor bedroom of the two-story, wood frame building. Kayla was sleeping on a couch in the living room, while Christopher Walters, 12, was in his upstairs bedroom.

About 11:00 p.m., a fire broke out in the kitchen, possibly caused by one of the family's dogs turning on a burner on the stove while trying to get at some food in a pot. Mrs. Garrigan woke to the fire, and at first tried to extinguish the flames. Then she roused the two children downstairs, and called the fire department. Grabbing Todd Jr., she carried him out of the house.

Meanwhile Kayla dashed upstairs to warn Walters about the rapidly spreading fire. He met her at the bedroom doorway, and then stepped into the hallway where he could see flames at the front door. They both retreated into the bedroom. Smoke billowed into the room, and Walters opened a window. Assuming that his half-sister was right behind him, he jumped out the window, spraining both ankles in the fall. But Kayla didn't follow.

The firemen who arrived shortly afterward found the young girl unconscious in a corner of the bedroom and took her to the hospital, where she died shortly afterward. Her sacrifice made Kayla the youngest recipient of the Carnegie Medal. FILE NO: 69755

On July 15, 1912, **LUTHER B. WEAVER**, part owner of a clothing cleaning and dye shop in Dallas, Texas, was fatally burned in an attempt to save an employee from fire.

C. H. 864

George Mabern, 25, was working in the back of the two-story brick building, where a gasoline still was located in the cleaning room. An explosion of the still shook the building, and Mabern was knocked to the floor. Gasoline fumes began to spread.

When Weaver, 35, heard the explosion, he ran back to the room where Mabern lay, his arms upraised. Just as he stepped into the room, however, a second terrific explosion occurred, filling the room with a mass of flames that extended through the open door. Running through the flames, Weaver, his clothing on fire, reached Mabern and dragged him out of the room and away from the flames. Both men then fled the building to the street, where the flames on them were smothered by blankets. They were then taken to the hospital. Unfortunately, they had been too badly burned. Mabern died later that afternoon and Weaver the following day.

In addition to accepting a Carnegie Medal on behalf of her husband, Weaver's widow received a monthly grant from the Commission until her death 62 years later. FILE NO: 10516

On April 11, 1978, **JOHN C. WOOD**, a 30-year-old prisoner at a state penitentiary in McAlester, Oklahoma, saved a guard from being mauled by a Doberman Pinscher.

C. H. 6359

About 2:15 that afternoon, James Martin and another man were training attack dogs on prison grounds. Wood, a former marine serving a 20- to 60-year sentence, was to act as an agitator for the dogs. He was waiting in a Jeep while Martin was working with a dog. However, when Martin stumbled and fell to the ground, the 75-pound dog leaped at him and began tearing at his head and arm.

Wood got out of the vehicle, grabbed a short length of hose, and began to beat the animal. The dog turned and tried to jump on Wood, who continued striking it with the hose. At that point, the other trainer arrived, snatched the dog's leash, and started swinging the animal in circles until it became unconscious. Martin was driven to the hospital where he received more than 200 stitches for his lacerations, but he eventually recovered.

Wood was not injured, but in addition to receiving a Carnegie Medal, for coming to Martin's aid he had his remaining sentence reduced.

FILE NO: 56256

C. H. 3474, 3475,
3476

MARGARET RICE, 15, saved a fellow student from drowning when their school bus swerved off the road during a blizzard and plunged into a deep, frigid lake. Her brother and father soon entered the scene and rescued another passenger.

On November 26, 1945, Rice was one of 20 students who, with Glenna Brown, 38, were passengers on the bus when the driver lost control on a highway that ran along Lake Chelan in central Washington. The vehicle careened over the steep bank and began to sink slowly some 20 feet out, in water 30 feet deep. Brown, Rice, and four other students managed to escape the bus. Three of the students, boys, swam to safety, but as Rice surfaced she noticed Mariette Archer, 17, floating helpless nearby. Rice swam to the bank, quickly removed her galoshes, shoes, and coat, and then swam back out to Archer. Taking hold of the unconscious girl around the neck, Rice paddled back to the steep bank and managed to lift her up onto a rock.

In the meantime, Rice's father and 17-year-old brother, who had been in a car following the bus, arrived on the scene. The brother, **ALAN HERBERT RICE**, entered the water and swam 40 feet out to Brown, who was unconscious and nearly submerged. With great effort, he towed her toward the bank, calling to his father for help. Although he was a poor swimmer, **ALAN RANDOLPH RICE**, 45, entered the water, swam to Brown, and aided in getting her the rest of the way in.

Fifteen students and the driver were drowned, but Archer and Brown were saved. FILE NOS: 40573, 40574, 40854

C. H. 2252

On October 11, 1926, **MARY EVELYN BROWN**, a 15-year-old schoolgirl, risked her life attempting to prevent an "ill-natured" father from murdering his 5-year-old son.

The father, a tailor in Woodstock, New Brunswick, was known to be a neighborhood bully, especially when he was drinking. That was the case when he came to a hotel, where his wife was the proprietor, about 6:30 that evening. When his wife became fearful for herself and her son, who was with her in the hotel's office, she tried to take the boy away. The father suddenly snatched the boy from his mother, dragged him from the hotel, flung him to the ground, and began attacking him with a razor.

Brown, whose home was across the street from the hotel, was washing dishes when she heard the mother scream, "He's murdering my child." Brown had often played with the boy and was familiar with the father's rages. She immediately ran out to help, thinking the father was choking the child and unaware he had a razor. Grabbing up a used, 10-pound lard bucket that had been filled with dirt, she came up behind the father, who was bending over his son. Three times she hit him on the back with the bucket, which fell from her hands on the last blow. She then kicked the father hard in the ribs once or twice, and he rolled away.

A man soon arrived and picked up the child. The young boy's throat had been slashed, and he died moments later. The father had also cut his own throat, but lingered three weeks before he died.

Although not physically injured in the rescue attempt, Brown required a few weeks to get over the emotional shock and was unable to attend school regularly for nearly two years following the incident. FILE NO: 26891

24 Sept. 2002
APARTMENT COMPLEX
DALLAS, OREGON

On September 24, 2002, 74-year-old **MARGUERITE ZACHARY** went to the aid of a woman who had been shot multiple times by a deranged gunman.

C. H. 8739

Charlotte Woods, 59, was manager of an apartment complex in Dallas, Oregon, where Zachary, a retired nurse, lived. Just after 7:00 that evening, Woods was turning on the sprinkler system in the courtyard of the four-building complex when a male resident, 60, confronted her. When Woods refused to speak with him and turned her back to him, he pulled out a .40-caliber, Glock semiautomatic pistol and fired at her repeatedly.

Zachary was in her ground-floor apartment when she heard what sounded like firecrackers. Not seeing anything from her window, she stepped outside and saw Woods lying on the ground, her midsection covered in blood. While walking to the stricken woman as quickly as she could, Zachary looked up and saw the man, now on the balcony of his second-floor apartment, brandishing a gun. Overcoming her fear, Zachary continued to Woods and knelt beside her. Conscious, Woods said she couldn't feel her leg and was afraid she was going to die. The assailant then fired again, one of the shots hitting Woods in the shoulder. Zachary told Woods to lie still so the assailant would think she was dead.

For five minutes Zachary comforted Woods in the courtyard, not knowing if more shots would be fired. None was. Then several police officers arrived on the scene, summoned by a 911 call from another resident. One of the officers spotted the man and told him to drop his gun, but the man retreated into his apartment.

The officer then called to both women to crawl to safety. When Zachary answered that Woods could not move, he told her to go alone, which she did. While one officer covered the assailant's apartment, another ran out and dragged the injured woman to safety. After a five-hour siege, during which time the assailant fired several shots in his apartment, he surrendered to the police without further incident.

The man eventually pleaded guilty to assault charges and was sentenced to 13 years in prison. Despite being shot 11 times, Woods recovered after several months. Zachary was not injured. FILE NO: 76401

C. H. 209

On January 11, 1907, **MARIE V. B. LANGDON**, a 20-year-old housewife living in a wilderness settlement in the Cascade Mountains, braved sub-zero temperatures and snow six feet deep to aid neighbors fleeing their burning cabin.

Langdon and her 25-year-old husband, Jesse, were settlers in the thickly forested area by Lake Wenatchee, several miles from the town of Telma in central Washington. The Langdons lived three-quarters of a mile from their nearest neighbors, Charles and Sophie Jacques, and their three children, Henry, 4, Gertrude, 2, and Estella, 7 months. The previous day, the two men had hiked into Telma to get supplies, but the weather prevented them from returning to their homes that night.

Early that frigid morning, Sophie Jacques had lit a fire in the stove that warmed their two-room, cedar-framed cabin. Sometime afterward, she noticed flames smoldering on the cabin wall near the stove. At first Jacques tried to extinguish the flames and then to gather up a few of the family's possessions. Unfortunately, the fire spread quickly, forcing her to flee the blazing structure with her three children, all barefoot and clad only in thin clothing.

Carrying the infant, the mother began trudging through the deep snow toward the Langdon cabin, pushing the two young children before her. After a short distance, however, Gertrude refused to go any farther, saying she was cold and tired. Removing her skirt and wrapping it around her young daughter, Jacques plunged on with her other two children.

It was 9 a.m. when Langdon heard cries for help. Rushing outside without snowshoes, she plunged through the deep, cold blanket of snow for 600 feet before encountering the now-crawling Jacques and her two children. Langdon took the infant and carried her back to the cabin, followed by Jacques. She then went back out and brought Henry to safety. Langdon built a fire and tended to the three for half an hour, then ventured into the snow again. She covered nearly three-quarters of a mile before she found Gertrude lying in the snow. The slightly built Langdon carried the limp child halfway back to her cabin before she realized Gertrude was dead. Langdon covered the child with her coat and left her in the snow, and after a hard struggle was able to make it home herself.

Though suffering from frostbite and exposure, Jacques, her son, and baby daughter all survived the incident. Langdon also required several days to recover, but otherwise suffered no long-term injuries. FILE NO: 1566

The Commission assigns each awarded rescue to one of 17 types. As the table below shows, a significant number of the rescues took place in burning buildings and vehicles, and in water. Some rescues fit no category, such as those where multiple threats are presented, or those in which the threat is unusual.

Rescue from an attacking animal	117
Rescue from human assault	341
Rescue from a burning building	874
Rescue from a burning vehicle	931
Rescue involving a moving vehicle	742
Rescue from submerging vehicle	165
Rescue from water	3,249
Rescue from water involving ice	521
Rescue with the use of a boat	296
Rescue from being electrocuted	155
Rescue from falling	88
Rescue from exposure to elements	46
Rescue from avalanche	176
Rescue from being struck by object	14
Rescue from an anticipated explosion	124
Rescue from confined spaces	813
Rescue that fits no other category	112

Males performed 7,986 of the rescues, and females, 778. The youngest rescuer was a 7-year-old girl, and the oldest was an 86-year-old woman. Eight thousand and seventy-three of the rescues were performed in the United States, and 691 in Canada. The states and provinces with large populations tend to be where the most rescues occur: Pennsylvania, 724; California, 583; New York, 581; Ohio, 519; Texas, 460; Ontario, 290; and British Columbia, 110. The states where the fewest rescues occurred are Nevada and South Dakota with 18, and Hawaii with 20. Two rescues were performed in Canada's Yukon Territory, and three in Nunavut.

About 500 ft

COMMISSION
INVESTIGATOR'S
MARKINGS ON A
PHOTOGRAPH OF
THE AMERICAN
FALLS SHOWING
COURSE OF THOMAS
CONROY'S AND
JOSEPH H. BATTS'S
RESCUE OF A
MAN 15 FEET
FROM THE BRINK.

(NEXT PAGE)
THE WOODEN
EXTENSION
LADDER USED
IN THE RESCUE.

ON THE BRINK

The Niagara Falls region of New York and Ontario attracts millions of visitors every year, most to view the spectacular falls of the Niagara River from safe vantage points. But by accident, through suicide attempts, or just for thrills, some witness the awesome power of the river firsthand. Carnegie Medals have been awarded to 15 individuals for rescues performed on the Niagara River.

C. H. 171, 172

PRIOR TO BECOMING
A FIREMAN, CONROY
WAS A NIAGARA FALLS
POLICEMAN AND A
TOUR GUIDE AT THE
CAVE OF THE WINDS,
AND IN THOSE THREE
OCCUPATIONS HAD
REPORTEDLY SAVED THE
LIVES OF MORE THAN
20 PEOPLE. ONE OF
HIS RESCUES TOOK
PLACE ON JUNE 1,
1874, WHEN, BEFORE
A CROWD OF MORE
THAN A THOUSAND
ANXIOUS ONLOOKERS,
HE VENTURED MORE
THAN 200 FEET INTO
THE NIAGARA RIVER
TO A MAN WHO HAD
FALLEN FROM A BRIDGE
A THOUSAND FEET
UPSTREAM. A GREAT
CHEER AROSE FROM THE
CROWD WHEN CONROY
AND THE MAN REACHED
THE RIVER'S BANK.
A FEW DAYS LATER, THE
"BUFFALO EVENING
NEWS" SAID OF
CONROY: "HE IS A
MAN OF MORE THAN
ORDINARY COURAGE,
AND POSSESSED OF
A NERVE THAT NO
DANGER CAN DAUNT.
HE IS A HERO, AND
HIS NAME WILL GO
DOWN TO POSTERITY
LAURELLED WITH
THE FEW WHO HAVE
BY SINGLE ACTS OF
HEROISM AND COURAGE
GAINED A NAME THAT
IS AT ONCE SUBLIME
AND IMPERISHABLE."

After midnight on June 5, 1906, a police officer patrolling the Niagara River about 500 feet above the American Falls observed a man on the bank acting strangely. He told the man to leave the area, but the man waded into the river. He slipped and was carried farther down the rapids but miraculously gained a foothold on the river's bottom. Two other men arrived. One tied a rope to his waist and started toward the man, but before reaching him, the man stepped back and was again carried closer to the falls.

All thought the man was doomed, but to their surprise he regained his footing about 30 feet from the bank, in waist-deep water just 15 feet from the brink of the falls. A rope was repeatedly thrown to him, but he brushed it away. The police officer fired his pistol to arouse the man, but to no avail. He had now been in the water for nearly an hour, and the crowd that had gathered was "dazed by the stolid indifference of the man in the face of what they had always believed to be certain death." The responding fire chief ordered a wooden ladder be placed under the iron fence along the bank and extended to the man. The ladder was not secured to the fence but was anchored there by several men.

At over six feet tall and in excess of 250 pounds, city fireman **THOMAS CONROY**, 57, could not swim. He was the one who volunteered to wade into the river and extend the ladder from the bank. Holding one end of a rope, which he refused to have tied to his body, Conroy supported the unsecured end of the ladder as he waded out. Extended to its full length, the end of the ladder remained three feet short of the man. Conroy tried to induce the man to reach out his hand, but he refused. Had Conroy lost his footing, the 30-foot length of rope between him and the bank would have permitted him to go over the falls.

Police sergeant **JOSEPH H. BATTS**, 44, a strong swimmer, crawled out on the extended ladder. At its end, he talked to the man in kindly tones but could not get him to move toward the ladder. The crowd begged Conroy and Batts to return to the bank, as the ladder creaked and sagged under Batts's weight. Batts put his legs between the last two rungs of the ladder and told Conroy to hold fast. He then lunged forward and grabbed the man with one hand. The man struggled to get free, but Batts retained his hold, and Conroy, holding the ladder with one hand, grasped the man with the other.

The weight of the two men at the end of the ladder and Conroy's weight and the rush of the water against it caused the ladder to sway. Batts shouted to the men on shore to pull the ladder in. Slowly it was dragged in, Batts holding to it with only his legs while his one hand held the man and the other a rope he had taken with him. Conroy pulled the ladder upstream against the river's flow. When the bank was reached, men grabbed Batts and the man and pulled them over the railing. Conroy made it to shore otherwise unassisted. FILE NOS: 1261, 1260

On May 19, 1912, Henry J. Lutz, 51, fell into the Niagara River and was being carried rapidly toward the American Falls. Although he could not swim, **IRAM KEVORKIAN**, 24, laborer, entered the river and waded out about 18 feet to a point in knee-deep water about 150 feet from the brink. Having been handed a pike pole, Kevorkian attempted to snag Lutz as he approached, but the attempt failed. Kevorkian waded farther out into deeper water, and, on his second attempt, the hook on the pole caught on one of Lutz's shoes. Others formed a human chain and helped them to safety. FILE NO: 8584

C. H. 746

Peter W. Langgaard, 24, was hired by a motion picture company to shoot the Whirlpool Rapids of the Niagara River in an 18-foot motorboat on October 23, 1913. He passed through the rapids safely, but then a piece of driftwood caught in the boat's propeller as it entered the pool and left the boat powerless. For the next several hours, during which darkness fell, the boat drifted around the whirlpool, Langgaard calling out for help. **FREDERICK G. PRESTON**, 41, painter, had witnessed everything from the bank of the pool. As hundreds of onlookers witnessed, the scene lit by a powerful searchlight, Preston jumped into the river and swam to the boat as it swung in the outer swirl of the pool. He secured a rope to the boat, then men on the bank pulled them to safety. FILE NO: 12053

C. H. 1036

While wading in the Niagara River on June 3, 1931, Bertha M. Schmidt, 55, was swept from her feet. **EDWARD A. C. DiRUSCIO**, 21, ran to the bank and entered the water at a point 335 feet from the brink of the American Falls. He waded to Schmidt, who was unconscious. Just before reaching her, he stumbled and momentarily went under the surface. They drifted toward the brink, but DiRuscio was able to get a hold of her. He then waded toward the bank, another man giving them a hand. FILE NO: 31167

C. H. 2591

C. H. 2996, 2997

John A. Probash, Jr., 10, and two other boys were in a rowboat in the Niagara River on the first of July, 1936. As they were jumping from the boat to land, Probash fell into the river and drifted to a point 300 feet from the riverbank. Fully dressed, LESLIE R. DAVIS, 25, dived into the river and swam to Probash, who then was five feet below the surface. Davis tried to tow him toward land, but Probash threw his arms around Davis's neck, and both were submerged. Probash struggled against Davis, who then called to SIGMUND HARRISON SKIBA, 19, for help. Skiba swam to the pair and grabbed Probash's hair. Probash continued to struggle, but Skiba, with great effort, swam and waded with him against the current to land, Davis following. FILE NOS: 35946, 35947

C. H. 4229

Nine-year-old Joseph E. Mack, Jr., fell into the tailrace of a power plant at night on August 24, 1958, and was carried into the Niagara River. In shallow water over a rock shelf, he caught hold of a projecting rock at a point about 75 feet from the bank and 400 feet from the brink of the Canadian Falls. The screams of his mother attracted PATRICK KELLY, 23, who, in dim light from the electrical illumination of the falls, made his way 135 feet along the base of a wall at the river's edge toward Mack. Wading into the river, Kelly lost his footing, then scooted in a seated position the remaining distance to Mack. Securing the boy, Kelly remained seated as he pushed himself backward on the rock shelf. He then got to his feet and, twice losing his footing on the slippery shelf, waded with Mack to the bank. FILE NO: 44527

C. H. 4394

On September 4, 1959, a 29-year-old woman was being carried downstream in the Niagara River several thousand feet above the American Falls when EDWARD C. OSWALD was notified. Oswald, 54, a deputy fire chief, was holding a drill with other firemen near the bank of the river. When he reached the scene, he entered the water and made a shallow dive, then swam and overtook the woman, who was about 40 feet from the bank. Oswald secured her but was prevented by the swift current from taking a direct return course. Instead, he towed her 260 feet to within several feet of the bank. The woman struggled with him there, but Oswald maintained his hold and towed her farther. Obtaining his footing, he pushed her into the arms of a man at the water's edge. FILE NO: 44840

JAMES P. MACNEIL, 29, a police officer on duty, detected something suspicious about a 59-year-old woman as she walked toward the Niagara River at a point about 500 feet from the brink of the American Falls on May 16, 1959. When the woman reached the edge of the water, MacNeil called out and started running toward her, but she walked into the water without hesitating and lay down with her arms at her sides. The current took her downstream. Without removing any of his uniform or gear, MacNeil jumped feet first into the river, landing in water four feet deep. He kicked his way over the rocky bottom to overtake the woman, and when he was within a few feet of her, he stretched out an arm to grasp her. He missed. The distance between them increased rapidly, and the woman was swept over the falls to her death. MacNeil managed to make his way back to the bank, where he grasped an overhanging bush to help him climb from the river. FILE NO: 50806

C. H. 5639

Visiting the falls with friends on May 30, 1983, Sherry L. Vyverberg, 20, fell into the Niagara River and was swept by the strong current toward Horseshoe Falls. Driving by, JOHN C. MARSH, 37, and two coworkers were flagged down and alerted to the situation. Knowledgeable of the river, and in fact an employee of the power company that had a plant at the scene, Marsh tied a rope around his waist, dived 15 feet into the river from atop a concrete icebreaker along the bank, and swam to Ms. Vyverberg, who was then about 450 feet from the falls. He grabbed her by the hair, and then yelled to the men on the icebreaker to pull them back. They were lifted by rope to safety atop the icebreaker. FILE NO: 59049

C. H. 6764

On August 14, 1992, Herman E. Townsend, 42, and a friend were scuba diving from a boat anchored in the Niagara River several miles upstream from Horseshoe Falls. When the friend became incapacitated, Townsend went to her aid, but he lost his hold on her and was carried downstream by the strong current. Having just bicycled about 17 miles along the river, KAREN B. SCHLACHTER, 28, a teacher, heard Townsend cry for help. She and others followed him about 800 feet downstream as he attempted to return to the bank. Fearing that help would not arrive in time, Schlachter partially disrobed, entered the water, and swam to Townsend, who was about 200 feet out. Grasping him by the hand, she swam toward the bank with him as the current took them farther downstream. A firefighter who had responded to the scene also entered the water, and he aided in taking Townsend to safety. FILE NO: 67152

C. H. 7716

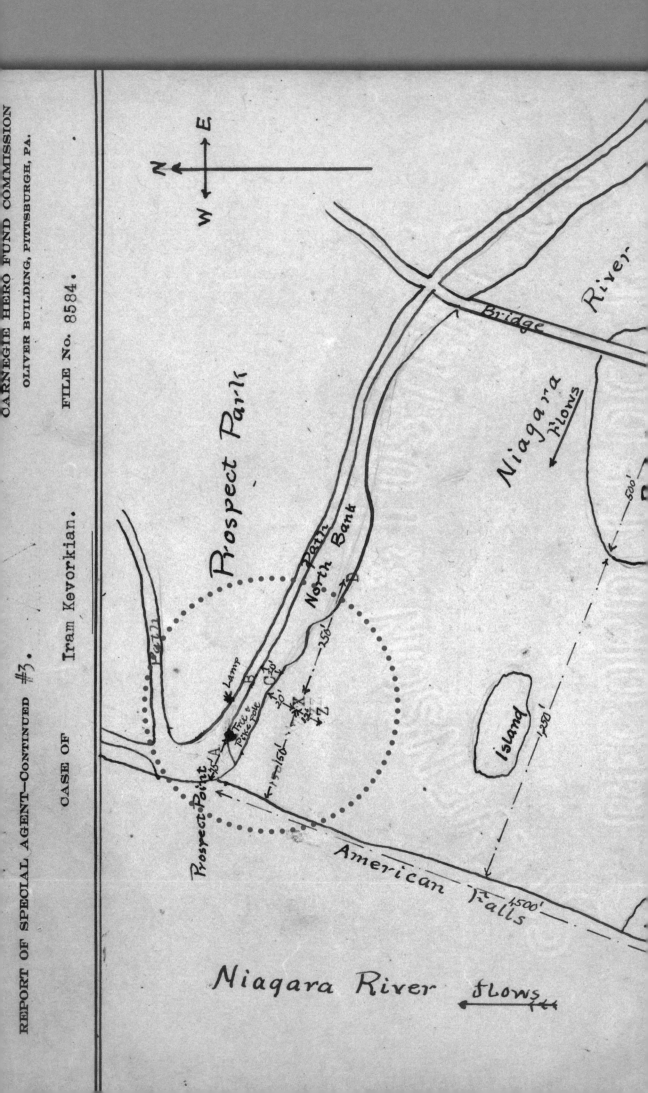

Z   X

Island

Goat Island

A = Where rescuer learned need of rescue.
B = Where rescuer removed shoes and started toward scene.
C = Where rescuer entered the river.
D = Where rescued entered the water.
X = Where rescuer stood during act.
Z = Where rescuer caught rescued with pike pole.

C. H. 5176

A 36-year-old woman intent on suicide entered the Niagara River 300 feet above the American Falls on June 14, 1993, and was quickly carried downstream. **FRANKIE J. KENNEDY**, 36, and his family were sightseeing behind a railing at an observation area at the falls when they saw the woman, who was just off the bank. Kennedy immediately jumped the railing and ran to the water's edge. He reached for the woman, but she was beyond his grasp. Kennedy ran farther downstream and, in a second attempt, got a hold of her by the arm. He maintained his hold while others who had followed him pulled her from the river at a point only eight feet from the brink of the falls. FILE NO: 67887

C. H. 8467, 8468

In the early evening hours of August 25, 1999, a woman attempting suicide was reported in the rapids of the Niagara River off Goat Island, above Horseshoe Falls. The sheriff's department was notified, and it dispatched members of its aviation unit, including **JEFFREY D. MILLER**, 39, who located the woman by helicopter. As the craft was not equipped for water rescues, the aviation unit of a neighboring sheriff's department deployed one of its helicopters, which was equipped with pontoons. Chief pilot **KEVIN R. CAFFERY**, 52, no stranger to situations of the type, responded. Caffery had earlier been nominated for the Carnegie Medal for the midwinter rescue of two boys stranded on the ice in Lake Erie.

Miller and Caffery located the woman by searchlight. She was sitting atop a submerged rock, holding to a branch of a tree growing from an exposed mound, about 100 feet off the island. Caffery lowered the helicopter to water level downstream of the woman, holding the craft by one pontoon against a submerged rock and working to stabilize it further against the extremely swift current by opening the throttle to full power.

KEVIN CAFFERY AND
JEFFREY MILLER

With no line secured to him, to avoid compromising the craft by his movement, Miller stepped into the waist-deep water and waded through the rapids toward the woman. Stopping 15 feet short of her at the edge of what appeared to be deeper water, Miller gestured to the woman to release her hold of the tree and be carried by the current to him. The woman did so, and Miller caught her. He waded back to the helicopter and pushed her onto one of the pontoons, then pulled himself onto the pontoon. Caffery later said that the jostling by Miller and the woman threatened to destabilize the helicopter, which could cause it to topple. Miller pushed the woman into the helicopter and boarded himself, and Caffery lifted off and flew to safety.

For their efforts, Miller and Caffery were recipients of the 2000 Deputy of the Year Award from the New York State Sheriff's Association.

FILE NOS: 74504, 74724

Caffrey, and Miller (not pictured), revisit the area of the rescue in the summer of 2004.

THE QUESTION OF WHY PEOPLE UNDERTAKE LIFE-RISKING ACTIONS FOR THE SAKE OF OTHERS IS ONE FREQUENTLY ASKED OF THE HERO FUND. IRONICALLY, THE HERO FUND IS NOT THE BEST SOURCE FOR A DEFINITIVE ANSWER — IF INDEED ONE EXISTS — AS IT HAS TRADITIONALLY FOCUSED ON THE FACTUAL ESTABLISHMENT OF THE HEROIC ACT RATHER THAN ON THE MOTIVATION OF THE RESCUER. "NO BOGUS HEROES," ANDREW CARNEGIE TOLD HIS FRIEND JOHN MORLEY. "MUST BE REAL THING."[1]

THE FUND'S GUIDE FOR ITS CASE INVESTIGATORS IS EXPLICIT IN HOW THEY MUST APPROACH A CASE UNDER CONSIDERATION AND WHAT THEY MUST DETERMINE TO UNCOVER THE "REAL THING." "YOU WILL BE REQUIRED TO MAKE THOROUGH INVESTIGATIONS...TO REPORT THE FACTS CLEARLY.... YOU ARE CHARGED WITH GATHERING COMPLETE AND ACCURATE INFORMATION TO PROVIDE...DATA SUFFICIENT IN DEGREE TO PERMIT A FAIR AND JUST DECISION." INVESTIGATORS MUST ASK THEM-SELVES IF THEIR REPORTS COVER ALL PERTINENT ASPECTS OF THE EVENT AND IF THE GIVEN FACTS ARE PROVEN BY EVIDENCE. SINCE ABSOLUTE OBJECTIVITY HAS ALWAYS BEEN THE IDEAL, SCANT ATTENTION IS PAID TO DATA OF A SUBJECTIVE NATURE. NO QUESTIONNAIRES SENT TO THE RESCUER, THE RESCUED, EYEWITNESSES, AND OTHER PRINCIPALS ASK FOR ANY DEEP MOTIVATION BEHIND THE DEED. NO PERSONAL INTERVIEW BY THE INVESTIGATOR SEEKS MUCH MORE THAN A DETAILED ACCOUNT OF THE INCIDENT.

STILL, 'WHY DO THEY DO IT?' IS A LEGITIMATE AND NATURAL QUESTION. BETTER QUALIFIED TO ANSWER IT IS SOMEONE LIKE SAMUEL P. OLINER, PH.D., EMERITUS PROFESSOR OF SOCIOLOGY AT HUMBOLDT STATE UNIVERSITY AND FOUNDER–DIRECTOR OF THE UNIVERSITY'S ALTRUISTIC PERSONALITY AND PROSOCIAL BEHAVIOR INSTITUTE. PROFESSOR OLINER, WHOSE SURVIVAL OF THE HOLOCAUST HE ATTRIBUTES TO THE COMPASSION OF A POLISH CATHOLIC FARMER'S WIFE, IS THE AUTHOR OF SEVERAL BOOKS, INCLUDING *DO UNTO OTHERS: EXTRAORDINARY ACTS OF ORDINARY PEOPLE* (PUBLISHED IN 2003 BY WESTVIEW PRESS). IN IT, HE DEVOTES A CHAPTER TO "ANDREW CARNEGIE'S HEROES" AND HIS FINDINGS FROM EXTENSIVE INTERVIEWS OF 214 CARNEGIE MEDAL AWARDEES.

Why Do They Do It?

by SAMUEL P. OLINER
HUMBOLDT STATE UNIVERSITY

VI

ORDINARY PEOPLE,
EXTRAORDINARY ACTS OF COURAGE

We human beings can and often do extend ourselves with unfathomable degrees of caring and compassion. There are many people—ordinary folks, just going about the business of living—who risk their own lives in order to rescue others, often complete strangers, in emergency situations. I distinguish this 'heroic altruism' from conventional altruism, and Carnegie heroes, the Victoria Cross or Medal of Honor winners, and rescuers in other settings that involve high risk to one's life fall into the category. Conventional altruism, which involves little or no risk to one's life, includes hospice volunteers and thousands of other volunteers who give of their time without compensation.

Upon conclusion of my interviews with Carnegie heroes, my overall findings were that they were motivated by a variety of different factors. Some expressed having compassion for the victims, many of having a sense of social responsibility towards their fellow human beings. Though all the rescue situations were dangerous, some rescuers felt they could accomplish their mission, while others felt that they could not live with themselves if they walked away from a tragedy. A few did it for religious reasons. As one rescuer said: "I am certain that God wanted me to walk by this river with my girlfriend so that I would see a couple of people drowning."

NORMOCENTRIC BEHAVIOR

Normocentric behavior, or the beliefs and values learned from parents and the community, was by far the most significant motivating factor in driving helping behavior. In 78 percent of the interviews, rescuers mentioned the importance of parental guidance and their internalization of moral norms and values. Many talked about how they had been taught at some point in their lives that people are supposed to care for one another, and they felt that being a helper is intimately connected with their own sense of who they are. This included learned values of caring and social responsibility acquired from the moral community in which they lived, and from their parents during their upbringing. They modeled moral/spiritual values conducive to forming close, caring attachments to other people. Also included in normocentric behavior is guidance by professional codes or norms and a sense of feeling that it was their responsibility to take action.

For example, a 47-year-old male truck driver who rescued a woman from her burning car following an accident stated:

> I kept thinking that the car could blow up at any second [and] she was on fire also. I was raised to help people, and that's the first thing that came to mind.

A 35-year-old construction worker who rescued two children from a burning building further illustrates the influence of parental values on his act.

> It felt like I was trying to walk through black, greasy Jell-O; it was just thick. I couldn't see anything, couldn't feel anything, and my hand landed in what I thought was an air duct...I stuck my foot in that duct so I would know where the window was, used that as my focal point, felt around the room. And I felt one kid's leg and I just grabbed the leg and just chucked him out of the window; didn't wait for anyone to catch him or anything. And I had to leave the ductwork then...crawled around the room... found the second kid, who was unconscious, and I threw him out, and then I dove out the window.

In discussing the importance of his childhood socialization—representative of the type of responses offered by other Carnegie heroes—he commented on the strong sense of duty imparted by his adoptive father, a U.S. Marine, whom he knew only for a few years while still quite young: "I was only five at the time, but he instilled in me a sense of duty and a sense of responsibility to other people. It's just something that was in my heart."

Another Carnegie hero, a 48-year-old frequent surfer and seafarer, told us how he rescued a woman from drowning in the Pacific Ocean:

> The moment I saw her...the first thought was "somebody's in trouble." There's no second thought to it. And then once I got my board and launched, it's kind of like what surfers call "total commitment," you know, total involvement. Once you take off, you paddle into a very large wave, there's no other way around it other than to go straight down and give it your full [commitment]. You can't turn around and back off.... So once I was going in the water there was no sense of my own peril. "I'm going to get her out of here. One way or another...I'm going to do it." And that's all there is to it.

When asked why he did it, he continued:

> It is my knowledge and experience with the ocean. In some ways...it's a bred-in thing because fishermen — that is something about all seafaring people—you see somebody in trouble, you do what you can.... It's kind of that unwritten code.

SOCIAL RESPONSIBILITY

Sixty-six percent of rescuers identified social responsibility as a motivating factor that influenced their decision to help a fellow human being. The stories of the following rescuers provide good examples.

A 49-year-old man risked his life to save a paralyzed woman from being hit by an oncoming train after her wheelchair became stuck in the track. He was heading alongside the track when he noticed the woman attempting to cross while the gates were being lowered for the approaching train. Seeing her shaking the wheelchair and crying out for help, he just stopped his car and jumped out. He saw the train coming; it was about 50 yards away and fast approaching:

> The train was about 20 yards away and I just grabbed her by the collar in the front and pulled her out onto me, and then she kind of fell on top of me because she was paralyzed from the waist down. Then the train was there and hit her wheelchair and drove it into my leg. And what I thought, the train had caught my leg and cut my leg off, but it was the wheelchair just hitting my leg.

When asked why many others might not risk their lives in a similar life-threatening situation, he offered:

> I think there might be some liability they're afraid of; something might happen.... Well, I don't think that's right. I think you have a certain degree of responsibility, if you see something happen like that, to try and offer some kind of help.

In another selfless rescue, a man who attempted several times to save a woman from drowning in a culvert expressed his motivation in terms of an overarching feeling of responsibility for her welfare:

> I just felt like it was my duty as a person...a matter of being a human. You've got to help somebody if they need help, if they are in trouble.

A 41-year-old man who rescued another man from drowning highlighted the responsibility that goes along with being the only person available to help:

> Seeing [him] out there...and there was no one else there. I think in some situations, people...count on the people around them...but, in fact, when I was there, it was either me or nobody.

One man demonstrated the essence of social responsibility when he explained why he saved another man from being electrocuted:

> It's like something in your mind says "Go help".... It's like another person in me.... You know that that person is going to die or that that person needs help, and you know you've got to help them.

EMPATHY

Empathy is a salient motivating factor centered on the needs of another—on that individual's possible fate. It emerges out of a direct connection with the distressed other, or one's feeling the other's pain and not being able to live with that. Forty-two percent of the Carnegie heroes reported empathy as their motivating factor. We often use empathy interchangeably with compassion, sympathy, and pity—which are its characteristic expressions.

Reactions may be emotional or cognitive; frequently they contain elements of both. The following accounts illustrate both the cognitive and the affective traits (from our hearts *and* our heads). The driver of an 18-wheel truck told us of his very harrowing yet ultimately successful rescue of another driver. His is a story marked by a great sense of empathy for others:

> The other driver went across all three lanes, up on two wheels on one side and then two wheels on the right side, and you could tell he was out of control.... So I told my boss, who was behind about a mile or so, on the radio, I says, "Run back there, Davey, and grab the fire extinguisher." And I said, "I can see the guy hanging upside down inside the van, and it's on fire. Nobody's helping him." I said, "I'm going back, man. I'm going back to help him...."

Running to the van, it seemed like his legs were not moving fast enough:

> I was running as fast as I possibly could, but it seemed like I was in slow motion, am I gonna make it, can I make it to get to this guy?

Then he noticed that the front of the vehicle had started dripping, melting:

> Now the truck, mind you, was upside down, or up on its side, and that would be onto the right side. That meant that the driver was up in the air in his seat and kind of suspended.... And I really don't know how the harness even works, the safety belt system works on that, but he was doubled over and I remember he had a big gash in his neck and I was concerned about that— bleeding, and he [seemed to be] unconscious....

Inside, it didn't seem that bad, other than the smoke billowing out the windows and the victim taking fumes in. The van driver put his hand on the rescuer's shoulder and squeezed. And the hero continued:

> He said, "Please don't let me burn alive in here alone. Don't leave me to burn alive in here. I have a family." At that time I saw my whole life as a young man, even through my tour in the service. I saw my family. I could see my parents... [and] I said, "Listen, if I can't get you out of here, I'm going to sit right here

with you and I'll hold your hand, and we'll go together."…
I didn't want to lose hope, and I guess the old boy upstairs said,
"Hey, there's the button." I hit it and he fell over my shoulder…
like a bag of potatoes, perfect.… I said, "just keep your head
down, we're goin' through this thing…" But the second we got
outside, there were all kinds of people just dragging us, pulling
us away from it.

He later went on to describe the motivation for his actions:

We made it. We had just enough time and as far as me doin' it,
I just couldn't see this guy burn alive. I just didn't want to see
him burn up, because he had no reason to die, and I thought,
"Hey, I'm gonna mess somebody's plans up. You're not getting
him today. You get him, you get me. You're gonna take us both."
But I'll never forget him putting his hand on my shoulder and
when I looked at him and I could see blood on his face and
I could see tears when I said, "I won't leave you. I'll sit here with
you." I wasn't sure if he was going to let me go or not. I knew
I could get away from him and save my own self, but at that time
I just said, "Hey, you know what? You've got to die [eventually].
If it's a cause, it might as well be a damned good cause." And it
was a good call, I think, trying to help this man out.… What an
amazing man.

EFFICACY

Efficacy, which some scholars view as related to self-esteem, is
the sense that one has the power to produce effects or achieve
intended results. Throughout my research, I discerned the importance of efficacy and courage, and at 38.8 percent it was the next
most common motivational factor for Carnegie heroes. Many times
this sense of confidence was the result of prior life experiences or
training, which is why it is so important to impart this to our children and to remember it ourselves.

A belief in his abilities coupled with a strong sense of self-
reliance caused a 43-year-old Carnegie hero to crawl into a burning
house to rescue an elderly woman. When asked why he thought
some people help in these situations and others don't, he replied:

I probably thought I could do something, I thought I could
physically go in there and get her. Had I been on crutches or disabled, I probably wouldn't have even considered it. But me, the

age I was, I probably thought I could do something, I guess. Some people wouldn't dream, the house is on fire, and a common term that always bugs me is 'let the authorities do it.' Like, oh, that is what the fire department is for. But you know ... I look at it as we have to take care of ourselves ... that is my theory on this fire department stuff. I mean the fire department is going to come, but if you can pull someone out of a car or help stabilize the situation or something ... people have to help each other.

INSTINCTIVE

We found that an immediate *impulsive* or instinctive response was the motivating factor over 27 percent of the time in our interviews with the heroes. Frank Farley, an educational psychologist at Temple University who has been studying heroes for the past 15 years, stated that the actions of situational heroes are frequently impulsive and that oftentimes people just act before they think.[2] Correspondingly, some of the rescuers we spoke to could not find a reason for their behavior other than stating that they just reacted to the situation without thinking.

For example, a 34-year-old woman wrestled to the ground a prisoner who was going to shoot a police officer. While the hero was standing just outside of a hospital emergency room, a female officer was escorting a prisoner out, and the restraint on the prisoner, also a female, slipped below her hip. When the officer went to pull it up, the prisoner tried to run, and as the officer tried to grab her, the prisoner hit the officer in the chest and knocked her backward and came down on top of her. The officer hit her head on the pavement. The rescuer explained further:

> I could hear her hit, and so I was just going to pull the girl off the officer, and when I got over there and started pulling on the girl, the officer starts yelling, "My gun! My gun!" ... so, I am just trying to reach down there and trying to find the gun, and the girl already had it out of the holster .... So then I still couldn't feel the gun, and I am thinking, "Oh my God, she is going to blow my head off ...." Then somehow I had grabbed her wrist, and the gun sort of pointed away from us because I was still trying to bring her hand out and away from the officer so she wouldn't shoot the officer, and she fired a shot [which did not hit any of us]. Then she pointed the gun at me and ran .... I was running, but the officer's eyes caught mine and ... I couldn't leave her. It

was like her eyes were screaming for help. So then I ran back and jumped on the girl again and knocked the gun loose … and I was able to get the gun, and the officer was able to get up to her radio and [several officers responded].

When asked why she did what she did and why she didn't run when she had the opportunity to, she explained it as a "natural instinct. I knew she was going to shoot the officer. I couldn't let this happen."

Explaining his rescue of a woman being attacked by an assailant with a knife, one of the heroes attributed his actions to a gut reaction:

When I did get involved, I mean, it was just a reaction. I can't explain it, it was just response.

A 48-year-old mechanic rescued a four-year-old boy from a burning trailer. While others looked on, this rescuer responded, without thought to his safety, to a mother's shrieks that her babies were inside. He smashed the door open and rushed into the smoke and flames. Three children were in the trailer, and he was able to pull only one of them out before the roof collapsed, killing the other two. He said he acted on impulse alone:

I had to go in there and get them, or at least try to …. I didn't even think about it. That's all … it was just a natural reaction. I guess I would have done it for anyone if I saw somebody in trouble like that.

RELIGIOUS AND SPIRITUAL BELIEFS

Over 16 percent of rescuers talked about the importance of religion and spirituality and the belief in a divine as the source of motivation for their compassionate acts. Some said that God told them what they needed to do, and a few said that God or another higher power completely took over their bodies and they essentially had no control in the matter.[3]

A 29-year-old man was driving down the street when he saw a house on fire. He grabbed a blanket from his van and tried first to go in through the garage, and then through the front door, but in both places there was too much flame. He jumped a fence to the back yard. The patio door was locked, so he grabbed the first thing he saw—a barbecue grill. Swinging it by the legs, he broke the sliding glass door and told the people to get out. But they couldn't:

> I don't know where I got the strength from, but I did thank God that he gave me strength and the wisdom and the courage to go in there in the first place. And he gave me the wisdom to think and the strength and courage to lead them to safety.... I was going to go back into the house, but (moments later) it collapsed.

RECIPROCITY

Rescuers, like other people, have multiple values that overlap, such as caring and empathy, and any one of them might assume supremacy at any given moment. For some Carnegie heroes, norms and expectations dictate that they help others because they expect others to reciprocate when they are in need. Approximately 10 percent of those interviewed gave the reason for rescue as reciprocity.

A 21-year-old male student who rescued another man from a fiery automobile following a crash related this story: He and a friend were just about to cross the street when they heard the noise of an accelerating car approaching from down the road. The car soon slammed into the back of a car that had stopped and was waiting for the two men to cross the street. The car that was rear-ended spun around into the opposite traffic lane and left in its wake a gas trail twenty feet long. The gas ignited and the rescuer's friend froze, and then urged the rescuer away from the scene:

> I just kept thinking, What if it was me? What if I got smashed? And if nobody helped me I would just sit there and burn. I just hope and pray that if that ever happened to me, somebody would do the same thing for me.

The interviews revealed that all heroes had either a high or a moderate sense of self-esteem, social responsibility, and locus of control, the feeling that they are in charge of their lives and of the situation before them. We observed also that younger respondents and males were more likely to score as high-sensation seekers, people who may be motivated because the event is risky. Last, we noted that the majority of Carnegie heroes held either a high or a moderate sense of commonality with diverse others, meaning that they have much in common with all humankind.

Most rescuers reported that, although others stood by and did not get involved, a few onlookers did get involved later on in the sequence of rescue. A large percentage of rescuers are male, which can be explained in terms of cultural norms; even though women may be present when a tragic situation occurs, men are "expected" to get involved in rescue. However, when women are on the scene without males, they will act heroically to save lives.

Further, our interviews with the Carnegie heroes corroborate that these people are not "larger-than-life" individuals; rather, they are ordinary people who, through their socialization, have internalized a sense of responsibility and empathy for their fellow human beings. They have acquired caring norms in their lives and developed the skills that both prompt and enable them to respond in emergency situations. Their sense of self and the moral values they have acquired would not let them be bystanders. Each of us needs to learn more about compassion and caring ourselves and to teach these values to our youth.

Every person has the potential to be a rescuer, but the transformation is not one that occurs overnight. Parents and institutions have to take part in teaching and empowering the young to care. It is through a continual process of learning and practicing caring norms—internalizing the skills and values that we identified as the salient motivational factors of Carnegie Medal recipients—that one is able to respond heroically in emergency situations. It is also through this internalization that each of us has the potential for breaking through the bystander role and developing ourselves into compassionate people who help those in need.

Carnegie's European Hero Funds

On September 21, 1908, just over four years after the establishment of the Pittsburgh-based Hero Fund, Andrew Carnegie expanded the concept to his native land with the establishment of the Carnegie Hero Fund Trust in Dunfermline, Scotland. Carnegie's intention to export his model of honoring civilian heroes to European countries was revealed in a note written by him in late December of 1907, to Charles Taylor, president of the first Hero Fund. "I got the idea this morning in bed listening to the organ. Why not extend Hero Fund to my Native Land Britain & Ireland. Make the Dunfermline Trust take charge of it." In a postscript he wrote, "Im [sic] very happy over this revelation this morning." In the three years following its creation, he established hero funds in France, Germany, Norway, Switzerland, the Netherlands, Sweden, Denmark, Belgium, and Italy. All remain but the German fund, which ceased operating in the late 1930s.

THE CARNEGIE HERO FUND TRUST (United Kingdom) recognizes voluntary acts of heroism that involve risk to the rescuer's life performed in the United Kingdom and Ireland, the Channel Islands, or the surrounding territorial waters. Those selected for recognition receive a leather-bound certificate and citation, and in cases of outstanding heroism involving repeated efforts to save a life, a bronze medallion is awarded.

    The fund also provides financial assistance, if necessary, to heroes who have suffered physically or financially, or to the families of heroes who have been killed in their act. The name of the hero or heroine is also inscribed in the Trust's Roll of Honor, which is kept in the Andrew Carnegie Birthplace Museum in Dunfermline.

FONDATION CARNEGIE
FRANCE

THE CARNEGIE
HELTEFOND
FOR NORGE
NORWAY

THE CARNEGIE
RESCUERS
FOUNDATION
SWITZERLAND

FONDATION CARNEGIE *(France)*. In a letter dated February 9, 1909, Carnegie offered to France the gift of an initial investment of $1,000,000, which was intended to honor and reward those who perform acts of civilian courage, and to aid the widows and orphans of rescuers who die. French President Armand Fallières accepted it on July 23, 1909.

The Fondation receives articles from a newspaper clipping service that describe acts of bravery performed on French territory. Following investigations, medals of bronze, silver, and vermeil, as well as certificates, are awarded to those who deliberately risked their lives to save human life. In addition, a cash grant may be awarded to the rescuer. From its founding to the present day, the Fondation has made awards to more than 12,000 people.

THE CARNEGIE HELTEFOND FOR NORGE *(Norway)* was established on March 21, 1911. The fund grants awards to people who, on Norwegian territory, perform voluntary acts of civilian courage to save the lives of others "in peaceful pursuit and surroundings." For a heroic act to be recognized, it must involve risk to the rescuer's life.

A board of three members appointed by the Ministry of Industry and Commerce governs the fund. In addition to the chair, members are the U.S. Ambassador to Norway, and a Norwegian citizen. The fund awards bronze, silver, and gold medals, financial grants, and diplomas to those honored for their bravery. Awards are decided by judgment of the board, with reference, if possible, to reports and comments from a local police superintendent.

THE CARNEGIE RESCUERS FOUNDATION *(Switzerland)* was established on April 28, 1911, shortly after the Federal Council accepted Carnegie's gift of $130,000. The Foundation grants awards to people who, on Swiss territory, risk their lives in peaceful endeavors to save the lives of their fellows. For an act of heroism to be recognized, the rescuer's life or health must have been exposed to a real danger. Persons recognized by the Foundation receive a certificate; engraved bronze, silver, and gold medals are also awarded, as are wristwatches and monetary grants to the rescuers and their families.

Since the establishment of the Foundation, over 8,000 people have been recognized, and more than two million Swiss francs in subsidies has been paid to rescuers and their families. Awards and monetary grants are announced annually.

CARNEGIE HERO FUND
BELGIUM

CARNEGIE HERO FUND *(Belgium)*. On April 17, 1911, Carnegie informed the Belgian government of his donation of $230,000 in government bonds, the interest of which was to be used to support heroes of peace and the families of those who lost their lives as victims of their own helpfulness.

The fund was adopted by royal decree on July 13, 1911. It awards individuals who expose their lives to serious and threatening danger for the purpose of saving the life of another human being. An extraordinary degree of selflessness, the seriousness of the danger, and the exceptional circumstances in which the acts of heroism take place are taken into account. Awards include a medal of bronze, silver, or gold, and a diploma, or, in some cases, just a diploma. Financial support is also granted to relieve the material needs of destitute families, and to help finance the studies of the heroes' children. The fund recognizes about 50 cases a year.

THE FONDAZIONE CARNEGIE PER GLI ATTI DE EROISMO *(Italy)*. In a letter dated June 17, 1911, Carnegie expressed his satisfaction that the Italian government had accepted his offer of $750,000 to establish a fund in Italy to undertake work similar to that of the Hero Fund in the United States. The fund was recognized under Italian law on September 25, 1911. In addition to awarding gold, silver, and bronze medals to heroes and heroines, the fund also makes monetary grants in exceptional cases. In recent years, the number of awards has averaged about 30 a year.

THE FONDAZIONE
CARNEGIE PER GLI ATTI
DE EROISMO
ITALY

THE
CARNEGIESTIFTELSEN
SWEDEN

CARNEGIES
BELØNNINGSFOND
FOR HELTEMOD
DENMARK

STICHTING CARNEGIE
HELDENFONDS
THE NETHERLANDS

THE CARNEGIESTIFTELSEN *(Sweden)* was established on October 6, 1911, in response to a letter Andrew Carnegie had written to the King of Sweden at the beginning of that year offering $230,000 for a hero fund. The fund awards individuals who voluntarily, or otherwise beyond what may be deemed to be their duty, have, by some gallant action in the peaceful walks of life, risked their lives in order to save human lives in the territory of Sweden and on Swedish ships.

For many years, the fund offered money to those who had suffered when saving or trying to save lives, and also to the families of heroes when there was a need. Currently, the social insurance system in Sweden normally helps in such situations, and, according to the statutes of the fund, it cannot offer money if the social authorities are obliged to help. Today, the award consists of a gold watch, a diploma, and a monetary grant.

Carnegie initiated the establishment of CARNEGIES BELØNNINGSFOND FOR HELTEMOD *(Denmark)* on December 30, 1911, in New York, in a letter to King Frederik VIII. Royal Assent by the King affirmed the fund, endowed with $125,000, on February 24, 1912. It recognizes outstanding acts of selfless heroism performed in Denmark, Greenland, and the Faroe Islands, or in their territorial waters.

The award consists of a diploma and 10,000 Danish crowns, or more in special cases, and, in cases where the rescuers lose their lives, the fund may grant financial assistance to the surviving dependents. A medal may also be awarded in recognition of certain heroic acts. Awards are announced once a year, in December. For the past several years, the number of awards made annually has ranged from 15 to 30.

STICHTING CARNEGIE HELDENFONDS *(The Netherlands)*. In a letter dated March 23, 1911, to the Minister of Foreign Affairs, Carnegie expressed his pleasure that the Netherlands had agreed to establish the Heldenfonds. He endowed the fund with a gift of $200,000, saying that he felt the amount would "meet the cost of maintaining injured heroes and their families during disability of the heroes, and the widows and children of heroes who may lose their lives... ."

The Heldenfonds awards silver and bronze medals, together with a certificate. The number of heroic acts awarded has averaged 45 in recent years.

In a letter to the Commission in November of 1914, Carnegie wrote, "... the Hero Fund grows in favor in all countries... ."

HEROES AND
THE FOURTH ESTATE

The Carnegie Hero Fund and the heroic acts of Carnegie Medal awardees have long captured the attention of readers of a wide variety of magazines and periodicals. *Reader's Digest*, for example, has regularly featured accounts of "Carnegie Hero" rescues. The *Saturday Evening Post*, *Esquire*, *Harper's Weekly*, *McCall's*, *Redbook*, *Family Circle*, and *People* have published similar articles. *Life*, in a major story in a March 1979 issue, chronicled eight heroic acts. Several other but less widely circulated and known publications, such as *The Lion*, *Sandlapper*, *The Tower*, and *The Modern Woodmen* also have run accounts of Andrew Carnegie's "heroes of peace."

The public first became aware of the Hero Fund even before it was formally organized. A number of reports surfaced shortly after Carnegie's letter to Charles L. Taylor of March 12, 1904, in which Carnegie announced his plan for the Hero Fund, somehow made its way into the hands of the press. Only three parties were privy to the letter, and each was quick to point to one of the others as the source of the leak. The few in Pittsburgh aware of the leak concluded it must have been Carnegie's doing, even though when the press learned of the letter's contents he was onboard a ship in the Atlantic Ocean and largely out of touch. Carnegie was not against its publication, for in another letter to Taylor, dated April 3, 1904, he wrote, "There was no reason the letter should not be published, even if names of Commission came later." And later in the letter, "It does not do to have such new ideas fall still-born."

Some of the earliest accounts poked fun at Carnegie's newest philanthropy. Was he attempting to create heroism? Was he promoting heroes for hire? One newspaper gave the impression that the hero was to wear the Carnegie Medal as a badge of publicity and occasionally wave it above his head like a banner. Editorialists asked, "Must the hero go in head first?" "Should you take your shirt off to flag a freight, or would the handkerchief be enough?" "Did a man qualify if he had lived five years with his wife's people?"

The original Commission members and Carnegie had some reservations about the press being able to appreciate the idea of the Hero Fund, but they were largely unfazed by any criticisms. Carnegie in fact was confident that the recognition of heroic deeds would lead people to stop and think and appreciate them.

In the book *Heroes of Peace*, published in 1935 in commemoration of the 100th anniversary of Carnegie's birth, Thomas S. Arbuthnot, the Hero Fund Commission's third president, wrote, "Deeds of heroism were matters of live interest. They were personal; they were full of color, and they had thrill enough to catch the imagination of almost any reader. Let it be said for the Press that the reporting of heroic deeds with the betterment awards was the turning point in any attitude of criticism or uncertainty. From that day until the present, the Press has been cooperative and considerate."

ENDNOTES

THE DAY THE VALLEY WEPT

[1] Pamphlet written shortly after the disaster to raise funds for the families of the deceased miners, whereabouts unknown.

[2] F. W. Cunningham, Fourth Report of the Department of Mines of Pennsylvania, Part II "Bituminous," 1904 (Harrisburg PA: Harrisburg Publishing Co., State Printers 1905), 663.

[3] H. M. Bitner, "Night of Terror at Mine," *The Pittsburg Press*, January 26, 1904, 2.

[4] "Miners Entombed," *The New York Times*, January 26, 1904, 1.

[5] Carnegie Hero Fund Commission Website (http://www.carnegiehero.org/history.shtml).

[6] Correspondence from the Andrew Carnegie Relief Fund to George A. Bigley, chairman, Cheswick Relief Committee, February 9, 1904. Carnegie Hero Fund Commission Archives.

ANDREW CARNEGIE

[1] W. J. Holland, *Twenty-five Years of the Carnegie Hero Fund Commission, 1904–1929* (Pittsburgh: Carnegie Hero Fund Commission), 7.

[2] Andrew Carnegie, *Autobiography of Andrew Carnegie* (Boston: Houghton Mifflin Company, 1920), 263.

[3] Letter from Andrew Carnegie to Frank M. Wilmot, November 11, 1913. Carnegie Hero Fund Commission Archives. Translation from the Online Scots Dictionary.

[4] Carnegie. Andrew Carnegie came across this proverb in the newspaper the *Scottish American*, 258–259.

[5] Ibid., 7.

[6] Ibid., 18.

[7] Ibid., 6.

[8] Ibid., 24.

[9] Kathlann M. Kowalski, "An Empire of Steel," *Cobblestone* (April 1999), 14.

[10] Joseph Frazier Wall, *Andrew Carnegie* (New York: Oxford University Press, 1970), 224–225.

[11] Burton J. Hendrick, *The Life of Andrew Carnegie* (Garden City: Doubleday, Doran & Co., Inc., 1932), 49.

[12] Wall, 1034.

[13] Carnegie, 3.

[14] Ibid., 232.

[15] Ibid., 101–102.

[16] *Annual Report* 1987, Carnegie Hero Fund Trust, Abbey Park House, Dunfermline, 8.

[17] "Steel King Steps Aside; 5,000,000 For Mill Men," *Pittsburgh Commercial Gazette*, 1.

[18] Andrew Carnegie, *The Gospel of Wealth and Other Timely Essays* (Garden City, Doubleday, Doran & Company, Inc., 1933), 17. First printed in the *North American Review*, June and December, 1889.

[19] Holland, 5.

[20] "Steel King Steps Aside," 1.

[21] Hendrick, 255.

[22] Thomas S. Arbuthnot, *Heroes of Peace* (Pittsburgh: Carnegie Hero Fund Commission, 1935), 33.

[23] Letter from Andrew Carnegie, undated. Carnegie Hero Fund Commission Archives.

[24] Letter from Andrew Carnegie to Frank M. Wilmot, May 13, 1912. Carnegie Hero Fund Commission Archives.

[25] Letter from Andrew Carnegie to Charles L. Taylor, June 4, 1904. Carnegie Hero Fund Commission Archives.

[26] Hendrick, 350–351.

[27] Wall, 894.

[28] Ibid., 896.

[29] Ibid., 713.

[30] Ibid., 796.

THREAD FOR A WEB

[1] Joseph Frazier Wall, *Andrew Carnegie* (Pittsburgh: University of Pittsburgh Press, 1989), 792.

[2] In 1911, the Carnegie Relief Fund would merge into and become the nucleus of the U. S. Steel and Carnegie Pension Fund.

[3] Andrew Carnegie, *Autobiography of Andrew Carnegie* (Boston: Houghton-Mifflin Company, 1920), 256–257.

[4] Ibid., 266–267.

[5] Andrew Carnegie, "Wealth," *The North American Review*, CXLVIII, 391 (June 1889), 662.

6 Ibid.

7 John D. Rockefeller (1839–1937), Carnegie's philanthropic "rival," gave away $540 million during his lifetime. Rockefeller Archive Center (http://www.rockefeller.edu/archive/). Several historians of philanthropy refer to the early 20th century development of "scientific giving." One important example is Judith Sealander, "Curing Evils at Their Source: The Arrival of Scientific Giving," in Lawrence J. Friedman and Mark D. McGarvie, eds., *Charity, Philanthropy, and Civility in American History* (Cambridge, UK: Cambridge University Press, 2002), 217–239.

8 John W. Jordan, editor-in-chief, *Genealogical and Personal History of Western Pennsylvania* (New York: 1915), 31.

9 In 1968, the Carnegie mansion became the Cooper-Hewitt, National Design Museum, Smithsonian Institution. The gift shop is located in Carnegie's study, where visitors can still read the original painted quotations.

10 Hartley M. Phelps, "Making Heroism Profitable," *World To-Day* (March 1910, 18), 261.

11 Frederick Lynch, DD, *Personal Recollections of Andrew Carnegie* (New York: Fleming H. Revell Company, 1920), 144. Accessed through University of Virginia Electronic Text Center.

12 Ibid.

13 John N. Ingham, "Reaching for Respectability: The Pittsburgh Elite at the Turn of the Century," in Gabriel P. Weisberg, DeCourcy E. McIntosh, Alison McQueen, eds., *Collecting in the Gilded Age: Art Patronage in Pittsburgh, 1890–1910* (Hanover: University Press of New England), 48.

14 Herbert Newton Casson, *The Romance of Steel: The Story of a Thousand Millionaires* (New York: Barnes, 1907), viii.

15 Thomas S. Arbuthnot, *Heroes of Peace* (Pittsburgh: Carnegie Hero Fund Commission, 1935), 37.

16 Carnegie, Autobiography, 267.

17 http://www.carnegieinternational.org.

18 Reed information: Mary Brignano and J. Tomlinson Fort, *Reed Smith: A Law Firm Celebrates 125 Years* (Pittsburgh, 2002).

19 Porter information: National Model Railroad Association (http://www.nmra.org/library/Porterbook.html); *Biographical Directory of the United States Congress, 1774–Present* (http://bioguide.congress.gov/scripts/biodisplay.pl?index = P000441); and Weisberg, McIntosh, McQueen, 83.

20 William Bender Wilson, *Robert Pitcairn 1836–1909: In Memoriam* (Pittsburgh, 1913), 15.

21 J. B. Calvert, "Notes on Pennsylvania Railroad Operation and Signaling" (www.du.edu/~jcalvert/railway/prr/prrsig.htm).

22 Wilson, 26.

23 Tom Rea, "William J. Holland: The Man Who Brought Dinosaurs to Pittsburgh." *Western Pennsylvania History* (Winter 2001–02, 84, 4), 28.

24 *Pittsburgh Post-Gazette* (December 14, 1932).

25 William G. Lytle, Jr., "Dr. William J. Holland, 'Young Over 70,' Looks Forward to Many Projects," *The Pittsburgh Press* (Dec. 1, 1931).

26 Robert C. Alberts, *Pitt: The Story of the University of Pittsburgh, 1787–1987* (Pittsburgh: University of Pittsburgh Press, 1987).

27 Anderson information: Phyllis Dain in Bohdan S. Wynar, ed., *Dictionary of American Library Biography* (Littleton, CO: Libraries Unlimited, 1978), 7–11.

28 Blackburn information: *The Book of Prominent Pennsylvanians: A Standard Reference* (Pittsburgh: Leader Publishing Co., 1913), 111; *The Carnegie Magazine* (Jan. 1932).

29 Letter from Andrew Carnegie to Charles L. Taylor, March 12, 1904.

30 *The National Cyclopedia of American Biography*, 16 (New York: James T. White & Co., 1918), 88.

31 *The National Cyclopedia of American Biography*, 20 (New York: James T. White & Co., 1929), 96–97.

32 *Pittsburgh Gazette Times* (December 7, 1916).

33 *The National Cyclopedia of American Biography*, 33 (New York: James T. White & Co., 1929), 500–501.

34 Jackson information: George Thornton Fleming, *History of Pittsburgh and Environs, from Prehistoric Days to the Beginning of the American Revolution*, 5 (New York, Chicago: The American Historical Society, Inc., 1922), 175–178; *The National Cyclopedia of American Biography*, 16, 128.

35 Scott information: *Biographical Review, Containing Life Sketches of Leading Citizens of Pittsburg [sic] and the Vicinity, Pennsylvania*, 24 (Boston: Biographical Review Publishing Co., 1897), 395; Fleming, 306; Frank C. Harper, *Pittsburgh of Today, Its Resources and People*, 2 (New York: The American Historical Society, Inc., 1931-1932), 853.

36 H. K. Webster, "Just Heroes: How the Carnegie Hero Fund Works in Practice—The Heroes It has Rewarded—What It Means to be a Hero," *American Illustrated Magazine* LX, 5 (September 1905), 570.

37 Ibid.

38 Letter from Andrew Carnegie to Frank M. Wilmot, April 3, 1904. Carnegie Hero Fund Commission Archives.

39 "Certified Heroes," *The Independent*, 70 (May 11, 1911), 969.

40 Webster, 570.

41 Letter from Andrew Carnegie to Charles L. Taylor, June 4, 1904. Carnegie Hero Fund Commission Archives.

42 Webster, 571–572.

43 "The Roll of Heroes," *The Outlook*, 105 (November 1913), 565.

44 Cynthia Crossen, "Distinguishing a Hero from the Merely Brave," *The Wall Street Journal*, June 17, 1996, B8.

THE HERO HUNTERS

1 Thomas S Arbuthnot, *Heroes of Peace* (Pittsburgh: Carnegie Hero Fund Commission, 1935), 37.

2 Hartley M. Phelps, "Making Heroism Profitable," *World Today*, 18 (March 1910), 262.

3 Lewis Edwin Theiss, "The Sleuth and the Hero," *Harper's Weekly*, 56 (June 8, 1912), 9.

4 Theiss, 9.

5 *2307 Quarterly* (October–December, 1960).

CASTING A SAFETY NET: THE BENEFICIARIES

1 Andrew Carnegie, Deed of Trust, March 12, 1904.

2 H. K. Webster, "Just Heroes: How the Carnegie Hero Fund Works in Practice—The Heroes It has Rewarded—What It Means to be a Hero," *American Illustrated Magazine* LX, 5 (September 1905), 570.

3 Carnegie Hero Fund Commission Report, 1914, 217.

4 Letter from Frank M. Wilmot to William M. Pickett, May 5, 1919.

5 Memo from Frank M. Wilmot to investigator, September 9, 1913.

6 Deed of Trust.

7 Letter from C. B. Ebersol to Evelyn Elizabeth Sponsler, May 29, 1931.

8 Letter from Don C. Hamilton to Lawrence Wm. Haywiser, March 14, 1987.

9 Letter from Frank M. Wilmot to Elizabeth J. Lawrence, July 23, 1919.

10 Clayton C. Hoskins, *A Jump in the River* (Wooster, OH: The Wooster Book Company, 2000), 159.

11 Letter from Mrs. George D. Hemphill to David B. Oliver, January 11, 1969.

12 Letter from Mrs. George D. Hemphill to Myrna Braun, March 5, 2000.

13 Letter from Ralph Kelley to the Commission, December 20, 1989.

14 Letter from Karen Nordin Seymour to Walter F. Rutkowski, June 17, 1997.

15 Letter from Keith M. Krumenacker to David B. Oliver, March 14, 1966.

16 Letter from Maryland Wilson Shytles to Robert W. Off, December 28, 1989.

17 Quoted by Maryland Wilson Shytles in a letter to Walter F. Rutkowski, August 7, 1992.

18 Letter from Maryland Wilson Shytles to Robert W. Off, December 28, 1989.

19 Letter from Maryland Wilson Shytles to Walter F. Rutkowski, February 5, 1990.

20 Letter from Clinton and Cynthia Oberholtzer to Commission, January 20, 2002.

21 Steve Bingham, telephone interview with Eliza Smith Brown, November 19, 2003. Bingham's father-in-law, Strickler Mullins, was awarded a Carnegie Medal in 1980 for helping to save a man from suffocation in a coal mine in April of 1978.

22 Letter from Paul J. Lessard to Walter F. Rutkowski, February 27, 2004.

23 Note from John J. Brosnan to Walter F. Rutkowski, July 8, 1995.

24 Letter from Clementine H Brown to Lawrence Wm. Haywiser, April 3, 1996.

25 Letter from James Robert Ussery to Commission, January 15, 2001.

26 Letter from George D. Hemphill to David B. Oliver, January 18, 1958.

27 Letter from Mrs. Wava S. Hellenga to Commission, November 29, 1916.

WHY DO THEY DO IT?

1 Joseph Frazier Wall, *Andrew Carnegie* (New York, Oxford University Press, 1970), 896.

2 Bob Calandra, 1999. "Why they do it." in R. Jerome, S. Schindehette, N. Charles, and T. Fields-Meyer, "Heroes Among Us," *People Weekly* (November 22, 1999), 141.

3 Ibid., 141.

All photography, diagrams, and clippings courtesy of the Carnegie Hero Fund Commission with the exception of those listed below:

page 10, Photo of Mark Laskow by Tom Gigliotti

page 23, Photo of Harwick Mine memorial by Dennis Marsico

page 24, Photo of Andrew Carnegie courtesy of Pennsylvania Department, Carnegie Library of Pittsburgh

page 38, Photo of Louis A. Baumann, Jr. courtesy of *American Illustrated Magazine*

page 40, Additional photos of Commissioners courtesy of Pennsylvania Department, Carnegie Library of Pittsburgh

page 61, Photo of Luigi Badia by Doug Chambers

page 62–63, 67, Photos of Air Florida crash by Charles Pereira, U.S. Park Police

page 64, Photo of Don Usher, Lenny Skutnik, Gene Windsor, and Roger Olian, by Howard Korn

page 70, Photo of map by Tom Gigliotti

page 82, 84–85, Newspaper clipping and photos of Brookwood miners courtesy of Sheriff Edmund M. "Ted" Sexton, Sr.

page 84, Photo of Dennis R. Mobley courtesy of Linda Mobley; Photo of Charles J. Nail courtesy of Janice Nail

page 104–105, 108, Photos of Jimmie Dyess and wife courtesy of Perry Smith

page 110, Photo of Carolyn Delaney by Shelly Katz

page 117, Photo of George Hemphill by Rob Amberg

page 120, Photo of Robert P. Stchur by Preston Mack

page 128–129, 131, Rudell Stitch boxing poster and family photo courtesy of Donald Stitch

page 135, Photo of Daniel Stockwell by Andrew French

page 155, Photo of Dorothy Kochs courtesy of *Front Page Detective*

page 156, Photo of Elsie H. McEvoy courtesy of *Weekend Magazine*

page 162–163, Photos and clippings of Captain Casto and crew, courtesy of Mark J. Casto

page 193, Photos of the St. Paul Coal Company mine courtesy of Chicago Historical Society

page 210–211, Photo of Kevin Caffery and Jeffrey Miller by Bill Ivy

page 223–226, Medal photos by Melinda McNaugher

ACKNOWLEDGMENTS

The idea for a book to commemorate the 100th anniversary of the Carnegie Hero Fund surfaced at the initial meeting of the Commission's Centenary Committee in August of 2000. The committee, which was chaired by Benjamin R. Fisher, Jr., also included Elizabeth H. Genter, Ann M. McGuinn, and Alfred W. "Burr" Wishart, Jr. Ben, quite unexpectedly, passed away in September of 2002. Burr was then named chair, and Mark Laskow, Nancy L. Rackoff, and Thomas L. Wentling, Jr., joined the committee. All are most heartily thanked for their many hours devoted to this major undertaking, and also for their wise counsel and support on the many other centennial projects.

Special credit, naturally, goes to our writers. Mary Brignano, wrote the wonderfully crafted chapters on the early history of the Commission and the investigators, and also helped with several other aspects of the book. Carol Bleier, whose initial and only role, at her insistence, was to put a focus to the book, could then not resist and eagerly and most capably tackled the Andrew Carnegie biography and the Harwick Mine story. Eliza Brown's chapter on the beneficiaries captured well the Commission's commitment to fulfilling Carnegie's vision, but, more important, revealed how profoundly that vision has so positively affected the lives of so many. David Bear, who doggedly dug through the Commission's files and grudgingly accepted our insistence for not much more than just the facts, nevertheless massaged our economical, some might say laconic, writing into even more compelling profiles of heroic acts. These writers in turn send their thanks to the many others who helped them in their research.

We also were fortunate to obtain the contributions of three other noteworthy individuals, especially Peter Krass, author of *Carnegie*, the outstanding biography of the founder, for the foreword. Professor Samuel P. Oliner, a leading authority on altruistic behavior, gladly shared his research on the factors that prompt ordinary people to risk their lives on behalf of others. Major General Perry M. Smith (Ret.) graciously found the time in a very demanding schedule to write the profile of Jimmie Dyess.

Walter Rutkowski, who has been with the Commission for nearly 30 years, was of inestimable assistance and guidance. He knows more about the Hero Fund than any other person, and cares for it beyond description. Without him, this book would have met sure *expiry*. Among his many writing and editing contributions is the account of the Air Florida disaster.

Of immeasurable help was the Commission's staff of Gloria Barber, Myrna Braun, Jeff Dooley, Eileen LoCasale, Susan Marcy, Marlin Ross, Paul Snatchko (no longer with the Commission), and Barbara Youngerman. They did research, suggested topics, and proofread, among several other chores. Most of all, they were supportive throughout. Thank you all for coming.

We are deeply grateful to the Carnegie Medal awardees, their families, and others who provided information, photographs, and memorabilia: Grace (Gunia) Abbs, Mark Casto, Glenn Bingham, Kevin Caffery, Carolyn Delaney, Bruce Gunia, George and Athala Hemphill, Ronald Hitchon, Ralph Kelley, Paul Lessard, Jeffrey Miller, Linda Mobley, Janice Nail, Roger Olian, Dr. Maryland Wilson Shytles, Lenny Skutnik, Dr. Robert P. Stchur, Dan Stockwell, Donald Stitch, Don Usher, and Gene Windsor.

Rick Landesberg, Joe Petrina, Kate Radkoff and Caroline Mengon from Landesberg Design put form and beauty to many thousands of words and hundreds of graphics in a way that only people of the highest level of creativity and caring can. They were outstanding, understanding, and great to work with.

Cynthia Miller and Dennis Lloyd of the University of Pittsburgh Press provided much-needed guidance on preparing the book for commercial distribution. We are grateful to them for helping us share with a wider audience the story of Carnegie's most treasured philanthropy, and especially the accounts of its heroes.

And thanks also to Lu Donnelly, dear friend and valued advisor. Finally, thanks to my wife Chris, who persevered through the project like the trouper she is.

To those whom we have failed to mention, please accept our apologies. We will make it up to you in 2104.

Douglas R. Chambers
Editor

COLOPHON

This book was designed and typeset by Landesberg Design, Pittsburgh, Pennsylvania. The text is set in ITC Charter, designed by Matthew Carter. Additional text is set in Eagle Bold, Scala Sans Caps, and Tribute. The book was printed by Broudy Printing Inc., Pittsburgh, and bound by The Riverside Group, Rochester, New York.